The Girl
on the
Balcony

The Girl on the Balcony

Olivia Hussey Finds Life After *Romeo & Juliet*

OLIVIA HUSSEY

WITH
ALEXANDER MARTIN

KENSINGTON BOOKS
www.kensingtonbooks.com

KENSINGTON BOOKS are published by

Kensington Publishing Corp.
119 West 40th Street
New York, NY 10018

All Kensington titles, imprints, and distributed lines are available at special quantity discounts for bulk purchases for sales promotion, premiums, fund-raising, educational, or institutional use.

Special book excerpts or customized printings can also be created to fit specific needs. For details, write or phone the office of the Kensington Special Sales Manager: Attn. Special Sales Department. Kensington Publishing Corp., 119 West 40th Street, New York, NY 10018. Phone: 1-800-221-2647.

Library of Congress Card Catalogue Number: 2018932845

ISBN-13: 978-1-4967-1707-8
ISBN-10: 1-4967-1707-4
First Kensington Hardcover Edition: August 2018

ISBN-13: 978-1-4967-1721-4
ISBN-10: 1-4967-1721-X
First Kensington Electronic Edition: August 2018

10 9 8 7 6 5 4 3 2 1

Printed in the United States of America

To:

*My beloved guru swami Muktananda, thank you
for saving my life.
Howard Wills, my dear friend and teacher,
thank you for your prayers of love and forgiveness.
I am eternally grateful to you both.*

*Thank you, Dean Paul, for our son, Alex.
Thank you, Akira, for our son, Max.
Thank you, David, for our daughter, India, for 28 years
of love and loyalty, and for being my rock. I love you.*

And to Kevin for . . . (Well, you know why.)

Contents

Part IV

Foreword

When I first glimpsed Olivia I saw—no, I felt—the true innocence and passion I was looking for in "my Juliet." During the testing phase I paired couples together amongst the hundreds of young actors who were auditioning. I was immediately drawn to the look of Olivia and the young Leonard Whiting. And so it began. They were laboring with the dialog of the "balcony scene," and as they stood there reciting their words, I thought, "Intense diction lessons would take care of that." For me, what was most important was the feeling: I wanted to see their true young passion. I remember Olivia began one of her long monologues and seemed nervous. I sat behind the camera rolling tiny bits of paper in my fingers and began flicking them at her while she was speaking. One hit her right on her forehead, and she immediately turned to me and said angrily, "Don't do that, I'm trying to act!" I burst into laughter and teased her. At that moment I saw the passion I needed!

Later I asked, "Do you like the balcony scene, Olivia?"

"Yes, it's all right," she replied.

"Is there another scene you would rather test with? One you love?"

"Yes," she replied, "the potion scene. That one is my favorite!" I told her to learn it and come back in three weeks. She returned as planned and did it for me. When she was done, lying there on the floor crying behind the prop bed, we were all just standing there in amazed silence. Michael York, who had come along to watch the testing that day, quietly turned to me and said, "You have to cast her!" But Michael needn't have said a thing: I knew THAT day I had found my Juliet! And, over the years, what fun we had working together.

Olivia, we have always shared a special bond. Even as the years passed, I thought of you and hoped you were well and happy—as you deserved to be. So, in closing, my dear Olivia, you have always been and always will be the image of that woman that you resurrected in my life . . . "the image of my own mother." I think you are the object of my adoration . . . Always alive!

God bless you!
Love, Franco Zeffirelli (2016)

Prologue

My oldest son's godmother was getting married, and Fifth Avenue was lined with light blue police barricades. As the long line of limousines inched closer to Marble Collegiate Church at West 29th Street, the crowds thickened. Through the tinted windows they seemed like exotic aquarium creatures: close, but a world away. I began to hear the familiar shouts of "Over here! Over here!" and catch the blinding white pop of flashbulbs.

I was getting nervous; I hadn't been involved in anything like this in years. It took me back to the premiere of *Romeo & Juliet*. My God, I thought, that was thirty-five years ago. (It was 1968, to be exact; now it was 2002.)

The limo stopped. I heard the click of the doors unlocking. My husband took my hand. "Okay, love," he said. "It's time."

I could feel the anxiety running up my spine and down my arms, making my hands tingle. I've always panicked when I feel I'm on display, and when I stepped out of the limo my vision narrowed and the muscles in my throat tightened.

"Olivia! Olivia! Over here! Over here!" photographers yelled, hustling for a shot. Across the street was a blur of waving arms and excited faces. David and I moved with the line of guests toward the cluster of policemen checking bags. It was only six months since 9/11, and New York City was on edge. I saw it in the stern expressions of the cops, in the deliberate way they moved through the crowd, scanning faces.

I felt a hand grab my elbow and tug for attention: an old friend, Sally Kirkland. "Olivia," she said, "you should step over here and say hi to people."

She pulled me out of the line and over to a small group of fans corralled behind a barricade, calling out to me:

"Oh my God, Mrs. Hussey, you look wonderful!"

"Olivia, where have you been?"

"Juliet, we've missed you!"

I smiled my automatic smile. I signed some pictures. I posed for some shots. And as I made my way up the church steps on David's arm, I repeated to myself, *"Where have you been? Juliet, we've missed you."*

Inside, the church was a galaxy of stars: Teenage supermodels sat in narrow pews fanning themselves, while old-guard actors like Kirk Douglas and Anthony Hopkins watched in stony silence, wondering perhaps why on earth they themselves were in attendance. A well-known singer, clearly drunk, lurched down the aisle, shadowed by her music exec partner. Above us in the balcony, I caught Donald Trump craning his neck over the edge, comparing his seat to others' and calculating his distance to the altar. All around us, people famous merely for being famous flittered between directors I had worked with and producers I had read for; some things, it seemed, never changed.

Liz Taylor walked in, leaving a hushed reverence in her wake. She wore a necklace of huge pearls and a birdcage veil of French netting over her legendary eyes.

"Do you think she'll remember me?" I whispered. I didn't think David had heard me, but he answered, "Of course, Livi, she'll be thrilled to see you."

I wasn't so sure; it had all been so long ago. I hadn't spoken to today's bride, Liza Minnelli, since Dino's funeral in 1985. That had been a hard day. Standing under a bright, cloudless sky with hundreds of other mourners, I kept my arm firmly around my young son as he was handed a huge, folded American flag. I remember thinking how small it made him look.

Liza had called me that morning: "I'm so sorry, Olivia," she'd said. "I just . . . I wanted to call."

"I know, Liza. Thank you."

"He was such a special man."

"He was Dino."

We hung up, not knowing what more to say.

Now, from our seats in the center pew, I saw faces from the past looking back at me. People I hadn't thought about in years waved as if it had been days and not decades since we'd last seen each other. What was more surprising, I found myself waving back.

If you knew me, you'd know I don't do trips down memory lane, but now I was really enjoying myself. My agoraphobia had apparently stayed at the hotel, leaving me free to relax and have a good time. I delighted in spotting old friends, people I had worked with, even a few old flames.

It helped that the wedding proved to be kind of nuts. The best man—Michael Jackson—struggled to maneuver Liza's dress down the aisle. The maid of honor—Liz Taylor—kicked off her shoes and stood barefoot during the ceremony. As Liza would say, "Go big, darling, or go home. I mean, why be boring?" Indeed, Liza, you crazy, fabulous star.

Toward the end of the night, after the balloons had

dropped at the reception and there was no more confetti to throw, I sat quietly, watching my nine-year-old daughter, India, as she moved from table to table, laughing, bits of half-eaten cake stuck to her fingers. The night had reminded me of something I had forgotten—or, perhaps, had told myself wasn't important: I had a story to tell, a story worth remembering. And I had a question to answer, asked long ago by a girl standing on a balcony.

I promised myself that when I got home, I'd tell that story and answer that question.

That was fifteen years ago. My promise to myself lasted as long as Liza's marriage. The voice in my head was too strong: "A memoir? Really, honey? And just who do we think we are?" I convinced myself that, if I was remembered at all, it was as a single image: Juliet standing on the balcony.

And that should really be enough. What more was there to tell?

Well, according to my family and friends, there was more. A lot more. And they urged me to start writing. Honestly, they insisted on it.

Mine's not been a simple story, but perhaps it's been about a simple girl. A life far from ordinary, but lived in an ordinary way. For sure, it's been a hell of a ride.

Now it's time to tell that story, time to answer the question that girl on the balcony keeps asking: *"Has the life I've given you been worth it?"*

Part I

A Rough Start

Alma Joy Hussey loved to dance the tango. She was twenty-three, the daughter of British expats living in Buenos Aires, and on Friday nights she would dance. Arm-in-arm with a couple of girlfriends, she would head to the *Avenida de Mayo* in the heart of the city. It was 1948, and the *milongas,* dance clubs, were packed with beautiful young people dying to see and hear their favorite singers. One of the best singers was a twenty-one-year-old man from Victoria, just outside Buenos Aires, who had moved to the city five years before. On one of those festive Friday nights, in one of those packed *milongas*, when the lights went down and the orchestra started up, Osvaldo Ribo walked out onto the stage to sing, and my mother fell in love.

At least, that's the story she told me. The truth may be very different. Memories are fluid; without firm context to anchor them, they can slip and slide. For my mum, that context shifted over the years, and she began to remember things as she believed they ought to have been rather than as they actually happened. As for me—at best, I think my parents were a pair of star-crossed lovers from disapproving families. At worst, I see them through the eyes of the girl who came from their broken home.

My father's real name was Andres Osuna. He was born in 1927, into a family that had originally emigrated from Northern Spain. His father died before I was born, but I remember my grandmother clearly enough: She disapproved of my mother.

I think there might have been quite a few disapproving faces in the Buenos Aires of the 1950s. As it remains today, the city was broken up into different communities: Spanish, German, French, Portuguese, and English. All Argentinean, of course, but each fiercely proud of its own cultural heritage. Before 1940, these groups mixed easily with one another. In marketplaces, Portuguese grocers sold to French chefs, Spanish families walked along boulevards chatting with German friends, and in corner pubs English bartenders poured glasses of Fernet for all.

But World War II changed everything. As Europe spiraled into darkness, the various ethnicities in Buenos Aires retreated into the security of their tribes. Lines were drawn, sides were taken. What's more, the war brought out old grudges and deep resentments. Words like "colonialism" and "assimilation" began to creep into conversations around the city, fostering an atmosphere of distrust and clannishness that lingered long after the war was over.

For my grandmother, who ruled my father's side of the family with an iron fist, even the idea that her grandson should love an English woman was not to be countenanced. She saw the English as nothing more than poor, vulgar potato farmers who should all be sent packing. For my mom's family, this condescension cut deep. First, they were not English; they were from strong Scottish stock. Second, they had been in Argentina for three generations

and felt entitled to call the place home. It was into these
dark waters my parents waded. They were in love and, despite their families' disapproval, they married.

I was born on April 17, 1951. I only have a few memories of my mum and dad together. I do know that they
were very different. My mother was all kinetic energy:
four feet ten, with a tiny hummingbird body and short
brown hair. She loved to party, and was always laughing.
In many ways, she looked at the world as a child might: as
a place of simple truths requiring direct action.

My father was, shall we say, more relaxed, with the indo-
lence that sometimes comes to those blessed with tremendous
good looks. In fact, he was striking, with hooded eyes; high,
chiseled cheekbones; a sharp jawline; and long, narrow
nose—noble features that could have belonged to the captain of a fifteenth-century Spanish treasure ship had they
not been softened by his kind, carefree expression and
deeply sensitive soul.

My father never drank. He never smoked. He loathed
parties. He was happiest sitting around his kitchen table
with his brothers, singing and playing guitar. He was a
gentle man.

Their marriage didn't last two years. They split when I
was one and my mum was pregnant with their second
child, my brother, Andrew.

At times I've thought, how sad to have your love destroyed by family pressure, Montague versus Capulet. But
maybe my father and mother were just too different.
There are parts of our parents that must always be a mystery to us. I can tell you, though, that I carried the pain of
their separation and the trauma of its aftermath for a long,
long time.

After my father left, my mother worked as a secretary
somewhere in the city. Six months pregnant, she would

leave early in the morning and come home after five, exhausted but uncomplaining. Most mornings, she would drop Drew and me off at her sister's on her way to work. I adored both of my mother's siblings: Uncle Bungie—a nickname for Barry—and Auntie Linni, short for Leonore. Linni was very much like my mother, small and strong. I remember spending hours snuggled up with her in the late afternoon, watching the headlights reflect off the blinds in her little apartment, hoping they shone from the bus that was bringing my mother home. The sisters even sounded alike; for years after my mother died, I would call Linni just to hear my mother's voice.

Some days, Uncle Bungie would come by Linni's flat. Tall and lean, he would walk through the front door carefully so as not to hit his head. I would throw myself over the back of the couch and rush to him. He never came empty-handed; as I bobbed and weaved around him, he would keep his hands firmly behind his back to conceal whatever little treasure he had brought me. Of all my early memories it's these weekdays spent with Bungie and Linni that I cherish most.

When he wasn't being "Uncle Bungie" to his hyperactive niece, my uncle was Captain Barry Melbourne Hussey of the Argentine navy, a dedicated, lifelong navy man. (In a huge historical irony, thirty years later, in 1982, Captain Hussey was a key negotiator in the surrender of the Falkland Islands to the British.)

On weekends, my mother and I would visit her parents. They lived in the English quarter of the city, in a lovely little house that sat snugly on a corner surrounded by hedges and tall trees. I loved spending Saturdays in the garden with my grandfather, watching frogs leap from hedge to hedge.

On occasion, my brother and I would visit my father. I

do have some sweet memories of him. Sitting on a vinyl-covered, steel-tubed kitchen chair with his shirtsleeves rolled up, he would speak in hushed tones about the beauty of tango or the simple pleasures of country living while I sat listening, lulled by the rhythmic way he rocked Drew from side to side, cradling him in one arm.

By 1954, though, the situation had become too hard for my mum. Between working for minimum wage and looking after two small children, she was riven with anxiety, faltering from stress, and deeply unhappy. Something had to change. Our aunt and uncle, wonderful and committed as they were, had their own families, and my mother felt it was unfair to burden them further. She decided to enroll my brother and me in boarding school.

I know that writers from Dickens to J.K. Rowling have sent their fictional children to boarding schools, and countless actual children have loathed or adored their experiences away at school. I was a little girl used to a tiny apartment in the suburbs of Buenos Aires; the idea of being sent away, separated from my family, was absolutely terrifying. I thought the school would be a cold and lonely place, full of mean, uncaring people. Worse, I thought, as children do, that my brother and I were being sent away because we weren't loved anymore. I was right on the former but so wrong on the latter.

All I remember of the first few months at school are the nights I spent wandering around dark hallways, looking for my brother—he had been placed in a separate wing, far from me. The nights I did manage to find him, I would climb into his little bed and cuddle up close, crying softly into the back of his head.

Mum would come every weekend. I remember her walking toward us one hazy gray morning, through the school's huge steel gates. She was wearing a red, white, and blue dress. She took us up in her arms and told us, "I love you both more than anything in the whole world." Pressed against her cheek, I tasted her sea-salt tears.

"But I can't take you home just now," she went on. "There's no one to look after you." Her arms were shaking. "I have to work. But you'll both be home soon."

We stayed for three years.

White Shoes

I was seven when we left Argentina. Mum had had enough: enough of being separated from her children, enough of struggling day by day, enough of a city that held nothing for her. In the fall of 1957, she had a plan: She would ask our father's permission to take us to visit relatives in England.

Though they never saw one another, Mum and Dad were still married, and Argentinean law gave the father full control of the children. One of the only images I have of them together is of the day my father signed the papers to allow us to travel.

A few weeks passed. My and my brother's simmering excitement began to bubble. This would be our first overseas trip; our first trip anywhere. We were visiting relatives in London, Mum would say; we planned to be there for two months. Naturally, we would miss our family—our dad—but no school for two months? Heaven. We would get to meet new family! We would see London!

Finally, the day came. Standing on the dock with our bags, we said good-bye to Auntie Linni, Uncle Bungie, my cousins, my granny, and my father, who had come down to see us off. All I could focus on, however, was my new white shoes. They were fancy dress-up shoes, shoes for a special occasion, and they were much too tight. They squeezed and pinched my toes painfully together and squeaked when I walked.

"Stop fidgeting and give your auntie a proper goodbye," my mother said.

"But my shoes hurt."

"Just do it, Livi."

We boarded the ship, and as it slowly slipped away from the dock, I turned around and saw my father waving up at us. He looked so sad. I concentrated on my shoes, on the pain in my feet—a child's way to block the sadness in her heart. I looked up at Mum; she had started to cry. I thought, "Don't cry, Mummy, we'll be back soon and see everyone again."

But Mum had kept her real plan secret from everyone. To this day, I don't know where she found the strength to follow through with it. We were going to visit relatives in England, she would say—but in reality, we were never coming back.

Under a Slate-Gray Sky

I love English television. My idea of a perfect evening is to sit curled up on my couch—surrounded by my daughter; my dogs; and, depending on the week we've had, my husband—watching British television: detective dramas, tongue-in-cheek comedies, period pieces with a touch of the macabre. I love their quiet confidence: They know how to take their time. The older ones are the best, I think. And what wonderful actors! Some—David Warner and Angela Lansbury, for example—I know, while some—like James Nesbitt and Helen Mirren—I admire. Others I know and maybe don't admire. But I could sit for hours and just soak them all in.

I also have, or so I've been told, a very English sense of humor: self-deprecating, leaning to the ironic. I swoon over deadpan lines. Give me Rowan Atkinson's forever frustrated Blackadder, or Edina and Patsy wrestling luggage on the airport conveyer belts in *Ab Fab*. I laugh out loud when life doesn't go Judi Dench's way in *A Fine Romance*, and tears roll down my cheeks every time Richard Wilson gives one of his curmudgeonly reactions to the modern world.

I mention my English sensibility and sense of humor because, fifty-eight years ago, when my mum, my brother, and I stepped off the ship under a slate-gray sky, I was Argentinean. My first language was Spanish. I had grown up with the sun and the heat and the warm winds that blow south of the equator. Here, everything was cold and damp.

We arrived almost penniless and not knowing a soul (good grief, this reads like *Angela's Ashes*). Our first few months were miserable. It was a time of tiny rooms and locked doors, endless tube rides and constant moving. We met a series of horrible, pasty-faced landladies who seemed to have stepped out of the pages of some dark fairy tale. Witchlike, they would stare down at my brother and me, their pale, distrusting eyes a warning that we were not welcome.

Before we left Argentina, my mum had arranged for us to stay with a distant cousin of hers, who turned out to be awful; she loathed us, and couldn't wait to see the back of us. We stayed long enough for Mum to meet another wretched woman who had two small rooms for rent in the house she owned. Mum found a job at the Argentinean consulate; she had legal-secretarial skills and was fluent in two languages. But to make ends meet, she also had to work evenings as a waitress.

As far as I can remember, there was nothing swinging about the London of the late '50s and early '60s. Thirteen years after the war, parts of the city were still a confusion of rubble and burned-out buildings. I remember the "Rag & Bone men" trolling the streets for discarded clothes and scrap metal and rubber to resell. Food rationing had ended only four years earlier, and the food we had was bland, simple, and colorless—the postwar cuisine for which Britain would become infamous. The city and its people were exhausted, and money was tight.

Working for the Argentinean consulate did have advantages. Mummy was able to get wonderful cuts of Argentine beef: *vacio*, *bife de chorizo*, and *bife de costilla*; different types of steak, including T-bone or porterhouse, virtually *unheard* of in England. They were prime cuts, and they were delicious—or would have been, if my brother and I had ever had a chance to try them. Our landlady, who was supposed to be looking after us while Mum was at work, kept them all for herself. She would simply lock Drew and me in a room all day. At noon, she would bring us a meal of beans on toast and leave again, locking the door behind her.

Her arrangement with my mother was simple: The landlady would take most of Mum's weekly wages as payment on the house. In time, the house would be ours. Indeed, she did eventually move out and we had a home. Then, weeks later, late one night, there was a loud banging at the front door. It was the woman. She had come with the "authorities." Announcing that the house was hers and that we were squatters, she had us thrown out.

Mum was so innocent, so naive. She had been giving away her weekly wages. She had signed no papers. She had been given no contract or title. She'd been conned, and we were out on the street.

My memories of what followed are a series of faded snapshots, images of difficult times: Penge Primary School, Miss Buchanan slapping a ruler across the back of my knees: "Don't think a pretty face will get you through life, Olivia." *Slap!*

"Yes, Miss Buchanan."

"Because it won't get you anything." *Slap!*

Earl's Court, central London. Then Wapping, on the north bank of the Thames, a dockland district hit hard during the Blitz. Wapping was like so many port areas, scruffy and forgotten.

Another school. A girl named Libby, who threatened to cut up my face with a knife. More moving. My mum having to get another job cleaning offices early in the mornings.

Through most of this period, I escaped to the movies. I had known that I wanted to be an actress since the age of four, though I didn't start to take my career seriously until I was eight—when, over breakfast one morning, I announced, "I think it's about time I started taking my career seriously."

Mum, bless her, reacted with all the solemnity and sincerity that her little girl demanded. She said, "All right, Livi, now how do we take your career seriously? Let's think."

We decided to begin at the cinema.

I loved going to the movies—I still do. Like children everywhere, I loved to project, to pretend to be those characters up there on the screen. I suppose I never really stopped. There in the dark, with Mum trying to catch a quick nap, I would *be* Debbie Reynolds in *Tammy and the Bachelor* or Doris Day in *Calamity Jane*. I was the great Albert Finney, filling the whole screen with mischief and wild, infectious humor in *Tom Jones*. I was Glenda Jackson in—everything! Even now, it's me solving the crime in *Prime Suspect* or standing on the table screaming in *Penny Dreadful*. Great acting has always had the power to knock me off my feet.

I would see these wonderful actors and it all seemed so natural, so effortless. They were just up there, on the screen. That's where they lived, and I was simply watching them. Though I did have a feeling, a suspicion, that there might be more to it than that. That perhaps Doris Day and Alan Bates knew what they were doing. I was watching them, certainly, but they knew I was watching. There was a technique involved, and I needed to learn it.

On the Boards

RADA, LAMDA, Central School, Webber Douglas School, Drama Centre, Guildhall, The Barbara Speake Stage School, the Aida Foster Theatre School: If you were going to be an English actor—a *serious* actor—you had to go to a London drama school, and the city had plenty to choose from. But how to choose? Where to start? Continuing to take my career seriously, Mum and I chose the school that was closest to where we then lived.

The Italia Conti School, 23 Goswell Road, was three miles from our flat. Founded in 1911 by the actress Italia Emily Conti, it was one of the oldest drama schools in London. By 1962, it was run by Mrs. Conti's formidable daughter, Ruth Conti, who personally conducted each new applicant's interview.

A monument to austere Edwardian taste, the Conti School's front entrance seemed designed to intimidate— London drama schools tend to take themselves very seriously. But to a ten-year-old girl who had stars in her eyes and was determined to become one herself, the coldness of the gray brick spoke of professionalism and commitment, while the white limestone pillars that framed the front stairway seemed powerful and secure. I loved it.

I remember running up the stairs for my interview with Miss Conti. She sat behind a fine, dark wood desk etched in gold leaf. She was elegant and poised, almost serene in repose. As she was about to speak, I leapt into the fray.

"Oh, Miss Conti, we don't have money, but if you just give me a chance I can really act."

Silence.

"So, if you would please let me come to your wonderful school, I'll do really well, and I'll pay back all the fees that my mummy can't pay right now—because, you see, I really *must* act."

Finished, I sat back in my chair and clutched the sides as hard as I could. A long pause, and then a smile slowly broke across her face, belying her previous cool detachment.

"Well, you have spunk, Olivia, I'll say that." She started to laugh, and then, "Welcome to the Conti School."

Looking back on that day, that interview, I'm at a loss to express my deep gratitude to Miss Conti. By giving me that opportunity she not only made me incredibly happy but afforded me a chance to belong somewhere, to make friends, and to take my first steps toward a new life.

That life began each day at nine a.m. with our required lessons: maths, English, history, and so on. Imagine how difficult it would be for a teacher to get a classroom full of ten- and eleven-year-olds to sit still and focus, let alone teach them multiplication tables—especially when those students know that the second half of their day will be given over to dance, song, improv, and movement. Our long-suffering academic teachers had an impossible job.

I loved our modern jazz and ballet classes. I would practice my singing up and down the halls, with the kind of abandonment only a child can have. I loved almost every afternoon class. I say almost because, as ironic as it may seem to me now, I loathed Shakespeare. I simply could not get my head around it. It was boring, and went on and on. Our Shakespeare class became an opportunity for me and my new best friend, Linda, to pop round to the pub and gorge on pork pies. (As you read on, you will find that food, and my love of eating, are reoccurring themes.)

Along with the marvelous training that London drama schools provided for a young actor, their relationships with film and television companies were—certainly for me, at the Conti School—a vital pathway to becoming a working actress.

Production companies based around London would inform the schools of the various child parts that needed to be cast. The schools, in turn, would assemble some of their more promising students to audition. This was how, at age twelve, I got my first real job.

In the 1960s, Charlie Drake was a well-known British comedian. His variety show, *The Charlie Drake Show*, was highly rated and appealed to both children and adults. I can still remember his catch phrase: "Hello, my darlings!" Since he was only about five feet one, he would end up delivering it at eye level to women's breasts! It was harmless, sweet, and funny in a Benny Hill sort of way.

He was looking for a young actress to appear on the show and play various small parts. Most thrilling was that she would be given one slot in each episode for her own little thing.

So there I was, standing onstage in a line of girls waiting to audition. Mr. Drake sat in the very back of the theatre in total darkness, just like in *A Chorus Line*. With the spotlight in our eyes, each of us stepped forward, said our name and what piece we'd prepared.

"You, little one. Step forward," the voice projected from the darkness. I looked around, Well, I'm the tiniest one here, I thought. He must be talking to me. I stepped forward.

"And what have you prepared for us today?"

"Well, I don't like Shakespeare, plus I'm too young for it, so I have 'The Owl and the Pussy-Cat' by Edward Lear." I could hear the girls start to giggle around me. A little girl's poem, they must have been thinking. I didn't care, though. Not only was "The Owl and the Pussy-Cat" one of my favorite poems, it also had the distinction of being the only poem I had memorized.

"Well, all right, then," Mr. Drake said, with what I swear was a new lightness to his voice.

Maybe it was my naïveté; my poem made him laugh, or perhaps he just liked the fact that I was a bit shorter than he was. For whatever reason, when the auditions were over, Mr. Drake came up onstage, thanked everyone, and took me aside. The press was then invited into the theatre, and I was introduced as the new girl on *The Charlie Drake Show*.

What a wonderful time! The reviews were positive, and over the next few months I appeared regularly on the show, as well as on another one called *The Crunch*. It was 1963. I was still attending the Conti School as well as going out on auditions most weeks. A month after President Kennedy was shot, I was cast in my first film.

I know, *everybody remembers where they were when they heard the news*. All I can remember, though, is how heavy and sad everything seemed. Kennedy was beloved in England, and his assassination cast a long shadow over the whole country. Though I didn't understand it, I sensed the shock and the disbelief in the adults around me.

The film was an American production, *The Battle of the Villa Fiorita*, starring Maureen O'Hara, Richard Todd, and Rossano Brazzi. It was shot in Italy. I was thirteen, I was making a movie, I was eating pasta in Italy; I simply could not have been happier.

After finishing *The Battle of the Villa Fiorita* and another film called *Cup Fever*, I was back in the United Kingdom, attending classes and going out on auditions again. One was for a stage production of *The Prime of Miss Jean Brodie*. It was going to be a huge show. Written by Muriel Spark and adapted by Jay Presson Allen, it was to be directed by Peter Wood and star Vanessa Redgrave.

My audition was awful. Truth be told, throughout my career my auditions almost always have been. I loathe them, and I think it shows—a shame, really, considering what I do for a living. At best, auditions are nearly tolerable. At worst, they can be exercises in extreme embarrassment. So I read for the part, badly, and, if not for Mrs. Allen's six-year-old daughter, I wouldn't have gotten the role. She had seen me in *The Battle of the Villa Fiorita* and had liked me. Apparently, she turned to Peter Wood and said something to the effect of, "Oh, isn't she wonderful. You must choose her."

Timing, luck and the goodness of people have, time and again, conspired to bring me through difficult moments in my life, and I've always been grateful.

The Prime of Miss Jean Brodie was a transformative experience for me—not a word I use lightly. Working night after night with Vanessa Redgrave, who to this day I consider one of the finest actors I've ever seen, was a revelation. We did eight shows a week, including two matinees, and she seemed to bring something new to each performance. Actors can be like that; some are just born to it. Their emotional life exists right beneath the surface. It never needs to be forced out or fought for. If anything, it is a struggle to keep it in check, to stop it from always being seen and felt.

The show ran for four years, and I worked in it for the first two. There were nights when nothing went right, and others when it was just perfect. One evening, the lights came up for the cast's curtain call, and sitting in the front row was the Royal Family: the Queen, the Queen Mother, Prince Charles, Princess Anne, Prince Phillip, and the Princes Edward and Andrew. They were all applauding, thank God. It seemed that the Queen Mum had been asked what she would like to do for her birthday, and she had said she wanted to see the play that had gotten all those wonderful reviews.

We toured throughout England, playing packed houses and enjoying the camaraderie that comes from being in a traveling troupe. I believe the best education a young actor can have is simply to work. Classes are useful, and for theatre, essential for learning technique. But for me, having to deliver the work when it matters is the best kind of school. *The Prime of Miss Jean Brodie* was my acting education.

A year and a half into the run, we learned that Vanessa had been cast in the film adaptation of *Camelot* and would be leaving the show. Called into her dressing room one night after a performance, I arrived pouting and plopped down on the well-worn couch opposite her makeup chair. Vanessa had just washed her face. She smiled into the mirror when she saw me. There was still eyeliner around her eyes, and some had smudged and run, making two long, black teardrops down her cheeks.

"Olivia, my love, how are we?" she said into the mirror, with a knowing maternal tone.

"Good . . . fine . . . I guess," I mumbled, not looking at her.

"Good," she replied.

There was a pause. I fidgeted, pulling my fingers, making the knuckles crack. Vanessa waited. Finally, I said, "You're leaving the show."

"Yes, I am."

"I'm happy for you." A fifteen-year-old's attempt at being passive-aggressive: I was disappointed that she was leaving *us* and jealous that she was going on to bigger and better things.

In the mirror, Vanessa Redgrave's aqua-blue eyes locked on mine. She had incredible eyes. There was a stillness to them, a pathos, as if they had glimpsed some inevitable tragic future. They seemed to take in everything and to understand it all.

"Come now, little one," she said after a time, "let's not have any of that." Though only in her thirties, she spoke with the authority of someone much older. "Now listen," she said, "you're a good girl and a fine little actress. If you can manage to keep your head straight and not let it change you, you'll do fine."

"What does that mean?" I said.

Her deep, exquisitely trained voice was measured and deliberate. "It means, my dear, not to worry. I have a feeling you'll be leaving the show, too, and soon."

Back in London, word was beginning to spread that an Italian director was in town, interviewing young actors for an adaptation of Shakespeare's *Romeo and Juliet*.

Part II

The Audition

Juliet: It's the defining role of my life, and most likely the reason you're reading this book. While it brought me fame—for whatever that's worth—and glamour, it also thrust me into a spotlight that, while intoxicating, was at times too bright and too revealing. It changed everything, and would define my life in ways I never could have imagined.

One thing is certain: Although the role brought me some terrible moments of grief and doubt and sadness, most of what I know about love and faith and joy, of the world and how I fit into it, I know because I played the part of Juliet.

But first, I had to get the part. Which brings me to 6566 Dean Street and my introduction to that wonderful, eccentric genius whose lifelong friendship I've treasured: Franco Zeffirelli.

Franco: I'm not sure where to begin. To say that he is the most talented person I've ever known feels, somehow, too small for him. I can hear him saying, "Oh, come now, Olivia *darling;* it's me, after all. You can do better. You *must* do better."

There has always been something operatic about Franco. He's grand, dramatic, and—like Florence, the Italian city-state where he was born—dignified and fiercely independent. What's more, whether at a dinner party, locking horns with someone over Italian politics, or thirty feet up on a camera crane about to get a shot, he's always in control.

He describes our first meeting in his wonderful autobiography, *Zeffirelli*. His story has a certain cinematic feel to it (you'll have to read his book for the details), but, with all due respect to the maestro, I think my version is more accurate.

In the summer of 1966, every actor in London was talking about Franco Zeffirelli and the casting of *Romeo & Juliet*. He had just directed Elizabeth Taylor and Richard Burton, two screen giants, in *Taming of the Shrew*. Now he was looking for two young unknowns to play the roles of a lifetime. I remember Miss Conti herself, coming into our class and making the announcement: "Girls, Franco Zeffirelli is looking for Juliet."

When I heard Zeffirelli's name, the strangest feeling rose up inside me: I *knew*. (I've since had these premonitions many times, but it's only recently that I've learned enough to take them seriously.) I *had* to audition.

Every other actress in every other play in the West End was also heading to north London to audition. Hundreds of other girls, from every school in London, were lining up at 6566 Dean Street. Clutching their copies of the four-hundred-year-old play, they were all reading for Juliet.

I was just one of those girls. And I was late. Sitting on the train, I had closed my eyes to lose myself in the soft *ch, ch, ch,* as it rolled over the tracks, and I'd missed the stop—typical. Arriving breathless and harried, I waited patiently at the back of the line. They were taking us in groups of five, and it was forty-five minutes before I reached the front. As I made my way up the stairs I was nervous but determined not to let the moment overwhelm me. Stepping into a large loft, I got my first glimpse of the volcanic presence that is Zeffirelli. He was directing a young actor in a scene from the play, but when we came in he stopped, looked over at us, and in his thick Italian accent said, *"Allora!* Everybody upstairs. Find a costume, put it on, come back down. *Fretta! Fretta!"*

Nervous and sweaty, we went upstairs. Reaching into bins, pulling heavy dresses off hangers, we did our best to ignore one another, locked as we were in our own private hells of anxiety and fear. There was only one dress left that fit me: a plain white dress very much like the one I ended up wearing in the potion scene in the film. I slipped it on.

"Oh God, let me do well," I thought as I looked at myself in a narrow full-length mirror. Then I pushed my hair in front of my shoulders and headed back downstairs.

We were to be paired with potential Romeos, interchanging partners as Franco saw fit. It was all very chaotic. Stylishly dressed Italian assistants were corralling actors into groups, using fast hand motions and broken English to get us all where they wanted us. I was standing quietly in a corner when Franco caught my eye. He steamrolled over with a young actor in tow and said, "You . . ."

"Olivia."

"Olivia, this is Leonard Whiting, I want you two to work together today." Franco stepped back, surveyed the two of us, said, *"Allora, molto bene,"* and strode off.

Leonard and I smiled at each other. Awkwardly, we shook hands. Then the actor who would play Romeo and the actress who would play Juliet went off to rehearse the balcony scene.

We liked each other immediately. I was a shy fifteen,

with long brown hair, a confusing Argentine accent, and a stubborn streak. He was seventeen, with a thick cockney accent and a brooding, vulnerable intensity. (Almost fifty years later, he still has impossibly green eyes—wonderful eyes, filled with kindness and caring, albeit now rimmed, like mine, with a few more lines of laughter and life.)

Our first rehearsal together was painfully awkward. I was uncomfortable with the famous balcony scene. It's about passion and falling in love, played with excitement and a sense of danger—a nightmare for a girl who knew nothing about boys, let alone love and passion. But we muddled through it, understanding maybe half of it, simply trying to get our tongues around the language. Then it was back downstairs to audition for Franco in front of the cameras—every audition was filmed, which made it all the more intimidating.

I think back on the pressure of that moment, on the desperate need I had to do well. There were so many beautiful, talented girls auditioning, and here I was. I had never been so nervous.

We began the scene:

But soft, what light through yonder window breaks?

Leonard was off to what I thought was a good start. He went on for a bit, and then it was my turn:

Ay me!

My first line; what a relief! A short line, to be sure, but at least I said it without fainting or falling over. Now Romeo again:

She speaks!
O, speak again, bright angel! for thou art
As glorious to this night, being o'er my head,
As is a winged messenger of heaven . . .

Rereading it now, I'm struck by the beauty of the language, the soaring analogy, and the emotion. Then, however, being fifteen and sick with nerves, I didn't have the foggiest idea what Leonard was going on about. What I did know was that the famous bit was next, and it was mine:

O Romeo, Romeo! Wherefore art thou Romeo?

Not bad, I thought; now, just keep going:

Deny thy father and refuse thy name;
Or, if thou wilt not, be but sworn my love,
And I'll no longer be a Capulet.

The man really did know how to turn a phrase, and I was getting swept up in his flowing words. Leonard and I were both moving fast, and the awkwardness and nerves were beginning to evaporate:

I am no pilot; yet, wert thou as far
As that vast shore wash'd with the farthest sea,
I would adventure for such merchandise.

Again, I had not the slightest idea what he was saying, but the feeling was there. Next came a big chunk for me. I breathed in and took the plunge:

Thou know'st the mask of night is on my face,
Else would a maiden blush bepaint my cheek
For that which thou hast heard me speak to-night . . .

About halfway through this twenty-two-line speech, I noticed Franco starting to fidget with something. I kept going:

In truth, fair Montague, I am too fond . . .

Tick!

Did something small just hit my face and bounce off?

I should have been more strange, I must confess . . .

Tick!

Something was hitting me on the cheek! I couldn't believe it; Franco was throwing little scrunched-up paper balls at me! I told myself to keep going:

But that thou overheard'st . . .

Tick!
. . . ere I was ware,
Tick!
My true love's passion . . .
Tick!

Oh my God, I thought, this is a nightmare! Who is this awful man? How could he be doing this to me? How dare he?

Somehow, I finished the speech. Leonard, panic in his eyes, came close to me for his lines:

Lady, by yonder blessed moon I swear
That tips with silver all these fruit-tree tops—

Back to me:

O, swear not by the moon, the inconstant moon,
Tick!
That monthly changes in her circled orb,
Tick!

THAT'S IT! Furious, I stopped the scene, threw my pages down, and turned on Franco, this terrible man who was embarrassing and sabotaging me. With tears in my eyes, shaking, I yelled, *"Would you stop!"*

The room went silent. Poor Leonard was rooted to the spot in terror. I stood glaring at Franco. He just stared at me for a long moment before his features softened. Then he smiled slowly and said, "Now, my darling, that was what I wanted to see. *Passion!*"

It became a weekly ritual to head to Dean Street and work with Franco. That first week, there might have been eight hundred girls and about as many boys. A couple of weeks later, it was down to a few hundred, then half that. Always Leonard and I were paired. I was, of course, thrilled to keep going back. Not only because I was in the running, doing well, and feeling confident, but also because I was seeing more and more of Franco's brilliance. I had, by then, developed something of a crush on him.

About a month after my first audition, I arrived at the

Dean Street loft and found that there were just three of us: Leonard, me, and a young actress with gorgeous, long blond hair. I felt the world might stop spinning. Three weeks before, Franco had asked me how I pictured Juliet. I'd said, "Oh, I see her as this ethereal, pale blond girl." And here she was, my last competitor.

The problem was that I was still having a hard time with the balcony scene. The intimacy conveyed by the language just didn't come easily to me. So it was a welcome surprise when Franco came over, took my hands, and said, "Well, darling, this is it. And I wanted to ask: Is there something else from the play you would like to do?"

There was: a monologue toward the end, in the scene where Juliet drinks the potion. A short piece, but I loved it. And, best of all, it would just be me.

When I told Franco, his eyebrows shot up and he took a deep breath. "Okay, darling," he said, "I'm going to Rome for three weeks. Learn the potion scene, and we'll see."

Traditionally, in the theater, the "potion monologue," as it's known, is what actresses playing Juliet were judged by. Franco had deliberately held off working on it during the auditions, thinking it might be too much and too soon for us. Nevertheless, I was determined to do it.

Memorizing has never come easily to me. I've always had a hard time just learning words. I need to connect them with an emotion, to feel what I'm saying. In Shakespeare, you almost can't find that emotion until you have the language locked away in your head. The poetry is what gets you there; the words are the road map to what the character is feeling. And for this scene those words came very fast and easily—one of the few times that has been true for me. There was something about it that felt natural, and in the end it only took an hour or so for me to get it down.

I was still performing in *Brodie*, and the girls in the play had made a deal: If you were about to audition for something, you could bring your audition piece in and show it to the group. We would give our reactions and offer feedback. So, after a Saturday matinee, a group of us gathered in one of the dressing rooms and I ran through the potion scene.

In the play, the monologue is around forty lines (in the final cut of the film it's much shorter) and builds to the moment when Juliet drinks the potion, imagines seeing the ghost of her cousin Tybalt, and collapses. I ran through the scene, and, just as when I was working on it by myself, the words poured out of me. The tears ran down my face as I thought about waking up in a tomb and seeing nothing but poor Tybalt, his body covered by his death shroud. I thought of Romeo never finding me, of love and death. I thought of silence and of being alone. Then, suddenly, it was done. I was lying on the floor, eyes closed, and all I heard was . . . silence.

"Oh God, they hate it," I thought. I opened my eyes and looked up.

One girl, I can't remember her name, was sitting on the arm of the couch, weeping. She wiped her eyes and smiled at me. A few others sat in stunned silence. Teresa, who was two years older, sat frozen, clutching the arm of her friend.

"Well? What did you think?" I asked. They told me it wasn't bad, but I knew it was better than that. I felt as if the scene were part of me; if I could just go deep inside myself and find a way of making the words real for Franco, I would be Juliet.

Typically, I've found, an actor does three auditions each time: First, there is how you play it at home, in rehearsal, before you step into the room. Then, there is how you actually give your audition, when it matters. And last, there is how you play it after the audition is over—usually in the parking lot outside or in the car on the way home. Sadly, for most actors, the reading you give last, when you are alone and there's no pressure, is the best. I had to fight my nerves and do the work I knew I could do, and I had to do it when it mattered.

Dean Street, two weeks later: a packed house. There were executives from the American studio Paramount Pictures. There was Franco, of course, with his assistants. Michael York, an established actor, was there as well. He was great friends with Franco, having played a role in *Taming of the Shrew*, and was set to play Tybalt in *Romeo & Juliet*.

Franco rushed over and said, "Olivia, darling, today is the day. Now listen, for this scene I want . . ."

"No, Franco," I said, "Just tell me where to stand. I want to do it my way for you."

"Well, darling, we are confident today, no? That's very good." Laughing, he turned to the assembled crowd and said, "Here is Olivia. She will be doing a monologue for us today."

A deep breath, a little prayer, and I began. When it was over, Franco found me behind the prop bed, crumpled up in a heap of tears, eyes closed and trembling.

"Don't worry, my little darling, don't worry," he said. He put his arms around me: "You are going to love Rome."

I knew then that I had won the part: I was going to be Juliet.

Romeo and Juliet
Go to the Movies

My dear mum, who had worked so hard and sacrificed so much, who had bundled up her two kids and left everything she had ever known for the promise of something better, was standing in the kitchen of our little house washing dishes when I told her I had just landed the part of Juliet.

"Oh, Livi," was all she said.

She took my hand and held it. We stood in silence for a long time. She was crying. I like to think that at that moment my mum felt that it had all been worth it. And that she was proud. There have been few moments in my life that have given me as much joy.

One of the conditions of getting the part was that I couldn't tell anyone I had it. Paramount Pictures was in the middle of negotiations to acquire the rights to the movie and wanted nothing leaked. So, whether it was in the dressing room above the *Brodie* stage, surrounded by all the girls who asked how my audition had gone—"Fine, I guess"—or with my friends down at the pub, I had to hold my tongue. No easy feat for a fifteen-year-old girl who felt as if she had just been crowned queen of the world.

A week or two after I had gotten the news, the intercom at the theatre where I was performing *Brodie* crackled out a call for me, "Miss Hussey, please come down to the backstage door." I rushed down the five flights of stairs and flung open the exit door behind the theatre.

Franco was standing in a pool of light. He was wearing an enormous fur-lined coat, with a cigarette hanging casually from his lips. Beside him stood a man who looked like a boxer who didn't mind losing: light brown hair brushed across a huge head; wide, thickset shoulders with what looked like a couple of sledgehammers hanging from them. But his smile was open, jolly, and without a trace of malice.

"Darling, I want you to meet Dyson Lovell," Franco said. "Now I want you and your Romeo to work with Dyson for a few weeks." And off Franco went, strolling into the night.

Dyson was a great friend of Franco's and would go on to produce his own films as well as work with Franco on multiple projects. His job now, though, was to work with Franco's two leads. Six hours a day, seven days a week he was to take us through Shakespeare's world: meaning and language, accents and rhythm, the monologues with their dreaded iambic pentameter.

The following Monday, I made my way to Dean Street— Franco had kept the loft space for rehearsals. Walking in, I saw Leonard. He had gotten the part—he was Romeo. I hadn't seen him for about a month. He gave me a timid hug and, smiling, said,

"Juliet, wherefore art thou, Juliet?"

His confident cockney accent always made me laugh, and his sweet humor banished all awkwardness. I was so happy it was him and that we would be working together. And work we did.

Dyson was a taskmaster. I don't think I've ever worked so hard in my life. We began by going through the whole text word by word and then, when we were done, we went through it again. We met with dialect coaches and voice teachers. We analyzed each scene. Always the emphasis was on the emotion: What are the characters feeling? How does that feeling inform their actions? Franco's simple instruction while he was gone was never to put technique before emotion. He had taken a risk in casting two age-appropriate actors for the roles; we were desperately inexperienced. But what we did have, in spades, was raw adolescent feeling—and that, I think, was what Franco was counting on.

Leonard struggled with his cockney, and I struggled with my shyness. We struggled together. It brought us closer, and I think that was also part of Franco's plan. Laughing and smoking cigarettes, Leonard and I came to know the text as well as each other.

One Sunday afternoon we decided to go see Franco's *Taming of the Shrew*, which had just been released in England. Its two stars, Richard Burton and Elizabeth Taylor, were, of course, household names. Their love affair had become the stuff of modern legend, and details of their lives were splashed across tabloids all over the world. (Years later, I would meet both, and believe me, they were indeed larger than life—more on them later.)

Leonard and I sat in the dark cinema. The movie began, and almost instantly we were overwhelmed. It just seemed so huge, so grand, packed with color and music—like all Zeffirelli's work, it was gorgeous to look at and listen to. Franco had come out of the Italian Opera and knew exactly how to fill the screen with sweeping pageantry and spectacle.

"What have I gotten myself into?" I thought.

Leonard took hold of my hand; his was as cold and clammy as mine. "Oh my God, Olivia," he said.

"Leonard," I said, "I think this is going to be a big deal."

I've always had a knack for understatement. Three weeks later, Paramount Pictures acquired the rights to produce and distribute *Romeo & Juliet*. On March 19, reporters gathered from all over the world, and at a lavish press conference Franco announced that he had his two star-crossed lovers.

The following weeks were a blur of interviews and photo shoots. There was a spread in *Life* magazine and newspaper coverage from Germany to Southeast Asia. When we weren't shut away in the Dean Street loft working, Leonard and I were sitting down to talk about what it felt like to be the two most famous lovers in the world. We hadn't shot a single frame of the movie. We hadn't even met the rest of the cast.

A Hollywood studio meant big business, and big business meant big money. This was reflected not only in the endless photo shoots and TV interviews but also in the subtle and growing pressures we both felt. For instance, the studio felt that there was, perhaps, a bit too much Juliet to their new Juliet and that, maybe, with their help, of course, I might want to slim down a bit. Now, I have never really had a slim body type. It's more, shall we say, buxom—or, rather, curvy. As Sophia Loren once said, "Everything you see I owe to pasta." Well, that's me: "Plump!" as my mum would say, and early on I never really had any problem with that. However, now somebody did have an issue with it, and calls were made.

I was sent to a "specialist" who, after a curt and not very thorough exam, prescribed me a plastic bottle of little white pills. They were appetite suppressers. I was to take two every morning and another two right before going to bed.

After three days I was shaking. After a week I was insanely hyper and strung out. It was my little mum who put a stop this madness.

I was fifteen; I couldn't imagine telling the studio they were crazy, that their pills were making me sick. But my mum had no problem with it. What happens when an "unstoppable force meets an immovable object"? Well, if that object is a single mother with a low center of gravity and fierce Latin maternal instinct, then the unstoppable force doesn't stand a chance. My mum took one look at the state I was in and announced, "They will have to take you just as you are, or not at all!" After flushing the pills down the toilet, she stormed into the living room and picked up the phone. She called the film's producer, John Brabourne. "My daughter is finished taking these hateful little pills," she roared. "You tell whoever it is that if they ever go behind my back again and try to force my little girl into doing something, they can go and find a new Juliet!" *Crack!* I can still hear the sound of the receiver as my mum slammed it down.

No more "specialists." I was to be my happy, healthy self again. However, a seed had been planted. I began to hate my body, and this warped body image would, in time, turn into a compulsion. Where once I saw food as a great joy, I now began to see it as the enemy.

Italy

Verdi said, "You may have the universe if I may have Italy." My love of Italy began in the summer of 1967. It's an excessively sentimental love, shaped in no small part by my experiences while filming *Romeo & Juliet*.

Even now, fifty years later, I can taste the Tuscan air. The countryside was a postcard picture of rolling hills. Like open ocean swells except deep green and yellow, they stretched out as far as I could see. Here and there little thumb smudges of brownish orange looked pushed into the tops of hills. Seen closer, the smudges took form: terracotta roofs packed around a church spire. Little medieval towns. This was the world of Romeo and Juliet, come to life just as I imagined it.

But Tuscany was yet to come. Now we were driving from Rome to Franco's villa along the Appian Way. My first night in Italy had been a disaster. The studio had booked me in a *pensione*. These small hotels are all over Italy. Like off-the-highway motels in America, they offer a bed, a cheap rate, and the promise that you can leave after a night. I took one look at my room and burst into tears.

Panicked that their Juliet might turn right around and head for home, the studio arranged for me to move to Franco's villa.

There were three of us in the car: me, the driver, and Miss Mayfair, my long-suffering, soon-to-be-gone chaperone.

Poor Miss Mayfair, seventy-five years old and hopelessly out of her depth. Everything about her was austere, a stereotype of moral rectitude. She was built thick and low to the ground. She had coal-black hair, streaked with gray, that she pulled back mercilessly and tied into a tight knot that never moved. Her eyes were close-set and always judgmental. Her lipless, tightly drawn mouth hadn't cracked a smile since before the Battle of the Somme. As you can tell, I had my issues with Miss Mayfair.

She had been with me since *The Battle of the Villa Fiorita*. Initially, because of her age, she had been hesitant to take on this new challenge, but I believe she saw it as her responsibility to protect me. Like a lone guardian standing at the gates, she would fight to hold back the onrushing enemy. That enemy, as she saw it, was the swinging 1960s, coming to engulf sweet, shy teenage girls in a miasma of marijuana smoke and free love.

Alas, it would prove to be too much for dear Miss Mayfair. It didn't help that her sweet, shy teenager was budding into a little diva. I saw my chaperone as this looming dark cloud—or rather, as a judgmental shadow that snored (we would come to share a hotel room). I was intensely focused on myself and my work, which made me a handful, I suppose.

When we drove up to the villa, Franco took me in his arms and spun me around, exclaiming, "My darling Juliet, she has arrived!" Putting me down, he gave one curt sideways look at Miss Mayfair and rolled his eyes. "Well, darling," he said, turning back to me and bookending my cheeks with his hands. "To work!" And he strutted off.

So, there I was, standing alone in the sun-drenched Roman countryside, now working for this mad Italian director and about to take on the role of a lifetime. I was nervous, to be sure, but I was also excited. This is what I'd wanted, and I was determined to work as hard as anybody there.

At Franco's villa I found a confusion of accents amid organized chaos. No people do anarchy quite like the Italians, to whom work isn't really being done, things aren't really being said, and life isn't really being lived unless accompanied by wild, dramatic hand gestures; furious, unintelligible yelling; and gallons and gallons of espresso. Every Italian knows that the trains need to run on time but also knows that things run better when fueled with a bit of passion and madness.

Filming had begun. Fight scenes were being shot some distance away, in a small Tuscan town called Bagno Vignoni. Meanwhile, preparations for the rest of the shoot were under way both at Franco's villa and at the legendary Cinecittà Studios, also close to Rome. Conducting all of this was, of course, Franco. Most alive in the heart of the chaos, he was the hub around which everything turned.

Cinecittà Studios

Cinecittà Studios looked exactly like what you'd want a movie studio to look like. Built as a monument to Italian fascism, it was opened in 1937 by Mussolini and his son Vittorio. After World War II, its huge lot was used as a refugee camp, housing something on the order of three thousand displaced people. In the 1960s, it was by turns grand and gaudy, bumptious and prosaic. An ancient Roman standing on its main lot would have felt right at home with its massive scale and its functional design. I thought it was magical.

The entrance was (and still is) a wonderful art deco I that made you feel as if you were driving straight into a movie; it seemed to be made out of celluloid. *Ben-Hur* and *Cleopatra* were shot there, and the magnificent set for *Gangs of New York* is still there and open to the public. But it was Fellini who, with his films *La Dolce Vita*, *Satyricon*, and later *Casanova*, cemented the reputation of the studio, dubbed "Hollywood on the Tiber," as the center of Italian cinema.

Now, Zeffirelli had come. *Romeo and Juliet*'s production would be huge and would require a legion of men and women to mount it. Battalions of hard-faced carpenters; platoons of camera, sound, and lighting men; squads of film veterans for the prop department, the stunt department, the hair and makeup department; for catering and driving, for logistics and organization. The enlisted rank and file who do the heavy lifting and never get the glory. They mustered, now, on Cinecittà Studios' massive lots and soundstages under the watchful gaze of their officers, the assistant director, the second assistant director, the gaffer, the key grip, the prop master, director of photography. And all overseen by the Generalissimo himself: Zeffirelli. It has always amazed me, the army of talented people that has to come together to make a film.

Temper, Temper

Past a lime-green steel door and down a twisting flight of concrete steps, you arrived at the basement floor of the Cinecittà Studios wardrobe department. Used as an air raid shelter during the war, the huge room felt cool and safe. Now it was the province of Danilo Donati and his sumptuous universe of costumes. God, the man was a genius, and I loved him. He would go on to win an Oscar® for his work on the film.

A small, round man with a huge, life-affirming passion, Danilo was bursting with talent, vision, and, more often than not, his favorite cream-filled pastries. He saw costume design as an art and brought an artist's mentality to it. From perfectly tailored satin cotehardies (long, buttoned, torso-hugging unisex garments) to the deliciously named wimples, every piece was one of a kind and gorgeous.

One day I was standing on a raised platform in Danilo's studio, being fitted for the dress I was to wear during the scene at the Capulet Ball, when Franco came downstairs. Tutting and grunting, he seemed furious; blowing smoke from his cigarette out his nose, he looked like a bull breathing through an early morning mist. Danilo was stitching pieces of fabric to the dress. I was standing motionless as he pinned and sewed.

Franco began to yell: "No! No! No! *Che cosa e questo? Questo non si puo andare qui.*" He grabbed a piece of fabric and tore it off the dress.

"Guarda come una puttana!"

Now, *puttana* was a word I knew; Franco was saying the dress made me look like a whore.

My God, I thought, what is happening? Here was Franco's temper, sudden and volcanic. I would come to know it well, and know to stay away from him when he was in it.

Danilo, who was no delicate flower himself and who, rightly, felt his life and his work demanded respect, began to give as good as he was getting.

"Non posso lavorare con vi!" ("I cannot work with you!") he bellowed. *"Sei un pazo!"* ("You are a lunatic!")

Today, I can close my eyes and remember, with startling clarity, standing between these two men as they screamed Italian obscenities at each other and tore away pieces of fabric from what I thought was a perfectly beautiful dress.

A sleeve gone! More yelling. My bodice pulled off! More yelling. Deciding, I suppose, that their fight required better acoustics, they exited, still locked in furious combat. I was left standing in my slip, pieces of the dress scattered on the floor around me. After three minutes of standing, frozen, I realized that the two gladiators were most likely not coming back. I slipped off the stand, had a good little cry, got dressed, and tiptoed out to find my lunch.

Later, I would come to realize that these fights, though huge and scary, were simply part of how the film shoot would run. These were passionate, temperamental men who lived and died for their art, and defended it at all costs.

Miss Mayfair and a Very Sick Girl

Because of the shooting schedule, I had about a month in Italy before my first day of work. I was working with a wonderful new speech and dialect coach brought in from London, Jeannie Scott. We would spend five hours together each morning, going over my lines. There were always reporters on set, so later Leonard and I would be trotted out for a spate of interviews and photos. And, of course, there were more harrowing dress fittings. Leonard had already begun filming, and every night we would talk on the phone. We gossiped and giggled. We whispered about how nervous we both were and how incredible and scary Franco could be.

Miss Mayfair and I were moved closer to the studio, to the Parco dei Principi Hotel in Rome. Even though I'd not yet begun filming my scenes, I was still working as hard as I could to prepare. I had memorized not only my part but the entire text—to this day, I can recite all of Friar Laurence's lines. Every morning I'd wake up and go over all of my scenes in bed.

Not that I did much sleeping those first few weeks. It hadn't taken long for Miss Mayfair's snoring to become something of a running joke among the crew; imitations of her low bass could be heard all over the studio lot. We shared a room, two twin beds not more than three feet apart, and her rumbling snore was an all-night siege on my senses. This went on until Franco noticed large dark circles forming under my eyes, at which point my chaperone was bundled up and rather unceremoniously moved. All of a sudden, and shockingly for Miss Mayfair, her nighttime duties were reduced to climbing three flights of steps, making sure I had locked my door, and saying good night. I can still hear the sounds of her slippered feet shuffling away and her bracelets clanking like the chains that Dickens wrapped around the ghost of Jacob Marley. Poor woman.

Miss Mayfair's snoring turned out to be the least of it. Two days before my first take, the pain began: severe cramping and sudden sharp stabs, starting from the lower left side of my stomach, lightning bolts of pain flashing through my whole body. I had always had a rumbling appendicitis. Brought on by stress, overexertion, or too much food, it had been a constant, albeit low-intensity irritation in my life. Now, it struck like a thunderclap. I was doubled over in pain, sweat pouring off me.

Franco was frantic. I remember lying in bed with a fever while worried shapes moved around me.

"I want her appendix out!" I heard him yelling. "We must not delay!"

A specialist was brought in from Rome, Doctor Silvestri, a very well-known American doctor. After his examination, he agreed with Franco: "We need to operate."

The thought of surgery, of removing my appendix, terrified me. Not only was I far from home and alone, but what about the film? How long would my recovery take? I had worked so hard, and I was so excited to be there. I thought about all the people on the crew, about their jobs; they were all counting on me. I thought of Franco and the shame of letting him down. I thought about my mum, holding my hand in our kitchen.

After a terrible night of self-recrimination and pain, I woke up feeling better. Not great, mind you—the cramping was still awful—but I could stand and eat a little. By the afternoon, my color was a bit more human. I was dead set on curing myself. I imagined standing on set, hearing Franco yell, "Action," and saying my first line. At seven o'clock I saw Doctor Silvestri again. He pushed and poked, then raised his head and said, "Incredible."

With that, the shoot was back on. Whether the problem had been stress, exhaustion, or too much focaccia I didn't know. All I cared about was that I was finally well enough to begin. I could be Juliet.

One-Take Hussey

On the twenty-sixth of April 1967, I arrived at Bagno Vignoni for my first day of shooting. The small town nestled in the Tuscan hillside had been invaded by Franco's enormous cast and crew. Some were living in the town, finding it easier simply to wake up, drink an espresso, and start working. Most of the boys in the cast were there, having a fine old time staying up late, working on the fight scenes, and generally being young in Italy.

Being on a huge film set can be exhilarating. All the people working together, focused on a single goal. A bubble forms, separating you from the wider world. Inevitably, cliques form and rumors spread, intrigue abounds. Friendships start and lifelong feuds are born. Future husbands meet future wives, and fleets of lonely ships pass one another in the night. You become, as it were, a family (a strange, dysfunctional one to be sure, but a family). You are a group of like-minded people coming together and taking on this massive project. It's so much fun.

My scene was simple: run down the stairs at Friar Laurence's church, say my line, and run off. It's the scene in which Juliet first meets Lord Paris. Most important for me was that I'd be wearing my favorite dress: a floor-length green velvet gown with gold lace down the sleeves. I loved the color and thought it made me look thin and my chest small.

The scene also called for me to be out of breath. So, while the crew set up, I ran laps around the small stone church. When the crew was ready, I came in out of breath and ready to go. Franco began to give me direction but, in what would become our modus operandi, I stopped him and said, "Why not just let me do it my way, and if you don't like it you can tell me?"

"Fine," he said, I could tell he was annoyed. "Just come down the stairs to here, say your line, and leave that way."

I took my mark and waited.

"*Pronto,*" Franco called from behind the monitor. "*AZIONE!*"

I bolted down the stairs, a streak of green and gold, mumbled at Lord Paris, and ran out.

"*Taglio! Stampa.*" ("Cut! Print it.")

For the rest of the shoot, one of Franco's favorite names for me was "One-take Hussey." I loved it.

Boobs O'Mina

"But Franco, I can't breathe in it! And it pushes my boobs up so high!"

"Darling, that is the point, after all."

"No, I want to look thin!"

"Olivia, you are a woman. Mustn't be afraid to look like one."

Franco and I were standing in a small, windowless dressing room somewhere deep inside Cinecittà Studios. Between us hung my Dreaded Bodice. Designed by Danilo, it had become a staple of my wardrobe and the bane of my existence. It was so tight that in between takes the laces running down the back had to be untied simply to allow me to breathe. The first time I stepped into the damn thing, it became the subject of a running argument with Franco. "It makes me look fat!" I would yell.

"Darling, no, no . . . *Voluptuous* is the word. You are beautiful. And my Juliet will break a million hearts."

"My chest, it's . . . it's . . . so embarrassing."

Franco would take my hands and smile sweetly.

"Oh, my little Boobs O'Mina," he would say, and walk out.

I hated the name. Franco coined it two weeks into the shoot. To call me onto the set he would use a bullhorn: "BOOBS O'MINA! BOOBS O'MINA!"

At the time, flat-chested was in fashion. Tall, flat-chested models like Twiggy and short, flat-chested ones like Edie Sedgwick were setting the standard. But I was short and top-heavy: voluptuous.

"BOOBS O'MINA!"

Mortified, I'd skulk onto the set, feeling as though everyone was staring at me.

"BOOBS O'MINA!"

Eventually, I was just mad. I thought, I don't care if everyone is looking at my chest, let them look. I would glare Franco's way.

"BOOBS O'MINA!" A few days later, I thought, So I have boobs? What's the big deal?

Then I got it. The nude scene! Leonard and I in bed. It was coming up. Franco suspected how nervous I was. He had been preparing me, chipping away at my shyness.

Clever man. By constantly calling attention to my body, he had drained away my embarrassment. Shock therapy, to be sure, and by today's standards not very PC. However, it worked for me. Franco always knew how far he could push me, and, by extension, how to get the best work out of me. We were of course very different people, but I like to flatter myself that at some deep level we understood each other, and that made us wonderful collaborators.

Late Nights

When a movie works, it can look effortless to the viewer. Performances seem so natural. You barely notice the camera work, the lighting, and the editing. The soundtrack swells right when it should to enhance the emotion of the action. It can all seem so simple, as though the movie could not have been made any other way. The reality is far different.

It all starts as an empty space. From the writer's blank page to a director's and editor's sifting through hours of shot film, a movie is made by making choices. Who should I cast? How do these people dress? What kind of mood does this melody evoke? How should I shoot this scene? What does this character say next? Do I cut to a close-up here? Every detail is a choice.

Think about your favorite movie. Imagine making it. You start with nothing, an empty soundstage. Now, bring it to life.

Romeo & Juliet was made by a group of the most talented people I have ever known. Having the opportunity to see these people work, to live with and come to know them as I did, was a gift beyond all measure. The days could be hard; I was so concentrated on my performance, so focused on the work I had to do, that it was impossible to take in what was happening around me. So it was only during the nights, after the days' shoots, that I got to open up and take it all in. No matter how tired I was, I would force myself to stay up and keep my seat at the adults' table.

After a long day of shooting that lasted deep into the night, Franco would hold court around a long, dark table in the rustic red-brick kitchen of his villa. His dinners were a carnival of laughter and conversation. Amid heaping bowls of amatriciana and puttanesca pasta, accompanied by the popping of corks, I listened as stories were told and told again, and filthy jokes, whispered between slow pulls of a cigarette, set the table roaring. I joined in singing songs, full-throated, at top volume. For me, these were magic nights, shot through with stardust.

What a raconteur Franco was! I remember him, arms outstretched like a symphony conductor, telling a particularly dirty story involving an Italian film actor. At the climax of his story—in which the actor was caught in a hotel lobby with his pants around his ankles—everyone at the table, including myself, exploded with laughter. Franco instantly focused his eyes on me.

"You speak Italian now?" he asked, raising an eyebrow.

Demurely, I answered, "Why, yes, Franco, of course I do."

For weeks, I had been using my native Spanish to fill in gaps and make translations of the Italian swirling around me. The two languages have so much in common, including a lexical similarity, that I found Italian came easily to me.

"Well, well, well. I must watch what I say from now on," Franco said. I could tell he was impressed.

* * *

Another night has stayed with me all these years. Inky black clouds had unfurled over Bagno Vignoni, blocking out the sun and threatening rain for the first time during our shoot. We abandoned filming and moved indoors.

By late afternoon, the darkening sky opened up and a light summer rain began to fall. I found myself in the lobby with Franco, Nino Rota, and our hotel's small upright piano. Nino was sitting next to me on the couch, hands folded in his lap, back straight. He was the very picture of calmness, like the Buddha beneath the Bodhi Tree. Franco, by contrast, was all arms and energy. Leaning in across the low table, he was trying to describe the music he wanted for part of the score.

Try to describe a song or a piece of music without using the melody or even naming the genre. Really difficult. Franco knew how he wanted the music to make the audience feel, what sort of mood it should evoke, but he was frustrated trying to put that into words.

Nino listened patiently as Franco became more exasperated. Finally, after what felt like a lifetime, Nino walked over and sat down at the piano. He played four notes.

"That's it!" cried Franco. "That's what I'm *feeling*."

Nino smiled and looked at Franco. "I'm happy you like it." He turned, looked at me, and winked. Magic.

Those four notes became the love theme in the film. Later, arranged by Henry Mancini and titled "A Time for Us," it would reach number one on the U.S. billboard charts.

Today I look back at my long life and am astounded by the people I have met, worked with, and, regretfully, in some cases taken for granted. The sixteen-year-old me knew Nino as the soft-spoken, always-smiling gentleman who played the piano beautifully. He was those things, of course, but what my younger self could not have known was that Nino had been a child prodigy in Milan, writing his first piece for an orchestra at age eleven; that in his career he would write the scores to more than 150 films, winning the Oscar for *The Godfather: Part II*. He wrote operas, string concertos, and ballet music. He was close friends with Fellini and director of the liceo musicale in Bari, where he taught for thirty years. Acclaimed as one of the finest and most prodigious composers of his generation, Nino was a great artist—but I knew none of this. Not that knowing would have mattered much as I laughed with him in the hotel that evening.

Nino could be quite funny. One night, working on music for the ball scene where Romeo and Juliet first meet, he was, again, sitting at the piano going through a beautiful piece of music. Franco, thrilled with what he was hearing, hovered just behind Nino with his eyes closed. However, something was nagging at Nino. He kept saying that the music seemed familiar and he was worried that, perhaps, this was an older piece of music that he was unconsciously replaying. Apparently, as Nino explained, this happened a lot to composers.

"I know I have heard this before," he kept repeating, "Someone *must* have written this a long time ago."

The hunt was on. People were dispatched to search for the copyright. It turned out that the piece did exist. It had been written by a young composer many years before. The name on the copyright was Nino Rota.

Nino had completely forgotten having written the music. When told that he had, he smiled, a hand-caught-in-the-cookie-jar kind of smile, and nodded to himself. "Well," he said, "I always loved his early work."

What a wonderful man.

Was There Anything Between Romeo and Juliet Offscreen?

Fifty years after making the movie, I still get this question. The simple answer is yes, but no. Not so simple, I know, but the truth almost never is, is it? Leonard and I shared an incredible experience. We were young and at the heart of something so huge and overwhelming that, naturally, an intimacy grew between us.

During the filming, it was all long telephone conversations, hand-holding, and some awkward adolescent kissing. I needed Leonard then, if only because he was the only other person who understood what it was like to be at the center of that mad circus. Also, we were cast as young lovers, *the* young lovers, and the romance of that was intoxicating.

We dated for a bit after the movie wrapped because, I think, we felt we had to. I remember we fought all the time. I loved Leonard and still do, but we were always meant to be just great friends.

This is not to say that I didn't have an absolute blast making *Romeo & Juliet*.

Roman Holiday

When I was young, I loved to party. I loved to have a few gin and tonics and dance the night away. During my days off, I would drive into Rome with Dorino, Franco's longtime personal assistant. We would head to a disco—it was the '60s, after all. Dorino was too cute. He was petite, like a delicate little bird, and always smiling or laughing. You can spot him in the film during Mercutio's Queen Mab speech, standing and laughing in the background. We always had a fabulous time together.

Franco was strict with Leonard and me during the shoot. He wanted a very particular image of us presented to the public: that of a pair of pure, innocent kids. So when photos of me dancing wildly, clearly a tiny bit intoxicated, found their way to him he was none too pleased.

Standing in Franco's bedroom one afternoon after a weekend in Rome, I was dreading the scene I expected. Franco took out an eight-by-ten envelope and began to lay out its contents on the bed. He had worked out an understanding with the Italian paparazzi: any pictures of his young lovers out on the town would come to him first.

"Now, Olivia, darling, this is not good," he said, laying out another black-and-white shot of me doing a good impersonation of a whirling dervish.

"Oh, Franco, I like this one!" I exclaimed. "Look at how skinny my arms look!"

"Darling, you are my Juliet! You can't be seen out dancing!"

"No! I'm Olivia, and I love to party!"

Franco just looked at me and started to laugh. In the end, what could he do? I was sixteen. I was working long, hard hours. Of course I needed to let my hair down from time to time. And Rome could be so much fun . . .

Eleven-thirty on a warm Thursday night found me speeding past the Spanish Steps and down Via del Corso on the back of a pea-green scooter. I had my arms wrapped around one of my new favorite people, John McEnery. He was playing Mercutio in the film, and I thought he was doing it brilliantly. I used to sneak onto the set when he was working and stand in awe as he thundered away. We had become friends late in the shoot, in part because I was intimidated both by his intensity and by how good I thought he was. Once I got past my shyness, though, we became good friends.

Following the scooter in a car was the actor Bruce Robinson, who was playing Benvolio. Bruce and I had gotten along right from the start of filming. He was a wonderful man.

The three of us had begun our night at a trattoria in the heart of the city. The boys drank wine and told stories while I sat smiling and soaking it all in. This was a life I had always dreamed of: Rome, the Eternal City, brimming with life; dinner with two handsome actors talking shop; and me, a part of it all.

Later, based on some questionable information, the three

of us went in search of a place to dance. Apparently, there was a disco that overlooked the whole city and, best of all, it was open all night. John and I took to the Vespa we had "borrowed" from the villa, and Bruce followed in the car. Making our way up the Esquiline Hill, we would stop and smoke cigarettes, ask for directions, or just laugh. No luck, so off we would go, up another one of Rome's famous hills. For the better part of the night we searched, carousing up and down thousand-year-old streets. We never found our fabled disco, but that was just fine by me. The evening was wild and special and, to me, perfect.

Meanwhile, Back on the Balcony

A few months into filming, some things had changed. Gone was Leonard's and my teenage fling; flirting took energy, and I had too much work and too little time. Plus, Leonard was busy with a plan that, as far as I could tell, involved dating every Italian girl between the ages of eighteen and thirty-five. We found that we worked best together when we dropped all the mushy teenage stuff and concentrated on our roles. Gone, too, was Miss Mayfair, my chaperone. Back in England, she was giving interviews to the press saying that I was difficult and something of a diva. Who knows, maybe I was.

Alas, for all these changes, the balcony scene and my struggles with it remained, frustratingly, the same. I'd never been comfortable with all the kissing and hugging, all the high emotion the scene called for. Worse still, now there were the camera, the lights, and a crew of 150 to contend with.

Franco had been scouting for months, trying to find the perfect location for the scene. After driving hundreds of miles, crisscrossing the Tuscan countryside, he had finally settled on a beautiful sloping hillside with an ancient wall running along its crest. Ideal for Romeo's ecstatic climb as well as his love-fueled farewell dash, the spot also contained many of the other elements that Franco wanted. The only drawback: There was not a balcony in sight. Never one to be thwarted by the inconveniences of real life, Franco simply had an entire plaster balcony built, along with a mock bedroom into which I would retreat. The set was magnificent; now, if only my performance could match it.

We shot during the nights, falling into our beds just before dawn and only after Pasqualino De Santis, our cinematographer, told Franco we looked too exhausted to continue. It was grueling work, and after two weeks of take after take Leonard and I were spent.

Poor Leonard, all that climbing had left him bruised and battered. What's more, on reaching the top he would come face-to-face with me. And I do mean face-to-face. Knocked heads, bloody noses, and bruised lips—how could kissing be this much work? We were trying to play—to live—one of the most romantic, most beautiful scenes ever written and we felt like a couple of bobblehead kids play-acting. Again and again, Franco would say, "I don't know my darlings, I think there is a little more in there." Later, Serena, our wonderful continuity lady, came over to me and said, "You know, Franco loved every take; he just wants it to be perfect." So did I.

Nobody pushed harder or demanded more of me than myself. If I felt I could do better, I would say so. Through bloodshot eyes, I would ask Franco for one more take. I desperately wanted to please him as well as myself.

Occasionally, the shooting of another scene would interrupt this work. I can't tell you how disorienting and emotionally draining it is to stab yourself to death on Wednesday morning, only to have to explode with life and fall madly in love on Thursday afternoon.

Late one night after a marathon of takes, Leonard and I decided we had had enough. Telling no one, we climbed into his little rented Fiat 500, pointed it in the direction of the nearest coast, and drove. Two and half hours later, we checked ourselves into a cheap *pensione* a short walk from the beach, bought three bottles of red wine, and headed for the water. Romeo and Juliet were playing hooky. Free of the expectations, the pressures, and the grinding schedule, we were just a couple of kids doing something we shouldn't.

We ran down the beach, carrying our shoes and the wine. We laughed at nothing, simply because we could and because no one was watching us. We cried our eyes out. We got good and drunk. We made out.

Actors

John McEnery was sick. He had pneumonia that caused one of his lungs to collapse. Arrangements were made to fly him back to London for treatment, but John insisted that he would not be going anywhere until he had finished shooting his final scene. Ironically, the scene was his death duel, where Tybalt—Michael York—stabs him and he falls down the steps of the town square.

I couldn't believe that John was doing the scene. In the days leading up to it he could barley stand. It is a testament to the kind of actor—the kind of man—he was that on the day of filming he was there in costume and ready to go. Actors can be fickle. They can be big, immature babies who never see beyond their own narcissism. That said, there is nevertheless something heroic in the lengths to which the good ones will go to get their work done. You can dangle them off the side of a building. You can yell at them, shoot them with rubber bullets, set them on fire, and generally kick them around. You can work them until four in the morning with nothing but the promise that the next take will be *the one*. You can tell them to swim across an icy cold river that may or may not be crawling with alligators (true story). And they will soldier on if they feel it is worth it for the project—and, of course, if they look good doing it.

So John did his scene—he was incredible—and was flown home to recuperate.

Meanwhile, for me the days blurred and bent into one another. It was as if I were living in two worlds, each inhabited by an identical cast of characters. The first was this make-believe wonder-world where everything was alive in "Words, words, words," the world of Shakespeare: high language, some of the most beautiful ever written, full of passion and meaning—set to a soundtrack of heavy, draped gowns swooshing across marble floors.

The other world was Franco's villa, no less remarkable for being real. It was at the villa that I first met Laurence Olivier, spent a marvelous evening chatting with the stunning Ingrid Bergman, and was beguiled by the Italian actress Monica Vitti. I ate dinner next to Jane Fonda and her then-husband, director Roger Vadim, who were filming *Barbarella* one stage over from us on the Cinecittà lot.

Milo O'Shea, Friar Laurence in *Romeo & Juliet* and one of my favorite dinner companions, was also in *Barbarella*. I remember him on the lot, constantly having to go back and forth between soundstages, changing costumes at an awkward jog. He was such a sweet man, and a fine actor. He always made me laugh.

At one of Franco's dinners, I was hit on by Paul Hardwick, who played Lord Capulet. Well, when I say "hit on," I mean he got drunk and said, "Frankly, Olivia, I would just love to fuck you," in front of Sir Laurence, Dame Maggie Smith, and Robert Stephens. Franco quickly hustled him from the room.

Acting

O n the whole, I would say that I can look back on 60 percent of the work I've done and say, You know what? I wasn't terrible in that. Sixty percent. And I'm proud of that number!

The camera captures everything. Every look, every nuance, every thought, whether it springs from a conscious choice or is simply there, welling up from the person you are. The camera sees it and grabs it and holds on to it forever. Some of the things it catches can drive an actor mad. What was I thinking there, you wonder. More frequently, you say to yourself, Oh God, you know what would have worked great there? At other times, though—and these are precious—the camera captures your perfect, authentic moment.

I have two such moments from *Romeo & Juliet* that have stayed with me; they are my favorites, and I think I know why. So much of what made the movie work was the fact that Leonard and I were so young. Speaking for myself—although I think Leonard would say the same thing about himself and Romeo—I had no problem understanding what Juliet was going through. Love: mad, crazy, wholehearted love. Confusing. Overwhelming. Selfish. Dumb. It all came naturally to me, young and innocent as I was.

During the ball scene, as Romeo and I moved around a circle of people, getting closer and closer to each other, it was so natural, so obvious, to look up at the older lady who was blocking my way and, when she gave me a rather snotty look, to think, Well, you may be tall and pretty, but I have love!

Then I looked away and another thought hit me: Besides, you're not really all that pretty. And I gave her my best evil eye.

Franco loved it. He loved it because it was real.

The other moment that means a lot to me is during the balcony scene. We had done it so many times, but Franco wanted one more little close-up, so back up we went. Off camera, Romeo says,

O, wilt thou leave me so unsatisfied?

I thought, Sex! But I said,

What satisfaction canst thou have to-night?

A beat as I waited for his answer, which was,

The exchange of thy love's faithful vow for mine.

Oh, thank God, I can relax, I thought, bless him. And I lifted my hand.

Small things, I know. But real little reactions—human reactions. I love them. They were born in the heart of a wide-eyed, innocent sixteen-year-old girl, and when I watch the film or think back on those two moments I remember what that girl was like and what she was feeling. And I can't help but cry just a little.

Live, to the World

In the summer of 1967, the BBC planned a huge, live TV broadcast. Various kinds of segments from nineteen countries would go out via satellite around the world. It was called *Our World*, and nothing like it had ever been done before. It was decided that something from *Romeo & Juliet* would be included. After some debate, Franco decided that the simplest thing would be to restage the wedding scene. So, on June 25, there—along with Pablo Picasso, Maria Callas, and the Beatles—I was.

I say "I," but of course it wasn't just me. Cut to: Leonard, Milo, and me, standing on our marks with sweaty palms and dry mouths, in front of an estimated 400 million people waiting to watch Franco take us through our small scene. At eleven minutes past ten the light on the BBC camera turned red, and Franco began to do what Franco did best: take over. He had brought in only a fraction of our crew for this re-creation, but in most other ways it was true to how we'd worked for the past four months. Yet, because Franco knew the camera was on him, the cheeky devil did command us a bit more than he otherwise would have.

He moved us through the blocking of the scene, all the while talking about what he wanted, what the scene was really about, and how best to achieve it. When he was directing, he would always speak to Leonard and me as adults; I loved that.

I remember standing in one of the church cloisters, waiting for the signal to come in.

"AZIONE!"

I was so nervous that I rushed in, flying right past my pre-arranged mark, and immediately began my lines. Franco, with a little smile on his face, stopped the scene and gently pulled me back to my mark.

Not too long ago my oldest son, Alex, sent me a link to the broadcast. There it was, shot fifty years ago in grainy black-and-white. Because the video is stripped of all color, it's hard to get a sense of the vividness of the moment. The church of San Pietro—where we shot—was (and still is) a remarkable place. It sits isolated on an ancient Etruscan hilltop. Its remoteness gives it a lonely, haunted feeling, making it a perfect location for the two doomed lovers to wed. The days we shot there left me feeling exhilarated if not a little melancholic, as if I had been touched by some deep mystery. None of that comes across in the BBC broadcast, though. Shame.

Teenage Heartbreak

I had won the role of Juliet with the potion monologue. It was my favorite passage in the play, and I had been waiting the whole shoot to film it. Franco had cut it to three lines.

I was devastated. I didn't understand. I cried my eyes out.

It had nothing to do with ego—I can say that honestly. It was deeper—something about the monologue itself; I connected with it. When I'd first read it, alone in my room all those months ago, something had clicked. Thirty-one lines and I'd known who Juliet was. That night, with tears in my eyes, I'd known how to play the part.

Now it was gone, and I was heartbroken. Franco explained that it was too much of a showpiece, that he needed the film to be a balance between Romeo and Juliet. He worried that, with the monologue, I would steal the movie. Whether true or not, whether his explanation was just a way of making a teenage girl feel better, I cannot say. Looking at the film now, though, I think Franco was right. I was pretty damn good doing it.

Last, but Not Least

Franco had saved the bedroom scene till the end. For months, he had been preparing me, working on my shyness. All those nicknames, all the times he would call attention to my body—which made me uncomfortable and then, oddly, comfortable. Treating me like an adult, inviting me back to the villa to stay up late with a who's who of European movie stars. He was protective of me, of course, but always in a nonchalant way. Still, I was just a young girl, and the thought of a love scene, of being naked in front of people, let alone in front of a camera, was terrifying. Until it wasn't.

On the day, the nude scene was supposedly left up to me. I was in my dressing room waiting to be called to the set, not really thinking about the scene at all. To be honest, it hadn't occurred to me that Franco would want a more "realistic" interpretation. We were doing Shakespeare, after all, and everyone knew that that meant traditional and dignified: "Yes, well, of course you must keep your clothes on, thank you very much."

It was only when Mauro Gavazzi, our eccentric makeup

artist, came in and announced, "I am here to make you up from head to toe, Olivia!" that I began to get nervous.

"No, no, Olivia, darling. You will be wearing your nightgown," Franco said, as I confronted him after a small panic attack in my dressing room.

"I will?" I asked. "Are you sure?"

"Yes, my darling, absolutely. No question. Although should things, you know, *flow* in another direction, I want you to be ready. This is all."

I had my doubts, but I was a professional—I told myself—and, after all, I trusted Franco. Plus, I wouldn't be doing it alone; Leonard was surely just as nervous as I was. I set myself, took a deep breath, and headed to the soundstage.

It was to be a closed set, which meant only the most essential crew members were allowed in. However, that didn't stop one crew member, whom I liked to call a "dirty old man" from trying to sneak his way onto the set. He was removed, and he was the exception. For the most part, our crew of older Italian gentlemen treated the day with total class, going so far as to turn their backs in between takes.

I can't say the same for Leonard. He loved it. Blessed with an extrovert's enjoyment of attention and a total lack of shyness, he cared not one bit about the world getting a good look at his bum. Spending the day naked in bed with a young lady was just fine by him, even if, to prevent unwanted shadows, he had to endure a piece of flesh-colored tape around his, um, manhood.

Leonard's breezy, careless attitude toward the whole thing helped me tremendously, and by the end I had forgotten about my shyness, the camera, and indeed my nightgown. I thought only of my Romeo and this one night we were having together.

The End; Now Comes
the Work

After six months and hundreds of hours of filming, principal photography was done. As I checked out of the Parco dei Principi Hotel, I tried not to think of that. I could feel a small, dark hole beginning to expand inside me. I was afraid that all the joy I had felt while filming would slide into it and drain away, leaving me empty and bored.

There is a terrible depression that waits beyond every wrap party. Actors are creatures of emotion—at least, I am—and after working so hard for so long, after investing your whole self and opening it up for all to see, after coming to love the people you are working with, to have it all just stop can feel like a terrible loss. Suddenly you're standing at the airport, suitcases in hand, feeling numb and alone. Days later, it feels as if you've got postpartum depression, or a kind of withdrawal that leaves you wanting nothing more than to be back—back with your true family, back in that vibrancy, back making a movie.

But, as I soon learned, my work was far from done. In the end, it would be another ten months before I would finally see the finished film.

The plane touched down at Heathrow Airport and a car drove me back to the two-bedroom house in Wimbledon where my mum, whom I hadn't seen since I first left for Italy, was standing in the doorway, waving. When she asked me how I was, all I could do was stare blankly at her. I was at a loss. How did I feel? How to even begin to talk about it? The kettle was on, heating water for a nice cup of tea. The little-flower-patterned curtains that framed the kitchen window were open, and outside I could see the little green lawn and the little wooden fence of our little home; everything was little. I felt little for noticing it. I felt ashamed. It had only taken six months to make all the bigness small.

But, although I was still only sixteen years old and could understand just a tiny part of it, I had in that moment glimpsed something important: All things pass. In the end, what you are left with is how you choose to live with yourself.

"Oh, Mummy," I said. "It was all very nice."

After the editing process, most of a film's postproduction work involves automated dialogue replacement, called ADR, or more commonly referred to as "looping." Simply put, when, for whatever reason, an actor's dialogue was not recorded correctly on the day of filming, it needs to be rerecorded.

For an actor, this involves standing hour after hour in front of a microphone in a darkened five-by-six booth, watching yourself on a monitor while becoming more and more frustrated.

Much of the movie had been shot using the newest Arriflex camera. Franco loved the clear, vivid images it recorded. Unfortunately, it had a nasty habit of making a slight clicking sound that the microphones could pick up. So, for example, the entire audio of the balcony scene where Leonard and I profess our love for one another was accompanied by a steady *click, click, click*. It was like water torture, and it meant that the scene had to be rerecorded.

Matching even simple dialogue can be difficult. You're standing in a booth watching the scene and waiting. Right before the line that needs to be recorded, you hear a *beep, beep, beep*. As you say your line, you have to match, perfectly, the movements of your mouth on the screen. With complicated dialogue—with Shakespeare, for example— the process is exponentially more painstaking.

For some, looping comes easily, whereas for others it can be more difficult than the actual filming. I was one of the latter. Imagine:

Love's heralds should be thoughts,
Which ten times faster glide than the sun's beams,
Driving back shadows over louring hills.

Again. Because I was late on "louring hills."

Love's heralds should be thoughts,
Which ten times faster glide than the sun's beams,
Driving back shadows over louring hills.

Again. Because I was too fast on "ten times faster glide."

Love's heralds should be thoughts,
Which ten times faster glide than the sun's beams,
Driving back shadows over louring hills.

Again. Because "Driving back shadows" didn't match up.

Love's heralds should be thoughts,
Which ten times faster glide than the sun's beams,
Driving back shadows over louring hills.

And on, and on, and on. Day in and day out. Leonard

was in his own booth one floor down, toiling away with his own dialogue. Franco moved back and forth watching us, giving us notes and keeping our spirits up.

On one particularly numbing afternoon, I found myself leaning against the wall of the dim engineering room as Franco argued with the sound engineer. Suddenly a voice whispered behind me, "You are absolutely brilliant in the film."

Without turning, I said, "Thank you."

The lights went up, and I turned to see Sir Laurence Olivier, smiling. I had met him briefly at Franco's villa one night, but we hadn't really spoken. Now, in this small room, I found I was overwhelmed. The story goes that Olivier had loved what he'd seen of the film and had come to Franco asking if he could, perhaps, in some small way be involved. Obviously, Franco was excited, and now here Olivier was, recording the opening prologue as well as the closing speech.

"Sir Laurence, ah . . . thank you so much." I noticed he was standing in his socks.

"It's Larry, please . . . and you were divine." Looking down at his feet, he went on, "Apparently, my shoes are squeaky. The things we must do for our art. . . ."

Franco and I had a fight. After nineteen takes, my voice was raw and my mood was worse. I said something about needing time to myself and stormed out of the looping booth.

I wandered around, opening doors and poking my head into rooms. We were recording in a huge brown block of a building on the Cinecittà lot. I was being shuttled twice a week across Europe: weekdays in Italy and weekends back home in Wimbledon. I was exhausted.

Passing an open door, I saw an old man sitting at an

ancient-looking mixing board. He was dressed the way you imagine your sweet old granddad would dress when he was off to church or a wedding: a comfy, loose-fitting suit with a green cable-knit sweater underneath. Just as I thought, Sweet, he looked up, saw me, and said, "Ah, Juliet. Come in."

We chatted for a while. He made me laugh. He had a wonderful Italian accent to his English: not that hurry-up-and-stop rhythm we think of, but more a low, smoothed-out tone. He sounded very dignified. When I left, I felt much better. I said to myself, What a kind, sweet gentleman. I wish Franco was more like that. But then I thought, Of course Franco has to be hard and demanding and temperamental; he's a director, after all.

I had no idea that my new friend was Federico Fellini.

I was frustrated by how difficult looping was, and I realized I was taking that frustration out on Franco. I told him as much, but I also told him that, even though he was stressed, he mustn't be so hard on me.

"Oh, Olivia, you think I'm tough?" he replied. "Just thank the Lord I'm not Fellini. He is *tough*."

We made up, and in two days we were working together happily again.

I went back to see my sweet old man. Once again, he invited to sit with him. This time, though, we were not alone. The room was packed, and I noticed that the word "Maestro" kept popping up. As in, *"Maestro, posso procurarvi tutto ció?"* ("Master, can I get you all this?") Or, *"Maestro, Vuoi che io a prenderlo?"* ("Master, do you want me to take it?")

Oh God, I thought, as I finally put it together. I blurted out, "Are you Fellini?"

"But of course I am!"

He was at Cinecittà editing *Satyricon*. Over the years, I would come to know him and his wife, the actress Giulietta Masina, well. He once drew a wonderful caricature of me while we sat together at a dinner party. I treasured it for years until it was stolen from a hotel room along with my Golden Globe and Donatello Awards.

The Tour

By November 1967, Franco had assembled his first rough cut of the film. All that was missing were a few edits and Nino Rota's score. Franco began screening the film at his home for friends and close colleagues. Meanwhile, promotion was gearing up. Paramount Studios had scheduled the first part of a massive world tour to coincide with the film's release. Leonard and I, and on occasion Franco, were set to travel to all the major markets: England, France, Spain, Germany, Canada, Russia, and the United States.

The thought of traveling to the United States filled me with the joyful anticipation of a child on Christmas morning. On a trip to Franco's villa, I had found a copy of Margaret Mitchell's *Gone with the Wind* and become obsessed by it. I went to bed dreaming of Tara, of the American South, and of what Rhett Butler should look like (Clark Gable was perfect).

New York: I almost fainted when I saw the lobby of the Plaza Hotel in New York. It was the grandest room I had ever seen, and about a million miles from the cheap *pensione* I'd stayed in when I'd first arrived in Italy nineteen months before.

The rooms for me and for Leonard were on the same floor, separated by the room for the third in our party, my new chaperone, Mrs. Marika Aba. She was Hungarian, and one of Franco's dearest friends. Leonard and I would come to love her and her stories involving everyone from JFK to the Gabor sisters.

On our first evening, at a party for the film, I was introduced to the famous American producer Hal Wallis. He very generously told me that he'd loved the film and that he had two projects he felt I might be perfect for: one was *Anne of the Thousand Days*, and the other was a cowboy picture called *True Grit* starring John Wayne. I mumbled something about being interested in *Anne of the Thousand Days*—but, as for working with Mr. Wayne, I was very clear: "I can't really see myself doing that. John Wayne doesn't really do anything for me."

Of course, Mr. Wallis was great friends with the Duke, so that conversation ended our relationship.

John Wayne went on to win the Oscar for his performance, and his costar, Kim Darby, was nominated for one. *True Grit* is a fantastic film, and it had taken me less than a minute to talk my way out of it.

Unfortunately, this scenario would repeat itself many times in the course of my working life. In this business, it's not just about the work you do; so much depends on putting yourself in a position to *get* the work in the first place. That means cultivating relationships, knowing how to play the game. But I was opinionated and I was young (and that night I was tired). I had nobody advising me, nobody whom I could even ask how to behave or what to do. Years would pass and many doors would shut before I came to realize that, for better or worse, networking yourself is as much a part of a career in show business as showing up on time, hitting your mark, and knowing your lines.

In the meantime, though, our glamorous tour was hard work. Leonard and I did *The Tonight Show* and we did *The Joey Bishop Show*. Standing before flashing bulbs with dozens of microphones in our faces, we smiled and did what we were asked to do. It was supposed to be a happy time, but I find that, looking back, the feeling I remember most was a slowly building anger that, at the time, manifested itself as a kind of moody detachment. Having a conversation with me then was an uphill battle, believe me. You might tell me how much you enjoyed the film; you might ask what it was like making it, or auditioning for it, or publicizing it; you might ask for a photo or autograph. And for your trouble, for all your polite small talk, all you would get in return was a slight nod of agreement and a well-practiced adolescent smile. But people mistook this laconic, detached manner as a flirty sultriness, which drove me crazy! I was just trying to be rude. Throughout the tour, which ended up lasting eight months, Leonard and I were always broke. While Paramount put us up at the Plaza, they made sure the press knew we were there, together. Yet we were given no budget for new clothes or hairstyling. I felt used. I find this difficult to admit, as it still fills me with anger, but for all the work I did on the film, and for all that the studio asked in promotion—for the two and a half years of my life that *Romeo & Juliet* consumed—I earned in total £1,500, or about $3,000.

Moscow: Franco was astounded. Paramount Studios could not believe it. Our producers were shocked. I wondered what the food would be like. We had been invited to Russia.

It was 1968, the height of the Cold War. East and West were locked in a battle of wills, staring each other down through the Iron Curtain. Somehow, despite all the posturing and saber-rattling, an invitation to open our film in Moscow had made its way through the Russian bureaucracy.

Initially, I found Moscow a sad place. We landed at Sheremetyevo International Airport on a Tuesday afternoon, and it was empty: completely deserted. It felt like an abandoned film set. We were met by a small cadre of government officials and one sanctioned photographer. Driving to the hotel, I was struck by the dated feeling of the city. I was still in a New York state of mind, and Moscow, with its endless gray and brown apartment blocks, was the last place I wanted to be. (How quick I was to judge. I had been in the city less than two hours and I'd already made up my mind.)

Then I started counting fur hats. Oh my God, I thought, they really do wear them! It had never occurred to me that the Russian fur hat wasn't just a stereotype. I cupped my hands against the backseat window and peered out: Everywhere Muscovites, crowned in their magnificent hats, were out and about, stepping over puddles, coming out of stores, carrying briefcases or bags of groceries. It was like watching Doctor Zhivago run errands. I resolved, right then, not to be so gloomy about the place.

On my second night in the city I embarrassed myself in front of the famous poet Yevgeny Yevtushenko. We were seated next to each other at a huge reception dinner. I'd been assigned a translator, a nondescript young man who had the uncanny ability to blend so deeply into the background you forgot he was there until suddenly his soft, heavily accented voice would start translating. So Mr. Yevtushenko and I began talking.

"Oh, and what is it that you do?" I asked.

"I write poetry," he responded (translated almost instantly).

"So do I!" And I launched into some maudlin free verse I had been laboring over in my off hours. There was a pause. I looked at my translator. If the boy could have disappeared, I think he would have. Instead, he gave me a bewildered look. His eyes said, "Please don't make me do this." But I offered no reprieve, so he turned back to Mr. Yevtushenko and began.

Let me say in my defense that I knew almost immediately I had blundered. The look on the great poet's face said it all. The exchange would have been hilarious had it not been excruciatingly embarrassing. But I wasn't done yet.

Later that night, I found myself chatting with another great Russian artist, the director Sergei Bondarchuk. From across the table he raised a shot glass of vodka and offered me a job, and I in turn raised my glass and, politely, said no. I told him I had no interest in spending three months in the far east of Russia, wrapped in blankets, ice-skating, and eating salted meats. All in all, quite an evening.

There were a few cloak-and-dagger moments. For instance, when you made a phone call on an international line—when at last it went through—you would hear a faint clicking sound in the background. When you learned that this was the sound of the government monitoring your call, it left you with a feeling of menace and foreboding—as though at any moment your hotel door would be kicked in and you would be hustled out and sent to some hidden gulag in the Siberian hinterland. It was totally irrational but completely exciting.

THE GIRL ON THE BALCONY 89

Three days later, we were (briefly) in St. Petersburg, called Leningrad in 1968. It's one of the most beautiful cities I have ever seen. Everywhere Leonard and I went we were mobbed. When we arrived, so many people came out to see us that the whole of Nevsky Prospect, which is one of the main streets of the city, had to be closed. They hadn't seen the film yet. They had no idea, really, who Leonard and I even were. All that seemed to matter was that here was something from the West. Something that had nothing to do with politics or power. Movies can do that: Even just the idea of them can transcend and transport.

London: The main event of the tour was, of course, the London opening. It was to be a Royal Command Performance before the Queen and the Royal Family at London's Palladium on March 4, 1968. The pressure was enormous. In the downstairs lobby of a hotel off Oxford Street a Royal valet took Leonard, Franco, and me through the forms and etiquette involved in a royal introduction: a bow of the head for the men, a curtsy for me. (Confusingly, we were told that, officially, there were no requirements, although most did observe the tradition.)

I could feel myself becoming increasingly nervous. Franco had had the fabulous Italian designer Roberto Capucci make a dress for me to wear to the premiere. It was low-backed and peach-colored and fell to the floor. I thought it was just about the most beautiful dress I'd ever seen, and I was about to ruin it.

At a quarter past seven a limousine turned onto Oxford Street and came to a stop in front of our hotel. Leonard and I had decided that the best way to cope with our anxiety was simply to descend into fits of giggles, and as were getting into the car I remember Franco warning us, "Now, you two kids need to behave!"

We arrived at the London Palladium to an explosion of flashing bulbs and twirling spotlights. Calm down, I told myself. Look around. This is a once-in-a-lifetime experience; it will be over all too quickly.

Hustled down the red carpet—everything happened so fast—I found myself standing at the back of the receiving line just inside the Palladium's splendid doors. That's when I saw her: the Queen. Her Majesty, the Queen. She looked stunning, regal, and radiant. I was reduced to a quivering teenage girl. (We were to receive our formal introductions backstage, after the movie, then head to a huge dinner that included Prince Charles.)

Leonard and I were shown to our seats directly behind the Royal box. I found myself looking at the back of the Queen Mum's head, and when the film ended she turned her head slightly to the side and I saw her wipe away a tear. I was over the moon.

But that's when the nightmare began. Franco, Leonard, and I were to walk out onstage and take a bow. I didn't realize just how nervous I was until I was shuffled into the wings and told to wait for my cue. Then we were onstage. Standing between Leonard and Franco, I felt as though the walls were closing in and the floor might drop open. All I could think of, as I stood there about to bow before the Queen, was that I might pee myself. It gives me no great joy to write this, but that is precisely what I did.

(Years later, I would be diagnosed with a severe form of agoraphobia: large crowds, open spaces, and uncontrollable social situations fill me with dread. The anxiety can induce paralyzing panic attacks. Not the best condition, given my profession.)

There followed hurried whispers. Leonard had to bite down on his tongue to keep from laughing; Franco told me not to move. I just smiled sweetly and, trying not to squirm, waved politely down at the Queen of England.

After an impromptu wardrobe change, I found myself seated—at his request—next to Prince Charles at the end of a long dining table. Charming to a fault and possessed of a fabulous sense of humor, the prince was completely the opposite of how he was portrayed in the media. We had an easy conversation. At one point, I told him how much my feet hurt; he immediately replied, "Oh, dear. Well, you must go ahead and rest them on my knees, then."

So there I sat, with my feet resting on the knees of the heir to the British throne while we talked about movies and music. I promised to send him the new Bee Gees album. I told him about making the film and how much I'd loved Italy. He told me his mother had enjoyed my performance in *The Prime of Miss Jean Brodie*. I was shocked and honored that she had remembered the play. In the end, he asked me to dance. It was a wonderful night. As far as I am concerned, the Windsors are a very regal family, indeed.

Boys

The first time I went to bed with a man was also the first time I smoked pot, and I kept my shoes on for both.

I was in Rome, a few weeks before heading back to the United States for the worldwide opening of the film, and my friend Lucianna had convinced me I needed a night out. She took me to the Piper Club.

Amazingly, it's still open today. Looking it up online, I see it also still boasts the tacky Toulouse Lautrec-esque sign above the door, and the stage seems to be about the same. But the images also show that the old place may be a bit past its prime and something of a tourist trap, a hollow echo of the place it once was.

In 1968, the club was cool—French New Wave cool. The boys in their slim-cut suits and thin black ties prowled and preened, trying to project their inner Jean-Paul Belmondo. The girls pouted, smoked Camels, and pretended not to notice. It was a bear pit of loud music, flashing lights, and dark corners.

I was self-conscious. Lucianna, concerned at what she

felt was my overly conservative style sense, had insisted on dressing me; the result was a form-fitting cream skirt and a tight, black button-down shirt with a popped collar. I felt frumpy and awkward, like a big piece of chocolate cake. All that was forgotten, though, when I looked up at the stage.

He was tall and thin as his mike stand. He was the lead singer of a band that had *two* sax players. He was French. Everything about Alain Jack said, "Look at me." And oh, boy, did I ever.

During a break in the band's set, one of the saxophone players found me giggling in a corner with Lucianna. "Er, hello," he said, in a thick French accent. "I am Gaston. My apologizes but one of my bandmates would like for him to meet you and because he thinks you are too much a lady, he did not want to come over uninvited."

"Which band member?" Lucianna said.

"The singer," he replied.

"Um, okay," I said.

Alain was polite, was well spoken, and stared straight down the front of my dress most of the night. He had an infectious, open laugh and a mischievous twinkle in his eye that seemed to say, "Yes, of course I'm nice, but really I only have one thing on my mind." In the end, though, I thought he was very sweet, so when he invited Lucianna and me to an after-hours party at someone's flat I thought, Why not?

I remember sitting in a semicircle of hypercool musicians and ultrafab models, trying to act older than I was by assuming as much ennui as a Wimbledon girl could muster. When I asked Alain what that odd smell was, he started to laugh and said breezily, "It's pot." When I asked, "What's that?" he really began to laugh.

"It's marijuana," he said.

"What's that?" I asked.

"Like a cigarette, only stronger and with good feelings." He said it just like that.

We talked and laughed, and later when Alain leaned in and said, "Would you like to spend the night with me?" I calmly replied, "Yes. Yes, I would."

I was quite happy with my "no big deal" performance. When he led me down a hallway to another room I sauntered coolly, nodding at the art on the walls, matter-of-factly saying things like, "Warhol is a genus," and "All this stuff in 'Nam, so not cool."

In the bedroom, Alain turned out the lights and got into bed. I climbed in after him, petrified but still trying my best to act nonchalant. It was only after he started to laugh so hard the bed shook that I realized my mask of sophistication had slipped. "Olivia," he inquired, "did you forget to take your shoes off?"

Alain Jack and I would go on to see each other, on and off, for about a year. The relationship ended—amicably—after he asked me to marry him. "Alain, I'm seventeen," I told him, "I'm just not ready for marriage."

One cold September night I met a man on whom I had had a crush for years. I was standing in a crowd of people outside a club called the Bag of Nails; I turned around and he was right in front of me. He smiled as he went past me, holding the hand of the woman who would become his wife.

Later that night, we met again in the lobby and began to talk. I lost track of the time, and it was only after his date had come over to say she was tired and was going home that I realized how late it was. They said their good-byes, she left, and a little later I found myself idly walking the streets of London with him.

A light rain fell, unnoticed, as we walked through Piccadilly, and although I will remember our walk for the rest of my life, I can't recall a single thing we said to each other. I do recall that it was easy talk, light and sweet, our heads huddled together against the rain. Eventually, we hailed a cab. I remember the cabby's eyes in the rearview mirror, their look of total disbelief.

An early morning mist had settled around Wimbledon as we pulled up in front of my house. He walked me to the door, bent down, kissed me gently on the cheek, and said good night. It was innocent and it was wonderful, and I wanted the moment never to end. As I watched Paul McCartney walk back down the path past my tiny lawn and step into the cab, I thought about how much of life is about coincidence—being in the right place at the right time.

A few weeks later, a story appeared in the British tabloids that Paul and I were romantically involved. We had been spotted at the Bag of Nails and seen leaving together. According to the article, we were having a secret affair and I was desperate for him to leave Linda and marry me. Journalist Jack Bentley, after pressure from both Paramount and Paul's people, eventually retracted the story. Years later, Mr. Bentley contacted me for some reason and I had the great pleasure of hanging up on him.

I will always have a warm spot in my heart for Paul McCartney, and for my little girl's fairy tale of what might have been. When we saw each other again a few years later at Apple Studios, he came bounding down the stairs, breathlessly saying, "Miss Hussey, so nice to see you again." *Miss Hussey*: He was such a gentleman. When I heard that Linda, whom I admired greatly, had passed away, I cried and said a little prayer for them both.

So I Became a Movie Star

At long last, on October 10, 1968, *Romeo & Juliet* was released and became an international sensation. It was universally praised by the critics, who declared it an instant classic and called Franco's casting of two teenage kids in the lead roles a masterstroke. Audiences everywhere fell in love with the film, and Leonard and I suddenly had two of the most recognizable faces in the world.

But all I knew that October was that my mum was driving me crazy. After a year in Italy making the movie and another six months touring the world to promote it, I was every inch the rebellious teenager. Living in Wimbledon again and with time on my hands, I felt caged in and misunderstood. My mum and I would fight constantly about curfews and cleaning up, about the dishes and the laundry. Of course, our fighting had very little to do with these mundane things and everything to do with my growing up and our growing apart.

Finally, after one particularly horrible fight, my mum said, "Well, Livi, if you don't like it, then you can just leave!" I packed a suitcase and without saying a word I left.

With no plan, no money, and nowhere to go, I ended up calling the only person in London I thought might help: Dyson Lovell.

"Of course, Olivia, you must stay with me!" he said without a moment's hesitation.

And so, three weeks after becoming a movie star, I found myself living out of a small suitcase in a friend's attic. But I didn't care. Dyson was always such fun; he had a wonderful life. He seemed to know everybody. There were always friends popping round his Bloomsbury flat to say hi, share a bottle of wine, and chat. Dyson loved music and good food, the theatre, and the latest art opening. Staying with him was frustrating at first since I was broke and couldn't pay even a few pounds in rent, but he didn't seem to mind. I tried to do my share of the chores around the flat, but I still felt uncomfortable about the situation.

Whenever I went out, which was most of the time, there was plenty to distract me. I had become—whether I liked it or not—part of London's "It" crowd. At night, I went to dance clubs or saw the next big West End play. During the day, I walked Carnaby Street wearing my white beret and huge oval sunglasses, window-shopping at amazing boutiques like Biba.

One night, I was invited to dinner by Justin de Villeneuve, who was managing the supermodel Twiggy. The dinner party was great fun, and I hit it off with both of them—they were also a couple. I thought Twigs was fabulous; I loved how she handled all the attention she got. Where I was closed off and shy, she was outgoing and free. Spending time with her, you would never know that she was the face—the symbol, really—of the new Mod generation.

Eventually, Justin asked if he might manage my career.

Seeing how well Twiggy was doing, I thought it might be a good idea. It proved to be something of a letdown for Justin, as for the most part his job was simply to turn down any offers for me. I was exhausted from *Romeo & Juliet*, and the last thing I wanted was to be back in front of the camera.

One phone call that Justin did take was from a seventeen-year-old American boy who, I was to learn later, had come to London with the express intention of meeting me.

I was sitting on the couch in Dyson's flat one Sunday afternoon when the phone rang. "Olivia, it's Justin. So listen, there is an American actor who is just dying to meet you."

"You know I don't have any interest in meeting any new boys right now," I said. It had been a few months since Alain and I had broken up, and besides, I was still in self-pity mode because of my lost Beatle.

"Why not?" Justin said. "He's right here and would love to say hi."

"Justin, no, I don't . . ."

"Hi. This is Dino." The voice was quiet, almost timid, and of course it had that jarring American accent.

"Hello," I said.

"I thought you might like to meet and have dinner."

"I don't have dinner with people I don't know." I was determined to slam the door on what I had decided was a pushy American kid.

"Oh well, that's good to know. How about breakfast, then, tomorrow?"

"I don't get up for breakfast." I really could be a right little brat when I wanted to.

"Okay, fine, how about brunch, then?" The note of frustration in his voice told me I was winning.

"What's brunch?"

"It's, ah . . . you have it before lunch but after breakfast."

Instantly, I shot back, "Oh well, in that case I don't have brunch."

The American accent was becoming more desperate: "Tea, coffee, a drink. Anything, please!"

There was something endearing about this last part; his tone was clumsily earnest but also held a hint of self-amusement, like a comedian who didn't mind that the crowd was laughing *at* him rather than *with* him. Dino was losing, but he was still having fun.

In the end, I relented.

"Tea, then."

The boy with the irritating American accent and I made plans to meet at the Dorchester Hotel, where he was staying.

"Great, this is great!" he exclaimed. "Can't wait. I'll meet you in the lobby and we'll have tea."

Still in disbelief that I had agreed to a blind-date tea party, I enlisted one of my girlfriends to go with me. While we waited in the Dorchester lobby, Linda had to tell me to stop looking over my shoulder and eyeing the two huge glass doors. An uneasy feeling had come over me that everything was about to change.

Ding. The elevator doors opened and out poured American sunshine. Dino was all blond hair, white teeth, and blue eyes; Gatsby without the issues. Wearing a powder-blue suit that had the largest lapels I'd ever seen, he strode over and with a California-sized grin told me how great it was to meet me.

I had a feeling in that moment that, over the years, I would come to know well. It started at the edges of my mood and slowly spread inward. It was triggered now, as it always would be, simply by being in Dino's presence: total irritation. Shaking his hand and looking up at that impossibly tanned face, all I wanted to do was hit him. He drove me mad right from the start.

He was nervous and blushed crimson when he asked where I would like to go. Not relishing the thought of being surrounded by photographers, I suggested we just have tea in his room. He said, "Great, let me order and we'll go up."

Walking into his hotel suite, I couldn't help but smile. He had ordered the way any nervous seventeen-year-old would, by simply getting everything on the menu. I was touched and, looking at all the food, famished. I sat down and went right to work on the finger sandwiches. As I later learned, Dino had a habit of talking when he was uncomfortable, so while I sat eating he went on and on. Occasionally I would say something like, "Oh, yes" or "Is that right?" but mostly I just stayed quiet and began to see, slowly, the warm, charming boy he was. He confessed that he had come to London with his manager, Bill, to meet me, and, now that he had, he hoped we'd stay in touch.

Later, Bill told me about the conversation he'd had with Dino after our tea party: "I'm going to marry that girl," Dino had told him.

"Um, I'm not sure she was all that interested, Dean Paul. In fact, I'm not sure she even liked you very much." Bill loved to tease Dino.

"Oh, give it a couple of years, Bill, you'll see."

It took four.

Christopher Jones

The first project I committed to after *Romeo & Juliet* was a small independent film called *All the Right Noises*. It had been about a year and a half since I was last in front of the camera, and I was only just beginning to feel like working again. So when a little-known director named Jerry O'Hara came to my door saying he was starting a film and promised it would be low-key and very little pressure, I thought it sounded perfect.

All the Right Noises was a strange choice. I was getting offers for so many films—big films—and perhaps a savvier actor, one with a view to long-term success, might have chosen differently. I can't say. What I do know is that I liked the actor Tom Bell and the comedian Judy Carne, both of whom would be in it. Throughout my career, I have only ever said yes to work that appealed to me, regardless of whether it was the best choice career-wise. Incidentally, although the film did nothing at the box office, it is now considered one of the standout independent British films of the '60s and '70s, and I'm proud of it.

Around this time, I saw a film with a young American

actor named Christopher Jones. He had caught the public's eye in a film called *Wild in the Streets* and was being talked about as the next James Dean. Two weeks after first seeing him onscreen—the film was *Chubasco*—I met him, and the course of my life changed again.

I received a call from Rudy Altobelli, who, along with Stuart Cohen, was Christopher's manager. Rudy and Christopher were in London, and Christopher wanted to invite me to have lunch with them. (I've learned that in show business this thing of having your representation call up people you might fancy is as old as the Hollywood sign.) I agreed, remembering how much I had liked him in *Chubasco*.

The three of us met at the London Hilton. Christopher didn't disappoint. He was shy like me, very quiet, and incredibly handsome. Also, I immediately took a liking to Rudy. We had lunch, and over the next few days Chris and I spent time together before he and Rudy left for Ireland, where Chris, who had been cast in director David Lean's film *Ryan's Daughter*, was to spend the next six months filming (ultimately, the movie would take a year to make).

Once settled in Ireland, Chris began to call and beg me to come visit him. He would talk about how much he missed me and how beautiful Dingle was. He told me Robert Mitchum, the star of the film, was dying to meet me. In the end, I agreed to go. I was young, and mad for a boy.

The town of Dingle, County Kerry, sits facing the vast expanse of the Atlantic on a stunning peninsula that gives the town its name. The whole scene is shockingly cold, tremendously green, and magnificently Irish.

I arrived completely unaware of the tensions mounting on the set. Chris seemed fine, fit and well. It didn't take long for us to pick up where we had left off: getting to know each other and doing all the things you do when you start to fall for someone. One night, overcome by our feelings, we searched the town for a priest or a judge who could marry us. (Fortunately, as it turned out, we didn't find one.)

I soon met Robert Mitchum, already a Hollywood legend, and he more than lived up to his billing. The crew loved him. As soon as I walked onto the set for the first time and met them, they began telling me about him. He was entirely approachable, they said—a must for any professional actor who values his reputation, but hardly a given considering who he was.

What endeared Robert to the crew above all else were the dinner parties he hosted for the old ladies of Dingle. On Tuesdays, the invitations went out, to *All the Esteemed and Venerable Ladies of County Dingle*. Mr. Mitchum offered his modest, rented home for *An Evening of Food and Lively Conversation*.

By Friday afternoon, the ladies of the town were a gaggle of excitement. They arrived en mass and were treated to a fine meal—cooked personally by the great American film star. Robert loved to cook; two of his favorite recipes—apple, onion, and cider sauce and American-style barbecue—never failed to make the menu. Both were huge hits. They came out of the kitchen smelling divine, cooked to perfection, and always brimming with Robert's special secret spice: hashish, finely reduced and in copious amounts.

The next day, the ladies of Dingle would all agree: They could not think of a better time spent with a finer host, and they couldn't remember ever leaving a party feeling as happy or laughing as hard. "How charming a man was that Mr. Mitchum," they would remark—nursing, perhaps, a slight headache.

I love that story; it never fails to make me smile. But beyond his irreverent, mischievous humor, I loved Robert because he seemed to care about me. I was then—as I have always been, it seems—open to, searching for, and needing a father figure. I remember sitting with Robert one afternoon at lunch. It was just the two of us, and he leaned in and, putting his hand on my arm, said, "You know, beautiful, I'm not sure Mr. Jones is really the best guy for you."

I laughed and teased him, telling him that even though he was a rough, tough movie icon he mustn't flirt with a shy, young thing like me. But he wasn't flirting.

I soon began to notice changes in Christopher: sudden shifts in mood, with flashes of anger. I was oblivious to the fact that his relationship with Mr. Lean was beginning to break down. His costar, the actress Sarah Miles, was having a horrid time working with Chris, who would sometimes sit staring off at nothing, glassy-eyed and silent. At other times, he would accuse a crew member of stealing from him and stomp furiously away.

Then, one night while Christopher and I were sitting on the edge of the bed talking, he suddenly punched me hard in the stomach. Doubled over in pain, I looked up and caught his dark eyes suddenly soften, as though he had been away and now he was coming back. He fell down next me and held me and told me he was sorry, that I was special and amazing; he told me that he loved me.

In his day, the poet Lord Byron was labeled "mad, bad, and dangerous to know." This was Christopher Jones; our relationship would prove to be one of the darkest periods of my life. But some good did come out of our relationship, and when I think back on it all, it is that good that I try to focus on.

A few days after that first incident, on a cold, blustery morning I walked alone down to the shoreline and stood close to the in-rushing waves. Closing my eyes, I listened to the ancient conversation between sea and sand and stone and began to cry. What was I doing, here in this lonely, wild windswept place, taking care of this fragile, troubled man? Shouldn't I be looking after myself? Shouldn't I be working? I should go back to London. I should take the first good film offer that came to me. I should get as far away from this man as I could. Looking back at that morning, it's very clear that I should have listened myself.

But I was in love. To a seventeen-year-old girl's way of thinking, leaving Chris would be the same as abandoning him; it would be a betrayal. Also, I felt sorry for him. Watching his deterioration, witnessing each morning his panic as the waves of paranoia washed over him, broke my heart, making it impossible to even consider leaving him.

To slow the tide of his unraveling, the production— cynically, in my view—decided to medicate him. It fell to me to see that he took his *meds*—that's what certain members of the production (who shall remain nameless) called them. I assume they must have been valium or some such thing. Not knowing what to do, I would crush and blend the things into his morning oatmeal.

Things settled down; Christopher was calmer and his mood swings abated, although on some days he was still so far gone he was unable to work. Then he got it into his head, correctly, that he felt too good, that he must be being poisoned. It was a nightmare. Rushing over, a wild snarl on his face, he would throw the bowl of oatmeal at me and scream, "I want you to eat this! I want to watch you eat this!" Then he'd laugh ghoulishly and storm off.

Over these hard months my one solace was Rudy Alto- belli. He knew Christopher and knew what I was going through. We became friends. Not long after I arrived, he asked if I might like to be managed by Stuart and him. They had some big-name clients, people like Sally Keller- man, John Savage, Tom Skerritt, and Valerie Harper. All were enjoying success. Although I didn't much care for Stuart Cohen, the thought of being with Rudy and, at that point, Christopher, appealed to me. Naively, I thought we would be like a family.

Two months into my stay in Ireland I received news that I was to be given the David di Donatello award for best actor of the year. The award is roughly equivalent to an Oscar and is given by the Academy of Italian Cinema. I was to travel with Rudy to the Academy's annual film festival in Taormina, Italy. Once there, I would make a little speech before hobnobbing with the notables of European cinema.

Although the thought of making a speech terrified me, I wanted to go; I had never won anything, and I wanted the opportunity to show my gratitude in person. But persuading Christopher to let me go was difficult. He was convinced that if I left I would never come back; he threatened to quit the film and follow me. Ultimately, it was Rudy who convinced him that there was no reason to worry.

The morning of our departure, I was sitting in Rudy's hotel room drinking tea. Rudy was on the phone; he had rented his home in the Hollywood Hills to a married couple and was making final arrangements with one of the two. Handing the receiver to me, he said, "Olivia, I want you to say hello to a lovely woman who's looking forward to meeting you. Her husband is the director Roman Polanski. Her name is Sharon Tate."

Sharon Tate sounded warm and friendly. She told me that she adored me in *Romeo & Juliet* and that I must come out to LA so I could meet her, Roman, and their new baby, who was expected any day.

Taormina, Italy: At the reception that followed the gala dinner honoring the year's best cinema, I stood holding my

Donatello Award and not really knowing what to do with myself. Through a throng of men in tuxedos and women in long gowns, Rudy pushed his way up to me. I think of Rudy as always pushing past people. Handsome in a strange Christopher Walken kind of way, he had large brown eyes that bulged a little from their sockets and were always moving, taking in information. He had an energy that grew out of his determination not to let other people's BS bog him down.

In his wake was a small, dapper Eastern-European-looking man whose bow tie was as big as his head. "Roman, I would like you to meet Olivia," Rudy said.

Roman Polanski, whose film *Rosemary's Baby* had come out earlier that year, was enjoying success as a young director and was at the festival to receive his own award. He was charming. He talked about Sharon and moving to Los Angeles, he talked about how beautiful Rudy's home was and how I must come and see it if I ever found myself in L.A. As I left that night, I thought how nice it would be to spend time with this couple.

Dingle, Ireland: Feeling guilty that I had taken a moment to focus on something other than Christopher, I boarded a flight back to Ireland, where things had gotten worse. Having discovered that he was being secretly medicated, Christopher now adamantly refused any help. He had become almost impossible to deal with. The whole production was being moved to South Africa for the final weeks of filming, and, again, Chris threatened to leave the film if I didn't stay with him. (God, I was so blind.) With assurances that things would be different, that I would be looked after, that we would have separate rooms, I agreed to go.

Things were not different; the nightmare continued. Some

nights, Christopher would force his way into my room and slam me against the wall, muttering horrible things into my face. Other nights he was near catatonic and would simply ignore me.

On the very last day of shooting, I stood on the beach and watched as David Lean tried desperately to pull a performance out of Christopher. Chris sat in the sand looking up at the great director and just laughed at him. It was one of the saddest things I have ever seen. The film was done. I was done. I wanted nothing more to do with Christopher Jones. Unfortunately, Christopher Jones was not done with me.

Part III

America

All through my time in Ireland and South Africa, all through my relationship with Christopher, I had been speaking with Dino. Wherever I was, he would find me and call. Just to make sure I was fine, he would say. Christopher hated it.

In our phone conversations, I would tell Dino what I was going through and he'd say, "Olivia, that guy is bad news. You have to get away from him." He would never tell me how he felt about me or that we should be together. We would talk like friends, nothing more.

He did keep telling me that I should move to LA. He would tell me to think about all the opportunity, all the freedom, and then he'd go on about the weather, the people he could introduce me to, and the fun we could have.

I was getting the same advice from Rudy. So, on returning from South Africa and after spending three weeks in London, I said good-bye to the few friends I had there and told my mum and brother that I would miss them and not to worry. "I'll be home again soon," I said, and I packed my bags and headed to America.

I've always had this kind of mind-set, like an on/off switch in my head. Even if it's a huge, life-changing move—breaking up with someone, or saying yes or no to a film—once I make a choice I turn off the part of me that looks back. I don't rethink, or wonder, What if? Instead, I think, Right, that's done: What's next? That's what coming to America was like: I made up my mind to follow my heart, and my heart told me it was time to leave London.

When I told him, Dino was beside himself with joy, so excited that I could almost hear him shaking over the phone. He immediately started to make plans: where I should go, who I should meet, how I would get around. I needed a car, he said. I needed to be close to the beach. I needed to meet his dad, Dean Martin, and I should not be intimidated or worried, because he was going to love me.

Mind you, as far as I was concerned Dino and I were still just friends, and I told him so.

"Olivia, I know, and that's good enough for me," he said. "But it doesn't mean I can't be excited that you're coming." He was always so charming—pushy and charming.

I arrived in Los Angeles in late September 1969. I was eighteen years old. In the entire city, I knew two people: Rudy Altobelli and Dino Martin. I never for one moment thought I would spend the next forty-five years there.

I needed someplace to live, and Rudy had invited me to stay with him. He owned a beautiful house off Benedict Canyon Drive, with a sweeping view of Los Angeles all the way from downtown to Santa Monica and the ocean. Surrounded by trees, it offered the kind of privacy Hollywood folks always look for; before Rudy bought it in the mid-1960s it had belonged to the actress Lillian Gish, and Rudy had subsequently rented it to people like Cary Grant and Dyan Cannon, Henry Fonda, and Mark Lindsay. "It was a gem of a home," Rudy would say, "full of good vibes."

But now it had a terrible story.

Five weeks before I moved in, the house and grounds had been the scene of one of the most notorious crimes in American history: the murders of eight-months-pregnant Sharon Tate and four other people by members of the Manson Family.

Rudy was still in Italy when he received the call with the news. Years later, he told me that one afternoon a few months before the murders, Manson had wandered onto the property asking for the music producer Terry Melcher, who had been a tenant in the main house. Rudy had ordered Manson away. Through the court proceedings, Rudy had learned that when Manson sent his brain-washed followers to the house he told them specifically not to forget about "the little Jew guy" staying in the back house. That, of course, was Rudy.

I didn't know Sharon, having only spoken to her on the phone that one time. I did know Rudy, and I saw how much it affected him: He had known Sharon. The crime was vicious and senseless, and had happened in his home.

Which would be my home for the next four years.

Let me say simply that the whole time I lived at Cielo Drive there was nothing strange or macabre about it. I was still very young, and by the time I arrived all traces of the crime had been erased. Certainly something awful had happened there—it was sometimes odd to stand in the living room and look out at the front lawn, knowing that those terrible things had happened *right there*—but it was not the house's fault. As someone once said, evil does exist, but it's always human.

For me, the real issue was that Christopher Jones was

still Rudy's and Stuart's client and he had nowhere else to live.

Rudy sat me down and told me that Chris would have to stay with us for a short time. That he would live in the back house, separate from the main house. That I was never going to be left alone with him. Finally, and most important, Christopher now understood that he and I were done as a couple.

I had my doubts but, seeing no other alternative, I agreed.

I've always loved Robert Redford's line about living in Los Angeles: "If you stay in LA long enough, you become an orange."

LA is a city of make-believe, and certainly there is something inherently shallow about the business of Hollywood. With so many people coming there to make or remake themselves, inevitably it sometime feels like a huge high school play. People try on new personas daily, and are prone to acting out each one. To top it off, everyone is deadly serious about this mad scramble for a new self, which leads to a kind of humorless sincerity; people know they're full of BS, but they expect you to take it as real. Yet for all of that, LA is a town that works hard, creates magic, and is full of creative—and beautifully flawed—people.

I arrived not really having any idea what to expect. As I sat, jet-lagged, in the passenger seat of Rudy's car, driving east along the 10 Freeway, I thought about London and Wimbledon, about all the dreary little houses we'd lived in when we first arrived. I felt I was stepping out from the long shadow cast by old Europe and into the endless California sunshine. I was so excited.

The first few days were a glossy, glittering blur. Dino had made plans; lots of plans. First, dinner at his favorite

restaurant, the Luau, then off to a members-only discotheque on Rodeo Drive in Beverly Hills called the Daisy.

With its exposed-brick walls and big leather booths, its
famous "see and be seen" patio (Mel Brooks held the cast
party for *Young Frankenstein* there, and it's one of Richard
Gere's favorite spots in *American Gigolo*), the Daisy was at
once comfortable, exclusive, and a Hollywood hot spot.
From Tony Bennett to Frank Sinatra, from Natalie Wood to
Paul Newman, you never knew which Hollywood
celebrity you might end up having drinks with. Dino loved
it, his younger brother, Ricci, spent the better part of his
late teens there, and I would walk through its front door
many a night.

The night I arrived in LA, Dino and I got to the Daisy a
little on the early side, around eight-thirty. The place was
half-empty, just a couple of beautiful people silhouetted
against the long bar's background light. We crossed the
empty dance floor to a corner booth. Dino was all smiles.
When we sat down, he immediately shot right back up, exclaiming, "Drinks!" and was off.

I sat quietly, my hands neatly folded on the table in
front of me, watching the place fill up. Dino was chatting
with the bartender, taking his time. Well, where are all the
stars? I was thinking. Just then Ryan O'Neal walked up to
the booth.

"Hi, how you doing?" he said. "Are you alone? Can I
get you a drink? I'm Ryan."

"No, thanks very much, but I'm with someone," I replied
in my most laid-back manner (i.e., not laid back at all).

"No problem, maybe a dance later," and he sauntered off.

Where am I? What a crazy town, I thought, shaking my
head and looking around for Dino.

An hour and a half later, the Daisy was packed with perfectly tanned people smiling, talking, laughing, and danc-

ing. I couldn't imagine any of them growing old. The atmosphere was one of careless invincibility, like steam rising. It enveloped the people, blurred them as they moved through it.

Where am I? I thought again.

Dino, it seemed, knew everybody, and everybody hustled and bustled to be around him. He didn't seem to mind; he didn't even seem to notice. I wondered how someone could be built like that.

Over the next few years, I was to learn that Dino did notice. There was much more to him than just a smile and a famous father. I came to understand that this apparent effortlessness, this ease, was just a cover for his relentless—reckless—drive to make of himself something more than just Dean Martin's son, the golden boy.

For now, though, he was a kid in a candy shop, showing me off and having a glorious time doing it. It was important to him that I love LA as much as he did—so I would never want to leave, I suspect.

He drove me around Beverly Hills: huge houses and perfect lawns. He showed me the spot where he and Ricci had run off the road in a full-size, working tank that their father had bought them.

"A tank!" I exclaimed.

"Sure," Dino said, "what little boy doesn't get to play with a tank?"

He was always so nonchalant about his family. He acted as if it were a completely normal thing to grow up the son of one of the most famous people in Hollywood.

One day, Dino and I were driving down Sunset Boulevard in his jet-black Porsche when suddenly he made a sharp left.

"I want to show you my room," he said. "I've just had it redone."

And just like that I found myself heading to 601 Mountain Drive and a meeting with Dino's mother, Jeanne Martin.

Dino's father no longer lived there. Some time before, Dean had apparently packed a small suitcase and, with his usual laconic charm, quipped something to the effect of "Well, that's about enough for me" and left. (His divorce from Jeanne after twenty-four years would be as amicable as a divorce could be; her settlement would set a Guinness world record. Their subsequent friendship would last for the rest of his life and make up a huge part of mine.)

The Martin house was one that the Cleavers might have lived in if the Cleavers had hit it big. It was a huge house, yet unassuming. It was friendly and impressive at the same time—a lot like the man who owned it, I think.

But first you had to get past the armed guard (not an unusual precaution in Hollywood). After that, you drove up a short, curving driveway to the front door. We hopped out of the car, and Dino took me straight into his room. He hadn't been kidding: I was assaulted by the strong smell of new paint. He had chosen a large black and white checkered pattern for the walls. I told him I loved it; black, after all, was my favorite color.

Just as I began to sit down, Jeanne came in. The shock of seeing her for the first time has stayed with me: Where I am dark-haired, moody, and pale, Jeanne Martin was blond, cheery, and tanned. Her golden hair perfectly framed her incredible blue eyes. She was stunning.

She was also so friendly it took me aback at first. She welcomed me, hugged me, and told me how wonderful it was to finally meet me. She radiated an airy confidence, an ease with who she was and how she lived. I loved her the moment I met her—perhaps exactly because she was so much my opposite in every way.

I spent the rest of the afternoon sitting comfortably outside in the Martins' backyard, drinking iced tea and thinking that this really was the good life. I didn't see any of the other kids that day—in addition to Dino, Ricci and their younger sister, Gina, lived in the house. The four older kids from Dean's first marriage—Craig, Claudia, Gail, and Deana, all in their twenties—were in and out all the time, though.

The Martin kids were all great fun to be around—a huge, life-affirming humor ran through everything they did. When they looked at you with their big, brown laughing eyes, you couldn't help but be enchanted (if you wanted to find them in a crowd, you simply listened for the group laughing the loudest). I would come to love them all.

A few days after meeting his mother, I was at the Hamburger Hamlet on Sunset Boulevard meeting Dino's closest friend, Desi, the son of Lucille Ball and Desi Arnaz (Sr.), Desi, like Dino, had grown up in a Hollywood fishbowl.

I have never been comfortable with my own fame. It's always felt awkward to me. It seems obvious but when you're famous, people treat you differently. People you've never met look at you as if they've known you all their lives. You can feel it, and, for me at least, that feeling has never been pleasant. For one thing, I've found it's much easier to disappoint people when you are well known. Between their expectations and your reality lies a minefield of misunderstanding.

With Desi and Dino it was different. Perhaps it was because they had grown up with it and knew nothing else, but being recognized never seemed to bother them. They were so easy with it, so natural. Never once did I see either of them be rude or dismissive to a fan. I loved that about them.

Desi is still a larger-than-life character. He sees life as a question, I think, something you have to wrestle with to understand. At that time he was also unbelievably loud: his laugh, his voice, his demeanor; everything about him was dialed up to ten. As a result, he was the center of attention wherever he went.

I would lean over to Dino and whisper, "I love Desi, but everybody looks at us when we're out with him." Dino would laugh and say, "Don't worry, Olivia, they look at us anyway."

Back at Rudy's, there was always something happening (another reason why living there didn't feel strange). People were in and out all the time. Sally Kellerman and John Savage would come by. Jack Nicholson, who intimidated me, would sometimes come up to smoke a joint and enjoy Rudy's view.

I remember Jack in a small scene on a rooftop with Barbra Streisand, the star, in *On a Clear Day You Can See Forever*. As we were walking out after the seeing the film, Rudy asked what I thought of it.

"Well, Barbra Streisand was fantastic as usual," I said, "but I thought Jack looked the way I feel whenever I meet him; he looked really nervous."

Rudy laughed. Later that night, he told Nicholson what I'd said. Rudy had a big Cheshire grin on his face when he told me that Jack had been offended.

I ran and hid in my bedroom I was so upset. How could he? I thought. He had asked my opinion and, innocently, I had given it. It had been for his ears only. I was embarrassed, so I decided that it would probably be best if I avoided Mr. Nicholson from then on.

A few days later, though, Rudy took me to a party at Jack's house, in part because he hoped to get me in front of Jack. He was disappointed when the opportunity never presented itself—Jack having left his own party to find a better one.

As we walked out, Rudy said, "Oh, don't you worry,

Olivia, I'll get you in the end." He loved to push my buttons, to make trouble and have a laugh. Rudy, I was learning, had a malicious streak and a medieval kind of humor: He laughed loudest at others' misfortune or embarrassment. It was not a pleasant quality, but more often than not it was obscured by his flamboyant, circus-act personality. He was a ball to be around, and I was young girl enthralled by it. I didn't see his antics for what they were.

One good thing did happen at that party: I ran into an old friend. I was, naturally, nervous and I felt out of place, so it was a godsend when I saw Victoria Turner, who had been in *The Prime of Miss Jean Brodie* with me in London; we were the two lead schoolgirls. It was so good to see her. Suddenly, I felt a link to England and the life I'd left behind. We started talking; she had married a fine American actor named Warren Oates and was now living between London and LA. We laughed, remembering how irritated she would get whenever I got the giggles onstage; she wore the most ridiculous wig for the show. We promised to stay in touch but, as happened so often in Hollywood, we didn't. I have always thought she was a wonderful talent, though.

Rudy also loved his pot. There were days when we would just sit at his huge antique desk overlooking the city and he would roll a joint and then another. As I became more paranoid he would laugh at me through the smoke. But after a time I'd start to giggle too. Then it would dawn on us that we weren't eating, and, good Lord, how much better this would all be if we were! So it was off to Musso & Franks for dinner. (The place was a mainstay of life in Hollywood.) I would dive spoon-first into a huge hot fudge sundae, and Rudy would slowly make his way through one of their famous steaks. Dino would sometimes join us. The three of us would spend the night laughing and gossiping and having a great time.

I had settled into a new life and I was feeling good, and all the while Christopher Jones was living in the back house.

I had some dates. Although Dino and I were now best friends, and not a night went by without our talking on the phone for a least an hour, we were not romantically involved. He had been seen around town with Candice Bergen (he was always careful not to talk to me about his love life), so I decided it would be fine if I dated as well. I began a very casual relationship with Terry Melcher—the same Terry Melcher about whom Manson had inquired when he visited the house a few months before the murders. Terry was the son of Doris Day. He was brooding and moody and always high, and after about a month our relationship fizzled out.

I went to more Hollywood parties and met more Hollywood people. They would always ask what I was working on, and my answer would always be "nothing." Between all the changes I had gone through and the laid-back LA lifestyle, work was the last thing on my mind. I have sometimes regretted all this lost time—time when I was at the height of my fame—but the truth is, I have never been very good at thinking about my career. However, I didn't entirely forget about acting; Desi convinced me that I should sit in on an acting class.

Lee Strasberg could only have been about five feet, four inches tall. I'm five feet two. He had white hair curled tightly above his ears, with a little left on top of a perfectly round head. His thick, black-framed glasses sat snugly on the bridge of his nose, looking as though they had lived there for decades. Behind them, his eyes were intense and highly intelligent and they never stopped moving. He was the most influential acting teacher in America, and it was hard to argue with his technique. Devoted students like Al Pacino and Robert De Niro were redefining what a leading man could be, and his most celebrated pupil, Marlon Brando, was, well, Marlon Brando.

Lee was so sweet when I arrived just before a Saturday afternoon class. He said hello, complimented me on my performance in *Romeo & Juliet*, and walked away to begin class. I sat in the back of the studio and watched. Forty-five minutes later, I quietly got up and excused myself. Nope, I thought, this is not for me.

I had watched Lee absolutely tear into the heart of a young actress as she fumbled her way through a monologue; he reduced her to tears. It had made her work better, no doubt, but it had convinced me that I was no Method actor. I couldn't imagine having to put myself through so much simply to give a good performance. I had enough trouble keeping my emotions in check off camera. The idea that I would have to dig up all my pain and insecurity, all my trauma, all my anger just to act seemed insane to me. It might work for others, but I felt that once my emotional dam burst, the flood would drown me.

I did enjoy my singing lessons, though. I took them with a teacher who lived in the hills above Sunset Boulevard; I wish I could remember her name. Sometimes I would see Goldie Hawn there, and we'd smile and wave as we passed one another.

That's what it was like. In 1970, Hollywood was a small community, and Beverly Hills, where so many actors and actresses, writers, producers, and directors lived, was just a small, quiet town, totally different from the homogenized shopping mall it is today. You would go into the pharmacy and see Steve McQueen flipping through the magazines and you would both smile and wave. When you came out of the market at the corner of Canon Boulevard and Wilshire, Jack Lemmon would hold the door open for you and you'd smile and wave. There were no paparazzi.

No big red buses packed with tourists. It was intimate and laid-back.

I had settled into this new, sunnier way of living. The people I met were for the most part interesting, talented, and fun. I stopped feeling the anxiety and the pressure that had often weighed on me in London. Things became lighter in LA, and I began to open up a bit more, laugh a little more easily, and be less hard on myself.

Then things, as they so often do, changed again.

The End of the Long Beginning

There was a standing lamp in the corner of my bedroom at Cielo Drive. When the door was pushed open, say by one of Rudy's two dogs, a shadow would slide slowly, like an eclipse, from the ceiling to the floor and from one end of the room to the other and blot out the light.

One night, I was almost asleep when the shadow began to move across the room. Out of habit, I dropped my hand down off the bed and waited for Lady, Rudy's German Shepherd, to find it and snuggle up. This time, though, it wasn't Lady; it was Christopher. And he closed the door behind him.

The next five-and-a-half hours were the worst of my life. Christopher was hearing voices. He was twitching. He was so far gone it was shocking. He began by whispering sweetly, tenderly, incoherently—but then, suddenly, his hands were on me, punching and slapping. He beat me for an hour, I think, all the while grinding his teeth and snarling, his spittle spraying me. Then he raped me.

As the hours went by, I went numb. I thought of nothing. Maybe I had a notion of staying alive; I don't really know. When it was over, and I was sitting on the bed with my back pushed up against the frame, my blood staining the sheets and pillows around me, I started to cry. In some way, I had always known that it would come to this; that it was only a matter of time before the dam broke and all of Chris's anger washed over me. If I felt anything at all that morning, it was pity. He was sick, sick in his mind. It wasn't his fault. When he left, at five thirty, he must have heard me say, as he was closing the door behind him, "I forgive you, Chris."

After a while, I managed to get up and walk gingerly into the kitchen, where Rudy took one look at me and started to scream. He ran out of the house and ten minutes later came back in saying, "He's gone, the fuck."

I didn't know what to do. I called Dino. When he arrived, his first words were, "I'm going to have him killed."

I asked him please not to do anything, that the thing had happened but now Chris was gone.

Christopher had split my lip open. There was dark bruising around my eyes and the side of my head. He had pulled my hair so hard that a clump had come out. My nose would not stop bleeding. It took two months to heal. During that time, I never left the house and Dino was there every day.

Once I had recovered enough to leave the house, though, I began to feel nauseated and ill. A thought worked its way into my head. Oh God, no, I thought. I told Dino, and he arranged for me to see his mother's gynecologist, Dr. Krohn, who confirmed what I already suspected: I was two months pregnant.

I spoke to Rudy. I spoke to Dino. I spoke to a psychiatrist. In the end, I decided that I could not have the baby. It had been conceived in an act of violence, and a child would bind me to Christopher for the rest of my life. I simply couldn't do it.

An abortion was arranged. I checked into Cedars-Sinai hospital under a false name. I was in shock, tortured by what I was about to do. That night, after Dino had left, I was lying in the hospital bed when the door opened and Christopher walked in—as silently as he had entered my room at Cielo Drive. I panicked: Somehow, I don't know how, he had talked his way in. He sat down on the edge of the bed. He apologized for what he had done but told me I should keep the baby. I told him I couldn't and that although I forgave him he must never come near me again or I would tell everyone what he had done. I pressed the call button for the nurse, and as she came in Christopher got up and left without a word. That was the last time I ever saw him.

It broke my heart to abort the baby, although I have never regretted it. I do sometimes think of what might have been, of who the baby might have grown up to be, and I'm ashamed. However, I know in my heart that it was the right decision, and I am ready to answer to God for it.

Love

I fell in love with Dino because of my experience with Christopher. Out of that horror came some of the brightest, happiest days of my life.

Dino stuck with me through the whole thing: never questioning, never judging, never expecting anything. His constant, caring attention got me through it. I cannot begin to express how wonderful he was.

March 1971 finds me feeling myself again (more or less) and sitting by myself at Rudy's watching Rona Barrett, a widely known LA gossip reporter, on television. Her segment was on the young and famous in Hollywood, and she mentioned that Dino and Candice Bergen might be heading to the altar sometime soon.

No, wait, I thought, this can't be right. I realized something that, deep down, I had known for a while but had been oblivious to in the day-to-day. I picked up the phone and called Dino. When he answered, I said, "Dino, I love you. I can't imagine spending any more time away from you."

There was a pause before he said, quietly, "I'll be there in ten minutes." I think he had been waiting a long time for that call.

He proposed to me ten minutes after arriving while we were sitting in his car in the Cielo Drive driveway. "Yes, of course." I said, instantly. We kissed and smiled at one another and then it became very Hollywood.

Dino was to appear that night on the *Merv Griffin Show* (Dino was something of a heartthrob; he was constantly asked to make appearances or play in celebrity tennis tournaments, and he was always in the tabloids). He asked if I would go with him to the taping and wait in the green room.

I was sitting backstage watching the live feed of my new fiancé when Merv asked him if he was seeing anyone. Dino flashed a cheeky smile and said, "Well, as a matter of fact, Merv, I am. Olivia Hussey and I are in love and we're getting married." He paused. "In three weeks."

What did he say? Three weeks! Where did that come from?

Within ten minutes Jeanne was on the phone with me, saying, "We love you, Olivia! Don't worry about a thing. I'll arrange everything. I love you, sweet girl!"

After the taping and flushed with excitement, Dino and I drove down to the Martins' Palm Springs house and spent our first night together. We were both so happy.

Over the next three weeks Jeanne was as good as her word. She planned everything. She has always been wonderful at putting events together and is a marvelous hostess. The whole family—my soon-to-be new family—were warm and welcoming, taking me in and making me feel so loved. The Martins are very special people.

Dino was in medical school—his father's dream was to see his son a doctor—and was spending most days at school. A few weeks before he proposed to me, he had decided to move out of Mountain Drive. He had found a little house for rent that belonged to Jimmy and Evy Darren.

Along with a nice view of the city it had a small pool with a little pool house attached and was cozy, warm, and bright. We had spent hours there decorating it. Together, we had shopped for furniture and bought curtains. Essentially, Dino had let me put together the whole house for him. It had never occurred to me that what he had been doing all along was letting me get comfortable in what would be my new home. He had always known.

Two weeks before our wedding, Dino and I were standing in the wedding band section of Tiffany's in Beverly Hills, choosing matching bands. It was my first time inside the famous store. Rudy, who had insisted on coming with us, had wandered off. Dino and I were about to pick out two thin gold rings when Rudy yelled from across the store, "Olivia! Dino! Get over here!" (Rudy would yell at full-throaty volume in a quiet cathedral if he felt like it.) He was standing over Tiffany's diamond ring cases, purring like a cat. "You know, kids, every girl must have a diamond engagement ring."

Dino laughed. "Oh no."

Together, the three of us chose a very simple ring for me. I cried, Rudy cried, and Dino stood there, glowing with pride.

Afterward we walked along Rodeo Drive and over to Nate'n Al's Deli for hamburgers and chicken soup. We sat in a big booth. I held Dino's hand under the table and couldn't remember a time when I'd been happier. The simple pleasure of the moment; everything feeling so right. Remember this, I thought.

Vegas, Dean, and a Wedding

Before the wedding, there was the small matter of meeting Dean Sr. for the first time. Dino loved his father; they shared the quality of being able to intoxicate a room simply by being in it. As I've suggested before, Dino's spirit, with his love of speed, was in part galvanized by his deep desire to earn his dad's respect, to be seen as his own man. I loved Dino for this, for how hard he worked. But it was plain to anyone who saw father and son together that Dino needn't push so hard and go so fast, that in fact Dean Sr. had always been proud of his boy.

Dino and I were meeting his father at Chasen's, the granddaddy of Hollywood restaurants. Instead of a check at the end of a meal, regulars like Walt Disney and Cary Grant (Dean Sr.'s hero) would sign their names and get a monthly bill in the mail. The place oozed class and glamour and old Hollywood.

Before we walked in, Dino took my hand and said, "Don't be nervous, he's great. You'll love him," then added, reluctantly, "once it wears off."

I said, "Dino, please, I've met famous people, you know. It's no big deal." Then we walked in.

It was like stepping out of a time machine into the 1930s, when Chasen's had opened: The interior was hushed and dimly lit, with a smell of old leather and a tuxedoed maître d' who knew Dino's name. Soft, red carpet muted our steps and wood-lined walls soaked up the glow from low-hanging chandeliers. Dean Martin sat, smoothly smoking a cigarette, in his favorite back-corner booth ("where Ronald proposed to Nancy," he told me later). When he smiled at us, I squeezed Dino's hand and said, "My God." Zeffirelli and Nino Rota are what Italian men really do look like. Dean Sr. was what Italian men *should* look like.

"Shush, Olivia," Dino said with a note of irritation. Then, "Yeah, I know."

Being with Dean Sr. was like watching a movie and knowing it would become one of your favorites. It wasn't just that he was charming and charismatic; everything he did, from the way he lit his cigarettes with his beautiful gold Dunhill lighter to the slow, sly manner in which he told jokes, was captivating. He sat easy and relaxed against the red leather booth, filling the space as if he had been poured into it. I loved his unhurried manner, his steady stare, the ocean of coolness he seemed to sail across. I was transfixed by the way he brought his glass up to his mouth, with his pinky finger, broken years before—boxing, maybe—shooting straight out.

It was a long dinner, full of stories and laughter. Though at times father and son were awkward with each other, their connection was palpable: Dino could make his dad laugh. For the Martins, humor was like breathing: essential. Every one of them—from Dean Sr. to Dino, his brother Ricci (who may have been the funniest of the lot), their younger sister Gina and their half siblings, and on down to the grandkids—processed the world through laughter. It was how they connected with one another, and it made for uproarious family get-togethers. I've heard my son, Alex, make the same jokes his grandfather would make. I've seen Gina leave a table of sixty-year-old business men in stitches. I've listened to Gail tell a story that made me laugh harder than I thought I could. They were—and are—the funniest people I've ever known, and it all came from Dean Sr.

He had that gift that only the extraordinarily talented have: He saw the world a little differently than the rest of us. Over the years, I'd catch him looking or listening to something and see a double-take, a quick reexamination. I'd see him connect that thing with something else. I wouldn't have the foggiest idea what he saw or heard or what it made him think of—but then, I'd think, that's one reason I'm not Dean Martin.

That first night at Chasen's, though, all I wanted was for him to like me, and by the end of the evening it seemed he did. I say "seemed" because, although he was always sweet and funny and unassuming, there was something distant about him. He was like a vast mountain range with peaks hidden in cloud cover; there were simply parts of him you'd never see. The mystique never left him, but eventually I did begin to see past that remoteness just a little, and glimpse the unaffected and genuinely kind man he was.

At the end of that night, he dropped his huge hand on mine and said, "Well, pretty girl, why don't you come up to Vegas, see my show, get hitched, and we'll have a party."

I'll always remember the cadence of his voice. It made me think of saloon doors swinging. That was Dean Martin.

With the wedding just a few days away, I was nervously making last-minute arrangements. Since I was not in contact with my father, Rudy would give me away. My mum had become angry and bitter toward my father over the years, and all that feeling had made its way into my brother and me. We were naturally protective of her, and in time I had found myself, also, angry at my father. It would be forty years before I picked up the phone and reached out to him. The sins of the parents. . . .

I called my mum (we spoke about once a week), and she was so happy. She was working hard and raising Drew, my little brother, and because it was all happening so fast there was no way they would be able to come over for the wedding. We talked for an hour, and I made plans to go to England for a visit afterward.

Jeanne had chartered a plane: The whole wedding party was flying to Las Vegas. Dean Sr. was playing at the Riviera Hotel, and Jeanne had turned the hotel's basement into a chapel for our wedding. It was a small affair: Desi was Dino's best man. The guest list included all the Martins, of course, as well as Terry Melcher and two friends Dino had made through tennis: the great Pancho Segura, whom Dino loved and admired, and Pancho Gonzales. Later, there would be a larger party at Jeanne's for the friends who couldn't make it to the wedding.

Dino had a small, tight group of friends whom he kept close, people like Chuck Roven, who would go on to become a very successful and talented film producer; Spencer Segura, Pancho's son; and Guy Finley, who today is a well-known self-help and spiritual writer.

The wedding itself, or what I can remember of it, didn't last long. I wore a lovely dress that Dino and I had designer Billy Zatz make for me in his little shop on Melrose Avenue. Before the ceremony, Jeanne came to see me in my room. She had three rings and said I should pick one as a gift. I was touched, and chose a small one that reminded me of a flower half blooming, its petals made of small diamonds. I wore it on my little finger for years, until it was stolen.

Looking at pictures of that day, I'm struck by how

young Dino and I looked; we were kids: Dino wearing his baby-blue button-down shirt that matched the color of Jeanne's dress, me standing next to Dean Sr., looking short and a bit moody. I wasn't, though. I was very much in love.

After the ceremony, the family all came up to the altar for photos. When I look at those photos I remember that it really did feel like the beginning of a whole new chapter of my life and that, even though I looked like a child, I wasn't anymore.

Homemaker

Dino and I returned to our new home and started our life together as husband and wife. On the first morning after we were married, he went off to the hospital and I wandered into the kitchen. Okay, I thought. Right. Time to cook.

I had been cast in a new role. The title of the movie was *The Good Wife*—I'm always ahead of the times—and I was the lead. I would act the part and, in time, become it.

But for me, learning to cook seemed like learning Latin or hieroglyphics: difficult, tedious, and almost entirely useless. I love eating food, not preparing it. I'd always wanted to cook, to be at home in the kitchen, but my appetite had always seemed to bully my patience. Nevertheless, I was determined that when Dino came home I would have dinner waiting for him. I threw myself into cooking, and it turned out to be so much fun.

I bought cookbooks that ended up well-thumbed and splattered with sauce. Lentil soup became a specialty, as did mashed potatoes. I learned to stem and sauté vegetables and grill steak that I served with an array of salads.

Dino loved lemon pie, so I learned to make it from scratch. With our new dog, Buffy, trolling for scraps around my feet, I spent hours in the kitchen, feeling grown up and having a ball.

We saw Desi all the time, and I had an opportunity to meet his parents. I met Lucille Ball, whom I had grown up watching on TV, one night at her home. Dino, Desi, and I had stopped by during one of her movie nights. All the lights were out in the living room, and people were sitting everywhere. The three of us started to move through, saying, "Excuse me, sorry," stepping over someone, banging into someone else. All of sudden, a gruff voice—it sounded like stone being rubbed across sandpaper—said, "Olivia! Come over here and sit by me."

I made my way over and plopped down next to a living legend. We spent the next hour telling secrets, gossiping, and laughing. Lucille was tough and funny, and had seen it all. She had made it in what was, and still to a large extent is, a man's business. She lived unapologetically and answered to no one. I loved her.

"You mustn't ever let them beat you!" she growled into my ear.

"Who?"

"Any of them," she replied, and nodded knowingly to herself. "Now be a love and hand me my cigs."

Desi Arnaz Sr., who was living in Del Mar with his new wife, reminded me of my own father. He had simple needs, was easygoing, and had that wonderful Latin charisma. He and I would sit outside, looking at the ocean and chatting in Spanish while Dino and Desi played in the water like a couple of kids. Lazy California days.

At home, Buffy had puppies—ten of them. Falling over themselves and, as they grew, barking and digging holes everywhere, the pool house became their playpen, and they had no trouble making themselves right at home. However, our little rabble did not sit well with Jimmy Darren, the actor and owner of the house. He threatened to evict us.

At dinner one night during one of our trips to Vegas to see Dean Sr. perform, I mentioned this problem to a couple of his friends. These particular friends happened to have given me a handgun for a wedding gift, saying, "Now, Mrs. Martin, this gun is special 'cause it's got no serial numbers." They were the type of guys other guys were afraid of; in short, they were mob guys.

As far as I know, Dean Sr. stayed clear of that tough-guy world; he was never impressed by all that. But it was Vegas, and even he had to play the game. So, after the show, a huge group assembled in a private dining room at the casino. Dean Sr. was sitting—his bow tie hanging loose, his shirt unbuttoned at the top—at the head of a huge, round table chatting quietly with whoever had worked up the guts to sit down next to him.

It wasn't an act. Dean Sr. was totally indifferent to affectation or rank. You could be a bricklayer or a veterinarian, drive a cab or be the heavyweight champion of the world—as long as you were a straight shooter, looked him in the eye, and, best of all, made him laugh, you were okay in his book.

So as the champagne flowed and an assortment of sycophants in all shapes and sizes fluttered through the cigarette smoke, I sat telling these friends of Dean's about my landlord problems. They sat there in their shiny, brightly colored suits and listened intently. When I finished, one of them said, "Now this is upsetting to hear."

He leaned forward on his elbows and stared off into space. Eventually, he said, "Those poor little puppies." As he continued to look off into space, I imagined he was thinking about their terrible plight. Finally, he looked at me with resolution writ across his face: "I'll tell you what, Olivia: I want to thank you for sharing this information, and I don't want you to worry yourself anymore. I'm personally going to take care of this."

A week later, Jimmy Darren called. "Hi, Olivia, Jimmy here," he said. "How are things?" There was a tightness in his voice, as though he were, I don't know, hanging upside down out a window or something.

"Listen," he went on, "if there's anything I can do for you, you just let me know, all right? And, oh yeah, your puppies. Listen, I overreacted. Of course they can stay as long as you want. Hell, let me know if you plan on giving any up for adoption. I'd be happy to take a couple."

Before I could reply, he hung up. I never heard from him again.

Dino, I learned, almost always got what he wanted. People loved him. They wanted to do things for him. They found it all but impossible to say no to him. When Dino put his mind to something, that was it—there was no stopping him.

In 1971, the Bee Gees were on the cusp of becoming the biggest band in America. I had met them briefly in London in 1968 when they were on the BBC show *Top of the Pops*. From there, they had gone on to enormous fame, churning out hit after hit and defining the '70s disco age. They were my and Dino's favorite group.

One late afternoon when we were at home, Dino's head shot up from the newspaper he was reading as he exclaimed, "The Bee Gees are in town playing a show!" He stood up. "Make dinner, Olivia, for five. I'm bringing them home with me tonight."

I laughed and said, "Dino, shut up. Stop being silly."

God, who does he think he is? I thought, as he walked
out the door—you can't always get what you want. I settled in for a night of TV watching.

Three hours later, I was standing in my pajamas shaking
hands with Barry, Robin, and Maurice Gibb.

The house was a mess: clothes everywhere, dog hairs
thick on the sofa, a pile of dirty dishes in the sink. Oh God,
this is a nightmare, I thought. As Dino fell into his familiar
Mr. Slick role, grinning wildly and letting loose a flood of
salubrious verbiage, I buzzed around the Bee Gees, tidying
things up.

I was, I felt, doing a smashing job of making a right fool
out of myself as I hurled a pile of shirts into the closet and
told Maurice I loved his hat. He smiled, thanked me, and
introduced his wife, who was standing next to him. She
was the singer Lulu. I was a fan. As I said, a nightmare.

Only the Bee Gees's class and manners saved the situation. They were so gracious, so unassuming, and so polite
in the face of my obvious discomfort that the whole thing
soon became funny. They stayed late, talking and drinking
coffee, relaxing into the night. Robin talked tennis with
Dino. I told Lulu where I liked to shop in LA. At one
point, Barry picked up one of Dino's guitars and started to
play Paul McCartney's "The Long and Winding Road." It
stopped me dead. It was the most beautiful version I had
ever heard. Can you imagine those words, that melody,
coming from Barry Gibb? (As an Aries, I secretly always
imagined Paul writing it for me.) By the time he had finished the first verse, all of us were rapt. I'll never forget it.

They left around eleven-thirty. As I closed the front
door Dino said, "Not bad, huh, Liv?" and flashed his California smile.

Oh, Dino, how I miss you.

* * *

A few months after Dino and I were married, Desi started seeing Liza Minelli. Liza and I would become close friends; she would be godmother to my first child, Alexander.

We met on a bright, cloudless Sunday morning at the Beverly Hills Tennis Club. Instantly there was a connection. I could see, clearly, my vulnerability, my fragile, sensitive nature alive in her. We were like two heart-shaped seismometers, attuned to the smallest of life's little tremors. But, unlike me, Liza was brimming with positive energy, dynamism, and spunk. She was, I thought, what I might have been if I had been born American and endowed with that particular American trait: optimism. Clear-eyed, devoid of irony, she bubbled with life and a passion for living so wide it spread sea to shining sea. I loved her.

The four of us—Desi and Liza, Dino and I—would spend a lot of time together. We'd fly to Vegas, see a show, have dinner at the Riviera, and fly back that same night. You could find us most Saturday nights at Madeo's in Beverly Hills, sitting in a corner booth getting tipsy and laughing far too loud. And Sunday mornings, to clear our heads, Liza and I would throw sweatpants on and whack tennis balls at each other up at Jeanne's.

I remember the night Liza won the Academy Award for *Cabaret*. I was at an Oscar party at Jeanne's when Liza came in. She was beaming and clutching the golden statue tightly to her chest as if she was afraid somebody would snatch it from her. I was so happy for her.

Jeanne's parties were legendary. You never knew whom you were going to meet. Dean Sr. hated them. Dino told me that his father once called the police from upstairs to have the party downstairs shut down. I can almost hear Dean Sr. on the phone: "Hello there, pal. So, there's a big ruckus over at the Martins' tonight. I'd appreciate it if you'd send someone out and shut it down." Then he'd hang up, chuckle a little, and finish his sandwich.

I remember once when, during a Christmas party, Dino and I had gone into the library to have an argument. We were going at it hammer and tongs when suddenly one of the French doors slid open and John Lennon popped his head in. He looked at us for a minute and said quietly, "Well, this looks familiar," and ducked out again.

Dino and I stood frozen for a long time, staring at the French doors. Then Dino slowly looked back at me. "Maybe we should give peace a chance?" he said, and hugged me.

Jeanne was so good at putting seemingly random people together. You'd have David Bowie sitting at a table with Elizabeth Taylor, drinking cocktails and listening to Truman Capote tell some insane story. Sean Connery might step outside with Sammy Davis Jr. to have a cigar and share a laugh. Jeanne always knew what would work, who would bring out the best in whom.

These were my first few months of married life, and as far as I was concerned they were perfect. I lived in a strange kind of balance between my newfound love of domestic life and the still-surreal glamor of Hollywood, and it was never boring. Plus, I was so in love.

So it was almost a disappointment when Rudy called and said I had an offer for a film. Called *Summertime Killer*, it would star Christopher Mitchum, Karl Malden, and me, and shoot in Spain for six weeks. I hadn't worked in months, and I knew it was time I did.

Partly I had been holding out for Franco's new film project to get off the ground. A few weeks after *Romeo & Juliet* was released, Franco had sent me a copy of Alexandre Dumas's *La Dame aux Camélias*, better known in English as *Camille*. He had always wanted to bring the story of Paris's most famous and beautiful courtesan to the screen. He had attached a note with the book that read, "You are my Marguerite Gautier."

But Franco was apparently having trouble finding financing for the picture, and I simply could not wait to work any longer. So I accepted the offer for *Summertime Killer*, and in the summer of 1971, in the international terminal at LAX, I said good-bye to Dino. He wiped the tears from my face and said he'd come visit.

Back to Work

I haven't seen *Summertime Killer* in forty years. The film wasn't bad at all—a solid box office hit, it made more money in Europe than *The French Connection*. For me, it was memorable for three things: Spain, Karl Malden, and my dinner with Brigitte Bardot.

I don't know much about politics, politicians, or ideology—the machinations of power have never interested me—but it was clear even to my young eyes that the nearly forty years that Spain had spent under the leadership of Franco had not been particularly good to her. After the romance of Italy and the energy of London, Madrid felt like something of a European backwater.

We would spend the first weeks filming in the capital, then the production would move to Barcelona. In Madrid we were staying in a rather drab hotel in the city center. The areas that recalled Madrid's glorious if checkered past were, I thought, beautiful. As an Argentinian, I found I slipped easily into the style and rhythm of Iberian city life. Knowing the language helped enormously.

From the beginning, though, Christopher Mitchum—

the film's star—didn't seem to like me. I had no idea why. An avid chess player, he hated that the first time we played together I took his queenside rook, but that couldn't have been the reason, I thought. Perhaps, it was my penchant for giggling during scenes. I know it's totally unprofessional, but once I get going it's almost impossible for me to stop. Only the wonderful David Niven, with whom I would work years later, was worse than I was.

It turned out, though, that Chris Mitchum didn't have a problem with anything I did. His issue was with all the things Rudy had put into my contract that would be commonplace today: my own trailer, special lunches to help me with my eternal dieting, a twelve-hour turnaround between workdays. Unbeknownst to me, these stipulations had put it into Chris's head that I was just another high-maintenance prima donna who needed constant coddling—something I'm very much not.

Life on a film set can be a delicate balancing act. Fragile egos abound. When actors feel slighted or underappreciated, they quite naturally tend to get upset. Often, they will gauge how they are being treated by having a look around at the perks and privileges other actors are getting. It can be very childish, and it easily leads to misunderstanding and tension. It took some time—Chris and I would end up working on two films together—but in the end I think (I hope) he saw past that initial impression and came to like and respect me.

Karl Malden, on the other hand, took to me immediately. He was a famous giggler himself, and we would sometimes have to do take after take because we could not stop laughing. Like Robert Mitchum, Karl was from the old school of acting: He always knew his lines, got along with everybody, and never put on airs. We'd sit in our cloth-backed film-set chairs and he would tell me stories about Brando and Steve McQueen.

After wrapping in Madrid it was on to Barcelona and the fabulous Monte Real, a five-star boutique hotel that was hidden snugly behind an ivy-covered wall just outside the old city. Days later, after a rather heated debate with the film's director, Antonio Isasi-Isasmendi, it was decided that even though my character had been kidnapped and was under duress she would still spend most of the picture in her underwear. For me, that meant a crash diet—only one plate of pasta a day—and hours at the hotel pool trying to color myself a nice dark brown.

I was down at the pool one day when Franco Nero, whom I had met briefly at Franco Zefirelli's a few years before, came swaggering up. Loquacious and charming, he had been all over the European tabloids because of his affair with Vanessa Redgrave. He mentioned that Brigitte Bardot would be arriving at the hotel any day—she was shooting a film—and that I should meet her.

I was a huge fan, so I called Rudy, begging him to arrange a dinner. My brother, Drew, to whom I was growing closer—albeit long-distance—flew out (I suspect more because of Brigitte Bardot than to see his sister).

My brother and I sat down to an early dinner with Brigitte Bardot and her entourage at a swanky little tapas place off Las Ramblas. She was so completely Brigitte Bardot: In a bad mood, she sat pouting at the head of the long table, barely noticing as people fussed and fawned over her. It was wonderful, like watching a movie. This is how it is to be a diva, I thought. I sat transfixed, munching on my garlic-fried shrimp and wishing Dino were with me so he could do all the talking.

Bardot ate very little and spoke even less, yet everything

revolved around her. I watched a waiter literally fall over his own feet trying to catch her eye. Old men sitting at the bar gawked, open-mouthed, silently toasting their good luck at walking in that day. When Bardot winked at the man I thought he would drop like a stone to the floor. It was a performance for the ages. My God, this is her real life, I thought.

I was nervous. Barely saying anything, I sat quietly next to Bardot, feeling small and frumpy. Later I learned that the way to her heart was to talk about animals. Like me, she was passionate about them and committed to their humane treatment. I wished I had said something. Then I felt guilty about the idea of using puppies and kittens to impress Brigitte Bardot. So silly.

Dino flew in halfway through the shoot. It was so good having him there. After my day of filming, we'd stroll aimlessly around, getting lost and making each other laugh.

It was after he'd left, and I was starting to feel lonely again, that I found my new little companion. She had been left to die in a filthy alley off a main street. Bundling her up in my arms, I decided that along with starring in the movie I was going to save this dog.

I named her Nena, and she must have thought she'd hit the jackpot. There was a trip to the vet. There was grooming. There were private walks by the hotel staff. Most days, Nena was my entourage on the set; I would lift her up and put her on the food service table so she could eat her fill.

Toward the end of filming I had a crate built for her. On my last day, I stood in front of my hotel with all my luggage plus the crate containing Nena: my street dog was going home with me.

Picking me up at the airport, Dino burst out laughing when he saw her. "Well, Olivia," he said, "you're going to love meeting Sofia! She's in the car. I found her wandering the streets of Beverly Hills and took her in!"

The six weeks in Spain had flown by, and as soon I was back in Los Angeles I told Rudy that now that *Camille* was off I wanted to do something high-profile. The producer Ross Hunter was in the middle of casting his new big-budget film, *Lost Horizon*. Apparently I was a front-runner for the one of the leads. The film was to be a musical remake of the 1937 Frank Capra movie, based on the novel by James Hilton.

Mr. Hunter had a reputation for making movies that made money, so Columbia Studios was fully behind the picture. It would have an all-star cast, a score by Burt Bacharach, and a lot of buzz surrounding it. Beating out Natalie Wood, I landed the role of Maria; I would star along with Peter Finch, Liv Ullmann, Sir John Gielgud, Sally Kellerman, and George Kennedy.

The film would shoot just over the hill from our house, on the Warner Bros. Studio lot. Because it was a musical, there would also be a long rehearsal time. Songs, dance numbers, and scene work would all be worked out before filming began.

The day after I signed the contract and a week before I was to meet everybody and start work, I began to feel sick. A quick trip to the doctor confirmed that I was pregnant.

Dino handled the news as you might expect of a twenty-year-old: He was happy, saying all the right things and looking after me, asking every half hour if I was feeling okay.

Our happiness was matched by Rudy's panic when I gave him the news: He was worried that I would lose the role. We decided it might be best if I didn't say anything for as long as possible. I wouldn't lie, of course; if anybody asked, I would tell them. But Rudy said it would be better to wait until I was well into rehearsals and knew everybody.

This proved harder than I thought. First, I have never been good at holding back; a lie, even a lie of omission, gnaws away at me. I hate it. Second, I was already getting bigger. During my fourth week, our costume designer, the Oscar-winning Jean Louis, took me aside to tell me, "Olivia, my love, you must try and watch what you are eating. I'm afraid your costumes are getting tighter and tighter."

Deciding to confide in him, I replied, "Oh, Jean, I'm sorry. Truth is, I'm having a baby."

"Olivia, that's wonderful!" he said. Then he whispered, "Not to worry, I'll make alterations. And mum's the word, my sweet."

Jean Louis was one of the classiest men I've worked with. In his long career he dressed everybody from Katharine Hepburn to Cindy Crawford, earning thirteen Academy Award nominations. He designed the dazzling, skintight dress Marilyn Monroe wore so breathtakingly when she sang "Happy Birthday, Mr. President" to John Kennedy on his birthday (I read somewhere that the dress sold at auction for over $1 million). He was an absolute dear to work with, and he knew how to keep a secret.

Weekday mornings, I rehearsed the dance numbers. In my baggy genie pants and tummy-covering sweat top, I listened carefully to our choreographer, Hermes Pan. Hermes was best known for his years of working with his close friend Fred Astaire. He paid me a huge compliment one day when he said I picked up steps faster than Ginger Rogers. I assumed he was simply being sweet, but I still took it as a compliment.

It was the singing that was hard for me. Although I still dream about having a great voice, at this point I'd settle for a fair one. I had started singing lessons as soon as I arrived in Los Angeles, and after my marriage you could always catch me singing a Bee Gees or Bowie tune while housecleaning or walking our dogs. But in *Lost Horizon*, the last high note in Maria's big song was way up there, and as much as I tried, as much as the great Burt Bacharach worked with me, I just couldn't reach it. In the end, my singing was dubbed. Which, I'm sorry to say, did not play well on the screen.

Fortunately, or rather unfortunately, my singing was hardly the most questionable element of *Lost Horizon*. Coming after a long string of hit Hollywood musicals, beginning with *The Sound of Music*, *Lost Horizon* would mark a sad end to that particular 1960s genre. The film was a ball to make, from Gene Wilder's coming in to audition and ending up improving a musical number to Karl Malden's stopping by with Michael Douglas to say hi. But it was such a bad film. It's now considered one of the fifty worst movies ever made (although one of the most enjoyable bad movies to watch).

Sometimes that just happens. So many different elements have to come together to make a film work. The planets need to align just right. You can have the best script in the world—ours was by Larry Kramer. You can have great music—ours was by Burt Bacharach. You can have a great cast, a world-class choreographer, and a producer who knows how to make a good picture. But having all the parts doesn't mean the whole will click. There is something magical in making movies. For all the experience you bring to bear, it's always a gamble. You either give yourself over to that or find another line of work.

Meanwhile, I was having a baby, and day by day I was becoming more excited. For Dino, the opposite seems to have been true. I began to notice that his showers were becoming a tiny bit longer. He worked through things in the shower; it was his time to think. I had always thought it was so sweet. Oftentimes I would hear the bathroom door shut and the water turn on and think, "Oh, Dino has something on his mind."

He had decided to take some time off from medical school to play semiprofessional football with a team in Las Vegas. (There was no end to the things he wanted to try; he was on a continual search.) But by that time I was well into my seventh month of pregnancy, and I wasn't too happy that he would be gone for about a month. I could never stand in the way of something he wanted to do, though—nobody could.

He returned from Vegas in late January 1973, around the time I wrapped *Lost Horizon*. I had managed to keep the pregnancy a secret from cast and crew through the entire shoot. It hadn't been easy, especially since I had been sick almost every day.

A few weeks later, Dino and I went to Jeanne's to watch a documentary, *Bigfoot!* Made by Peter Byrne, an Englishman Dino had met who had led expeditions searching for the mythical creature (I should mention that he had also run his own safari company in Nepal for 18 years, wrote books, and was a serious conservationist). As I sat there watching some incredible, if slightly suspect, footage I began to feel uncomfortable; my stomach began to cramp. Later that night, I finally had to wake Dino up.

"I think he's on the way," I said calmly.

"Okay," said Dino, and went straight into the shower.

As I sat quietly on my suitcase by the front door, waiting for Dino to wash away the shock of the moment, I thought about motherhood: Nothing was ever going to be the same again. Would I be a good mother? Yes, I thought, of course I will. A feeling of total love and readiness welled up inside me.

I remember telling Dino, as we were speeding down Beverly Boulevard, that I was going to be sick. He immediately pulled over, leaned across me, opened the door of his new, canary-yellow Ferrari, and said, "That's fine, Liv. Just, please, not in the car." Even at that moment, he was such a *guy*.

At 12:22 the next afternoon, after six hours of labor that turned Dino's face pasty white and sent him flying out of the delivery room, my first son, Alexander Gunther Martin, was born. A more beautiful baby I had never seen. I held him close while I smiled and cried and finally drifted off to sleep.

Alex's room was sky blue and bright yellow. Soft, white baby sheets lined the white-painted crib. A cream-colored carpet sprinkled with bright silver stars tied the whole thing together. A mobile of zoo animals—giraffes, lions, and elephants—turned slowly above his crib. It was just about the most darling little room you've ever seen.

Dino and I came home with Alex the day after the delivery exhausted, elated, overwhelmed, and arguing. We had been fighting a lot since Dino had come back from Las Vegas, and I had felt something wasn't right. I loved him: He had wooed and won me, he had been there for me after Christopher, and now he was the father of my boy. Even now, years after his death, there's a part of my heart that's his. But, I had discovered after he got back, he had cheated on me. When I was seven months pregnant, he had gone off and been unfaithful. As I laid Alex down in his eggshell-colored bassinet, all I could see was red.

For the next few months, we tried our best. We posed for happy baby pictures: the famous, loving couple with their beautiful baby boy. We talked and we laughed—nothing could change the fact that we were basically good friends. But a light had gone out, and we both knew it. If we'd been older, perhaps, we'd have gone to counseling. We would have worked to rebuild trust and learned to communicate. We'd have done all the things you do before you say it's over, walk away, and start again. But we were young, and it was a different time. So Dino started spending more time out with his friends. I hung out with Desi (Dino joked that I'd won custody of him) and the songwriter and movie composer Guy Finley.

During these difficult months I got hit with another piece of news that landed like an A-bomb. Dino sat me down one day and told me that Liza, having traveled to Rome to do some publicity, had met with Franco and tested for the lead in *Camille*.

I was stunned. Liza and I would often talk about work, and I had told her how excited I was to play Marguerite Gautier. How it was the role of a lifetime, and how Franco would bring it to life. I had said that he was a genius and I loved him and that he was adapting the work with me in mind. It was like I was handing it to her, the way I described it.

I felt betrayed. I understood that having an Oscar-winning name like Liza's attached would help Franco get the picture made. Directors, in my experience, will do anything to get a project off the ground, and I really couldn't blame him (although in my heart I did). But Liza? How could she go behind my back like that? She wouldn't even have known about *Camille* if I hadn't talked it up.

Not too long after that she called from Rome to apologize and smooth things over. It was big of her, but I found myself being nasty, telling her that Franco must be thinking of doing the film as a comedy if he were willing to cast her in the role. It was a terrible thing to say, and I felt awful afterward, but I was hurt and angry.

Ultimately *Camille* never did get made. Liza and I did find our way back to being friends, although it was never quite the same. She and Desi split up after she and Peter Sellers had too much to drink one night in London and got married (the marriage was annulled the next morning). Movies are a very strange business.

Guns

Dino had always had a passion for guns. Growing up, he had been surrounded by them—a strange 1950s cultural thing, very American and totally foreign to me. When the boys were in their early teens, Dean Sr. had presented them with a decommissioned World War II artillery cannon. It was kept out in the desert, close to their house in Palm Springs. The boys would spend summer weekends swimming, riding their bikes, and firing their cannon.

By the time Dino and I were married, he had acquired a huge gun collection. There were World War II guns of all types from every nation, including a U.S. grease gun, a British Sten gun with the famous clip on the side, and a 20mm antitank cannon that the Swiss had built for the Germans. He had two Thompson submachine guns and antique flintlock pistols and muskets. (I must confess that Alex, my son, had to help me with this list, as I know nothing about guns. But even then I knew it was a special collection and must have been worth a small fortune.)

Now that Dino and I were splitting up, I had a new baby in the house and was angry. I gave Dino an ultimatum: "Get your guns out of the house! Sell them, store them, give them away, I don't care. I just want them gone!"

Early one morning a week later, Dino walked into the house trailing behind him a five-foot, four-inch rat: squat and fat, with wide, awkward hips; thick, stubby legs; and a sharp, pointy nose jutting out over a small, thin-lipped mouth. He wore round, wire-rimmed glasses and a loose, ill-fitting suit. Sweat ran down his forehead. He refused to look at me when Dino introduced us. He would have been hilarious if he hadn't been so unpleasant.

"This guy's a creep," I whispered to Dino when the two of us went into the kitchen.

"He's here to buy my collection," Dino replied, and walked out.

I had a sour, sinking feeling; something was telling me that this guy was bad news. Dino began to pack up his smaller guns, putting the cases in the trunk of the beautiful Cadillac Eldorado convertible that had been my wedding gift from Dean and Jeanne. He was going to follow the rat man to his place, where the rat man would decide which pieces he wanted. It sounded shady to me, and as Dino left I thought again, this isn't good.

I made coffee. I fed the dogs. I went into the bathroom to take a bath. A little later I was standing over my bathroom sink, wiping the condensation from the mirror, when there was a knock at the bathroom door.

"Olivia, open the door, please." It was Dino.

"Give me a second," I yelled back through the door.

"No, Olivia, now." His voice sounded strained. I wrapped my hair up in a towel, put on my big robe, and opened the door. Dino looked deadly serious. I could see he was afraid. Behind him, standing in our bedroom, were six or seven men looking back at me. One of them said Dino was being arrested, and they had a warrant to search the house. They moved Dino and me and Norma, our housekeeper, into the living room, where they told us to sit and wait. Dino was in a lot of trouble, they said, and I would be too if I didn't cooperate.

I sat with Alex in my arms for two hours while the men searched our little house. Dino and I kept a couple of joints in a silver box on our antique coffee table; in a moment of high drama, when I thought no one was looking, I grabbed the box and sat on it.

The police—so they had identified themselves—found nothing, but throughout the search they were hard and, I thought, unnecessarily rude. I knew how difficult their jobs must be, and to have expected any consideration from them was perhaps foolish, but their attitudes, their barely concealed condescension as they moved about the house, struck me as over the top. We were hardly Bonnie and Clyde, I thought as I sat there in my bathrobe holding my three-month-old boy.

After the search, the men left, taking a very quiet Dino with them. There was not much that shook Dino, but this obviously had, and I remember thinking how much like a little boy he looked as they led him out.

The house was a mess, Alex needed to be fed, and Norma was in shock. I had tears running down my cheeks, and I didn't know what to do. Then the phone rang. "Olivia, I don't want you to be scared." Frank Sinatra's voice resonated with calm and authority. "I'm taking care of this. Dino has been charged with eleven federal counts of illegal weapons possession without a license, but we're on it. It will be okay, honey. Just stay put and Dino will be home in no time. Love ya, baby."

With that I started to relax. The Chairman of the Board was on the case, and nobody was better at looking after his own.

It took four hours before Dino was back, clearly shaken

but smiling. He didn't really go into detail. Later, I learned that his arrest had been the culmination of a huge LAPD investigation. It had been a setup; the police had wanted to make an example of Dino. A ridiculous amount of man-hours and resources had gone into something that was, in the end, nothing more than an opportunity for the DA to grab some headlines and for the police to humble and humiliate the son of a rich celebrity. They hadn't counted on Sinatra stepping in.

A deal was reached. I never saw my Cadillac convertible again, Dino's impressive gun collection—just a few of which had been illegal—was confiscated, and the DA had a chance to parade the son of Dean Martin in front of the cameras. But all charges were dropped.

The arrest had made a splash in the papers, and the story was good fodder for the gossip shows. More important, Dino seemed, all of a sudden, to have grown up. He became more serious. He dropped out of medical school, deciding a life in medicine wasn't for him. He laid low, passing on parties, avoiding all the usual hot spots. Perhaps the reality, the threat of jail—of losing so much—had left a mark somewhere deep inside him.

That change was especially reflected in our conversations; there was no more charm or youthful angst. It was clear we weren't going to make it, and we both had to come to grips with that fact. For Dino the transition would be easier; he had a home field advantage, after all. But for me, well, everything I knew about living in Los Angeles I knew through Dino: The places I ate were the places he had introduced me to; all my friends—except for Rudy—I had met through him. Then there was his family, which I thought of as my own. Were they now going to disappear from my life?

More than anything else, though, I was sick with grief

over losing my best friend. I spent more time at Jeanne's. Three, four times a week I would drive up to the gates of Mountain Drive and press the buzzer. I just wasn't ready to let go. To be alone.

Jeanne, of course, welcomed me in. "Regardless of what's happening between you and Dino," she would say, "you are my daughter-in-law and the mother of my grandson, Olivia. You are always welcome in my home." She was all class.

She had recently hired a new secretary. Young, sweet, and eager to learn, Sharon Heinz—one of the heirs to the Heinz family fortune—was also highly strung. She had a habit of scratching her neck raw whenever she became nervous. Needless to say, we got on. With Jeanne out and the house empty, I would sit with Sharon in her little office while she worked through Jeanne's papers.

Sharon was married to Nick Weinberg, whose brother, Henry, had just started dating Elizabeth Taylor. When I met Henry, he immediately said, "Would you like to meet Elizabeth? Because she would love to meet you."

Six years before, I had sat in a darkened movie cinema in East London watching with muted awe Franco's *Taming of the Shrew*. Elizabeth Taylor had been like a supernova on that screen, radiating energy. She seemed to possess an almost elemental quality, like gold or stardust. What's more, she was, in my opinion, the single most beautiful woman in the world. Now I was driving through Bel Air to meet her.

"Look at how *gorgeous* you are! Get out of here right now," she gasped when I walked in. She had a bad back— a memento from her first husband, Conrad "Nicky" Hilton, who, the story goes, had thrown her down a flight of stairs. She was lying in traction, surrounded by an array of soft, cream-colored pillows. "Much too beautiful," she said again.

Stepping farther into her room I replied, "And you are Elizabeth Taylor, and even lying in bed with no makeup on, with your violet eyes you are still the most glamorous, beautiful woman alive."

She stared at me for a heartbeat and then burst out laughing. "Oh, all right then, come sit by me." Her voice was a purr.

She reminded me of myself: naïve, but far from dumb. Open, almost childlike; she had no airs. Yet, I would realize, we both possessed strengths we might not understand but that could flash out to keep us safe when needed.

I remembered the time, years before, when Franco had taken me to meet Richard Burton in London. I had worn a bright, tight canary-yellow suit with a fabulous plunging neckline. Franco hated it, and as we walked into Mr. Burton's dressing room Franco had made some flippant remark about my dress being too loud and revealing.

"This old thing? I love it!" I'd retorted, "The colors are just so—outstanding. Don't you think?" And I had giggled into my hand.

"My God, she's a lot like Lizzy," Burton had said, and laughed his throaty Welsh laugh.

Sitting now at "Lizzy's" bedside, I could see why he had laughed. I recognized mischievousness in her. And playfulness. Again, I recognized myself.

I spent a few weeks sitting with her every day while she convalesced in bed. We talked about movies and men, actors we admired, and films we would have loved to have been in. We shared stories about growing up and coming to Hollywood. Mostly I just listened, and I always left feeling more in awe. She was one of the few who turn out to be bigger and brighter than the image. What a star she was.

Still, I grieved for my broken marriage and the family I was losing.

What do I do now? I thought. Elizabeth Taylor had battled back, but she was Elizabeth Taylor. There was only one of her. Nauseated and afraid, I would go to bed with an overwhelming sense of loss and the strange solace that comes from feeling very sorry for yourself.

At that difficult moment, an offer for a film came in. *Black Christmas* was going to be a classic horror film, the director, Bob Clark, told me. In the end, it became a good deal more, I think. I love it because it was one of the first true "slasher" films. Making it was scary and thrilling and fun. Ironically, Bob—whom I adored working with—would find his biggest success directing a comedy, *A Christmas Story*.

Filming in Canada, *Black Christmas* would take me out of LA for eight weeks and that, I thought, was just what I needed. The idea of sitting at home thinking about my marriage filled me with dread. Yes, it was selfish of me— Alex was just five months old. But he would stay with his father, ten minutes from Jeanne's. He would be surrounded by family. I decided to say yes to the film.

There was no pressure working on *Black Christmas*. It didn't have a huge budget. It was what we would consider today an indie film, and indies can be so much more enjoyable to work on than studio films.

I loved how Bob worked. Quietly and with great care, he went through each day's shooting. He involved us, the actors, in decisions about shots and scenes. I worked well with the two leads, Keir Dullea and John Saxon. Another of the film's leads was a young Margot Kidder. Margot was outspoken, brash, and up for anything. Totally fearless, she would interrogate Bob about each page of the script. "Why would my character do this here?" or "Do you honestly think my character would say this, right now?" For Margot, it was simple: We may be working on just a low-budget horror film but, dammit, if we couldn't make it the best low-budget horror film ever. Though I admired—envied, really—her volubility and dedication to the cause, I was intimidated by her style. I've always preferred to work quietly (hushed tones and clear, polite explanations bring out the best in me). So I tended to shy away from Margot on set. It was nothing personal, but when people work so differently, it's best, sometimes, to keep your distance. A film set can be a fragile ecosystem, and it doesn't take much to disturb its equilibrium. The reason I loved Bob was because we worked in such a similar fashion. Notwithstanding our differences, Margot and I got on well (if at a distance), as did everyone on the set. The film was just what I needed, and I was thrilled it had come along. A few years ago, there was a remake of the film, and the producers contacted me asking if I might like to do some PR for it. I declined. I didn't have anything against their remake—indeed, I hadn't even seen it—it was just that *my* version held a special place in my heart. To this day *Black Christmas* is the only horror film, other than *Psycho* and *The Exorcist*, I've seen. (And, naturally, both of those in their original versions.)

About three weeks into the shoot, Dino and I spoke. I had been checking in with him most days, but this was our first real conversation. It settled some issues: Dino and I would formally separate. We would put the house on the market, split the money, and go our separate ways.

After hanging up, I called down and ordered a bottle of wine. I felt like a failure. I cried, I drank, and I spent the night with someone. All very natural, but this was the point at which my grief began to lead me down a self-destructive path.

Dino moved out late on a Sunday afternoon. Monday morning, he was back at the front door, asking what was for breakfast. We couldn't help but laugh together while we cried. Through it all—our marriage, our baby, the infidelity, the arrest—our deep friendship had endured. It always would.

I had been home three weeks, and everything was happening so fast. I was now a single, twenty-three-year-old mother with a baby boy and three dogs. I was scared. I felt as though it was my fault, that if I had only been stronger I could have saved my relationship. I was frightened that I might not be a good mother. Alex was a beautiful baby boy, and I felt I was somehow letting him down.

These thoughts were toxic: I was depressed, and the power of my depression was in its self-fulfilling quality. I felt I had made nothing but bad choices, so I started to make bad choices. My eating became uncontrollable: binge eating, middle-of-the-night raids on the fridge and pantry. I began to drink more.

In today's self-help parlance, I began to treat the symptoms and not the cause. I started to take diet pills to offset the eating. When they kept me awake, I took sleeping pills, with white wine spritzers to wash them down. I have never been able to hold alcohol, so when I drank I got drunk.

A "cry for help," a "downward spiral." Name it what you like: I was in trouble, and I needed help.

An Apple and a Flower

A Santa Ana wind blew warm through the window of the Santa Monica bungalow. Outside, the huge blue Pacific barely seemed to move. The man who was about to become my guru was sitting in a big, comfortable white armchair hugging himself and laughing in a way that can only be described as jolly. He was dressed in bright orange and gaudy red. His lightly tinted glasses couldn't hide the sparkle in his eye. Everything about this man with the strange name radiated pure love.

I want to introduce Swami Muktananda, the guru who came into my life that clear, sunny California day and never left. Meeting him was the most important thing ever to have happened to me. I am the woman I am, the mother, the wife, and the actor I am, because of him. In fact, I believe I am alive today because of his presence in my life.

I really think that the universe led me to Muktananda. Slowly at first, step by step, until it set me down in front of him so I could be walloped by his energy right down to the base of my spine. I want to share that journey from when I was desperate, scared, and punishing myself to the moment when Muktananda, whom I would call Baba, spoke to me for the first time and my head exploded with light as tears streamed down my face.

My friend Guy Finley and I are both seekers, always open and ready to embrace new ideas. Guy had heard about a meditation group that met in Santa Monica, and thought that the two of us should go down and have a look.

Stories of how people came to find the thing that saved them often start with them having to be dragged, kicking and screaming, toward it. Not so for me. As I've said, I knew that I was in a bad place and needed help. Also, a new year, 1974, was right around the corner. It would be a chance to start fresh, I thought, to make some much-needed changes. So I jumped at Guy's invitation.

The group was a casual affair run by a man named Bob Raymer. Like so many of the people I was about to meet, he turned out to be wonderfully kind and patient with me. I knew nothing of India or meditation, and the idea of sitting still and doing nothing but breathing for any amount of time seemed absolutely crazy to me.

Inviting me into his little study the first time, he talked about meditation and eventually about how I might begin to be kinder to myself. He had a soft, sweet voice that you had to lean in to hear. He told me that he was a direct disciple of Paramahansa Yogananda, an Indian guru—the word means simply "teacher"—who had helped introduce meditation and yoga to millions of people in the West through his book *Autobiography of a Yogi*.

Soon I was seeing him regularly. During our meetings, which were always so relaxing, I would sit facing him on a small couch. On the wall behind him was a picture that I would find myself getting lost in. It was a photograph, clearly taken in India, of two men, one of whom, much

My parents
on their wedding day.
Buenos Aires, 1950.
(Author's personal collection)

This picture captures
so much of who I am.
I've always loved to eat.
Buenos Aires, 1952.
(Author's personal collection)

My dear mum loved to cut my hair.
She fancied herself quite the stylist,
but strangely, I always seemed to
end up with lopsided bangs.
Buenos Aires, 1955.
(Author's personal collection)

Drew and me with Olive Hussey, our grandmother on our mum's side. She may look stern but she was a total softy—again with the bangs. Buenos Aires, 195. *(Author's personal collection)*

My father conferring with his mother. She *was* as stern as she looked. *(Author's personal collection)*

My mum (far right) with my aunty Linni. They were so much alik *(Author's personal collection)*

I'm not sure when this was taken.
My father was considered one of
the last old-style tango singers,
although I never got to hear him sing.
(Author's personal collection)

y first professional headshot.
vas 10 and the photo was for
otlight magazine, which highlighted
·w actors in London. I thought
poked like a young Audrey Hepburn.
*hoto credit: Courtesy of
·otlight magazine)*

The Prime of Miss Jean Brodie, 1965,
Wyndham Theatre. Forever afterwards
I could say I worked with
the great Vanessa Redgrave.
I played Jennie, the "pretty one."
(Copyright: Central Press/Hulton Archive)

"The star-crossed loves." Leonard and me on the balcony. Oh, how we struggled with the scene. *(© Paramount Pictures Corp. All Rights Reserved. Courtesy of Paramount Pictures)*

Haggling with an Italian shop owner in between shooting (I thought if I shopped in costume I'd get a better price). Miss Mayfair, my "Dark Cloud," hovers just behind me. *(© Paramount Pictures Corp. All Rights Reserved. Courtesy of Paramount Pictures)*

Bicycling around Cinecitta
Studios between takes.
(© Paramount Pictures Corp.
All Rights Reserved. Courtesy
of Paramount Pictures)

Leonard and me sharing
a moment while filming
the wedding scene.
(© Paramount Pictures Corp.
All Rights Reserved. Courtesy
of Paramount Pictures)

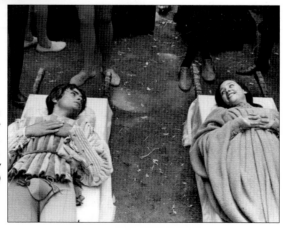

Leonard and me about to film
our final exits (I'm desperately
trying to make him laugh).
(© Paramount Pictures Corp.
All Rights Reserved. Courtesy
of Paramount Pictures)

Franco directing. The only true genius I've ever known.
(© Paramount Pictures Corp. All Rights Reserved. Courtesy of Paramount Pictures)

The love scene. Lord, I was nervous (of course, Leonard was anything but). *(© Paramount Pictures Corp. All Rights Reserved. Courtesy of Paramount Pictures)*

Leonard and me behind
the scenes, being artistic.

My favorite image of
myself as Juliet: young,
innocent, and in love.

The Royal command performance of *Romeo and Juliet*, 1968. This photo was taken after my unfortunate little accident. *(Photo Credit: Keystone Pictures USA/Alamy Stock Photo)*

Alan Jack, my first boyfriend. Talented, tender, and very French. Sadly, Alan passed away in 1995. *(Author's personal collection)*

Ireland during the filming of David Lean's *Ryan's Daughter*, 1969. A difficult time made worse by how young I was. *(Photo Credit: ZUMA Press, Inc./Alamy Stock Photo)*

Dino and me at the altar with the whole Martin family, 1970. What a larger-than-life group they were. I may look pouty and brooding but I was over the moon, I was so happy.
(© Ron Galella/Ron Galella, Ltd.)

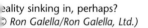
eality sinking in, perhaps?
© Ron Galella/Ron Galella, Ltd.)

Dean Sr. and me. Being with Dean was like watching an old movie and knowing it would become one of your favorites. Jeanne took this and I remember it was an unbearably hot day.
(Author's personal collection)

Dino and me in 1973, when I
was eight months pregnant.
Our dear friend Barry Bregman
took this. I'm thinking,
"I could murder a bowl
of pasta, right now."
*(Photo copyright:
Barry Bregman)*

Alex and me, 197.
Dino and his
mother, Jeanne,
were thrilled:
Alex was blond!
*(Photo copyright:
Barry Bregman)*

My dear friend Bonnie Moffet
took this of me around 1975.
I included it because
it's my husband David's
favorite shot of me.
*(Photo copyright:
Bonnie Colodzin Moffet)*

Jesus of Nazareth (1977).
The crucifixion scene.
A powerful scene and
I disagreed with Franco:
I thought the wine helped me.
*(Photo Credit: Ronald Grant
Archive/Alamy Stock Photo)*

Death on the Nile (1978) cast photo. This was the closest I dared get to Bette Davis.
She would've preferred, perhaps, that I sat in a dinghy tied to the back of the boat.
(Photo Copyright: Michael Ochs Archives)

Akira and me in Japan, 1981. I was totally, madly in love. I used to wait backstage for him at his concerts. (What on earth am I wearing?) *(Author's personal collection)*

I love this sweet shot of Akira and me in 1982. God, we were happy. *(Author's personal collection)*

In 1983 my oldest became a big brother Akira and I named our son Maximillian Hussey Fuse. *(Author's personal collection)*

My guru, Swami Muktananda, 1985.
(© 1977 SYDA Foundation®)

My third—and last—husband, David. He's rock and roll down to his bones. He swept me off my feet, literally, by taking me for a ride on the back of his Harley on our second date.
(Author's personal collection)

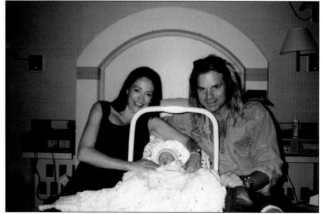

In 1993 David and I welcomed to the world our daughter: India Joy Eisley. Joy, after my mother.
(Author's personal collection)

In 2003 a dream of
mine came true.
Playing Mother Teresa
was not only an honor
but it rekindled my
love of acting.
*(Photo Courtesy of
LuxVide S.p.A.)*

The Maestro, Franco,
and me at the premiere
of his film *Hamlet*, 1990.
(© Ron Galella/Ron Galella, Ltd.)

Dr. Michael Castro. When you get to be my age and you've been through what I've been through, it's good to have a great doctor. (Photo credit: Alexander Martin)

Dr. Ari Gabayan. My second great doctor. Together they are my "Wellness Team." (Photo credit: Alexander Martin)

My son Alex, his wife Megan, and David and me outside the Aero Theatre in Los Angeles, 2016. The event was the premiere of the digitally remastered version of *Romeo and Juliet* (I wish Max and India were in the shot). (Author's personal collection)

Our daughter, India,
with our two great loves,
Baba and Lola.
(Author's personal collection)

The girl on the balcony.
(© Paramount Pictures
Corp. All Rights Reserved.
Courtesy of Paramount
Pictures)

younger, was sitting at the other's feet. They were half-dressed, and there was a calmness to their expressions that somehow moved me. When I asked Bob who these men were, he told me they were a student and his teacher. The older man was Sri Bhagawan Nityananda, a guru who had spent his life in India. The younger man sitting at his feet was Swami Muktananda Paramahansa, who was here in America. My heart, I remember, skipped a beat. Something about the second name resonated with me, and something about both of them, their aspects perhaps, spoke to me. I decided I wanted to know more.

At the end of the meeting Bob gave me a copy of a book written by a guru named Sathya Sai Baba. The picture on the back showed a man with big, happy eyes and a huge 1970s Afro. He was known for being able to manifest *vibhuti*—an ash that in Hinduism is used for worship and is considered sacred—from his hands in front of the large crowds that came for his blessing. In his book, he talks about finding your own guru: If you are sincere, your guru will find you in your lifetime. I loved the book; it was simple and straightforward. I decided to write Sathya Sai a letter because I had been told that he was known to put his hands down on piles of letters and bless them. I asked him to bless me and also, if there was a guru out there for me, please to send him; I needed him.

It was a bit like writing to Santa, only a Santa that you really believed in and expected to hear back from. A few weeks later, I learned that Bob Raymer was hosting an evening with Swami Muktananda, the man sitting at the feet of his teacher in the photograph on Bob's study wall. I asked him if I could attend.

"Of course, Olivia," he said, "just bring a piece of fruit and a flower." The fruit was an offering to show respect and the flower was to ask for a blessing. That didn't sound too bad, I thought; the idea of one of these spiritual men blessing me seemed nice.

I arrived late. Holding my apple and flower and feeling a little nervous, I made my way up the street to Bob's condo. Out in front, people were already waiting in a line to be let in. I pushed past the line and, once inside, immediately felt the energy in the room. I began to feel warm; beads of sweat started to run down my back. The room was packed; from where I stood at the back I could see very little, but I could hear the laughter, big bursts of it, erupting from up front and rolling like an ocean swell across the room to me. I craned my neck to see who was laughing.

Finally, I saw Swami Muktananda, sitting in his white chair as I described him in the first paragraph of this chapter, dressed in his orange and red; Swami Muktananda laughing and swaying like a happy baby; Swami Muktananda hugging himself in unrestrained delight. That was what I saw; what I felt was pure love. He radiated it: love for himself and for all of us in the room. It was so clear. How wonderful to be that comfortable with yourself, I thought, to be so happy and loving.

He spoke for about an hour, telling stories through his translator, Professor Jain. Funny stories, stories about India. He told jokes, too, and all the while he would lightly touch people near him on their foreheads. I was now sitting cross-legged against the back wall by the door, transfixed. Toward the end of the talk, when it was clear that I was not going to be able to get to the front and have a blessing, I slowly put my apple and flower beneath a cabinet so that nobody would step on them and whispered, "This is for you, and please give me your blessing."

Swami Muktananda got up to leave. As he rose, we all stood, smiling. He began walking to the door I had been sitting next to, laughing and winking at people as he went. When he was close to me, he stopped. There was a man between us, and I watched, hypnotized, as Swami Muktananda gently pushed him aside. He came right up to me and fixed me in his gaze. After a slight pause, he started speaking Hindi: "Baba says you do not meditate," Professor Jain said.

My head filled with light. Tears started from my eyes. Suddenly I was full of energy. Through an uncontrollable smile I replied, "No, I don't."

"Baba says everyone should meditate. It's the will of God."

I was aware that the entire room was looking at us; I didn't really care. Swami Muktananda lifted his hand to my face. He touched my cheek. He stroked my hair once, then twice. Suddenly he said, "I bless you!"

With that, he left the room. I had asked for a blessing, and he had given it.

People began to file out, but I couldn't move. A hot, rushing energy was moving up and down my spine. There was love, so much pure, new love rising inside me, and my head was saying, This is why you were born, for this moment. I wanted to live in this place forever. I wanted to see Baba again. I wanted to be near him.

Then a calmness descended on me. My eyes closed, and I sat down. It felt like what heaven might be like—a bright blue light in the center of my forehead and a stillness that was unlike anything I had ever known: bliss.

I was aware of sounds, but they seemed a long way off, and I was somehow floating far from them. Tears were streaming down my face and I couldn't move. Judgment had left. "Self" had left.

Ecstasy, that's what I was feeling.

After a time, my eyes opened and I saw Bob sitting across the room smiling at me. Slowly I stood and approached him. "That was the most amazing feeling I have ever had," I said. "That was the best twenty minutes of my life."

Bob looked at me and started to laugh. "Olivia, you've been sitting in meditation for two hours."

So it was that this gentle Indian man became the center of my life. There had been, to borrow a phrase, a God-shaped hole at the heart of me. More: a father-shaped hole and a confusion about who I was and who I wanted to be. Now, Baba would fill those empty places with his love, with his compassion, and with *shakti,* the divine force.

In May 1974, a few months after I had first met him at Bob Raymer's home, I took Dino to meet Swami Muktananda—now Baba to me—in Pasadena. Something new and powerful had entered my life and I wanted nothing more than to share it with those I loved most. I had no idea what Dino's response would be.

"I want you to come and meet this guru from India" is perhaps not what you expect to hear from your soon-to-be ex-wife. But Dino was game, so off we went.

I could see that Baba's energy was calming to Dino and he seemed really to enjoy the day we spent with him. A little while later, I gave Dino a small picture of Baba and he kept it in his wallet for years; I like to think that it was in his wallet the day he died.

Baba would always ask me, "How is your husband?" and I would always reply, "Baba, you mean my ex-husband."

To which he would smile and say, "Yes, yes, your husband." He felt the bond between Dino and me. Funny, Dino used to say, "Just wait, Olivia; when we're thirty-five or thirty-six, we'll get back together, you'll see." He died at thirty-five.

Another friend whom I wanted to introduce to Baba

was the actress Leigh Taylor-Young. Like me, Lee has always been open to an expanding spiritual world. We decided to take Baba's three-day intensive in the Catskills.

These retreats focused on meditation, chanting, and Baba's talks. You lived in a dorm and were expected to work: washing dishes, chopping food for meals, whatever needed to be done. It was called *seva,* selfless work in a place of prayer and meditation.

Every time I saw Baba, when he stepped into the room or simply turned his head and looked at me, I would burst into tears. He would laugh and laugh and say, "Look at this little actress, see how she loves to suffer!"

Nevertheless, for me those three days were charged with an ever-deepening feeling of compassion and holiness. Apart from one little confrontation with another woman over a bunk bed—a small reminder that I was still a long way off from total compassion and enlightenment—the experience was magical; I was grateful to Baba. I felt so good.

I received my spiritual name at a retreat in Oakland. Baba had just finished his lecture, and people were lining up for *darshan,* when they could go up to the guru and receive a blessing, ask a question, or seek advice. Sometimes people would ask to be given an Indian name. I was sitting close to the back and off to one side, thinking that if Baba had come into my life to be a kind of father to me, then I didn't need to ask him for a name. He would give one to me.

A moment later, Baba was peering over the many heads between us and looking straight at me. Professor Jain gestured to me to come close. I thought, Oh God, I'm in trouble.

I know it's hard to believe, but I felt that when he wanted to, Baba knew what you were thinking at any given moment. So, as I was making my way forward past the hundreds of people crowded around the front of the auditorium, I was panicking that he had seen something naughty or bad in my head.

I got to the front and knelt down. Baba leaned in close to me—when he was that close, his *shakti* could be overwhelming—and said, "Muktabai." As Jain translated, he said, "That is your spiritual name. Wear it well, for it is half my name: Muktananda." He smiled—he had the most wondrous smile—and said, "It means 'Sister Liberation'!"

As usual, I started to cry, and he gave me a sly wink.

I loved him so much. Not only for all that he was—kind and compassionate, utterly selfless and touched with a profound insight into this strange, confusing universe— but also for what he gave openly to me: a direct physical experience of what was inside myself. He let me feel an ocean of compassion, great rolling waves of love. Love for all things. Love for myself.

Later, I was sitting alone on the floor of the great hall where, twice a day, people would gather for a group meditation. Along the walls were paintings of saints: Sri Bhagawan Nityananda (Baba's guru), Anandamayi Ma (the great woman saint), as well as others. This was, in part, what had drawn me to Baba's teachings: It didn't matter what religion you practiced or what you believed; all were welcome because it was about love and compassion. That was it. There was no brainwashing or anything absurd like that; just meditation; chanting; and, again, opening yourself up to the power of love.

So there I was, eyes closed and just beginning to see in my mind's eye the pure blue sphere that can sometimes materialize as you move deeper into your meditative state, when a thought flashed across my consciousness: This is my destiny. This is what I was meant to do: find God within.

As quick as lightning I made a decision: I would give up acting and become a *sanyasini*. A *sanyasini* is like a nun: You take vows and you dedicate yourself to your guru and to self-enlightenment.

Having decided, I made my way back to my dorm room. Later that evening, I was sitting on my bed when I heard Baba's voice growing louder down the hallway. Suddenly he was standing in my room with two monks, Swami Tejo and Professor Jain, all of us crowded together in the small space. Baba came closer, took my shoulders between his hands, and began to speak softly to me in Hindi. Professor Jain translated: "Baba says he loves you very much, Muktabai. That he will always be with you, deep inside your heart."

I could feel the tears well up. Jain went on, "To be a *sanyasini* is not your destiny. You do your work for God through acting. You can awaken people to love and compassion just by being you. You are stronger now, and Baba blesses you forever!"

Swami Tejo handed Baba a beautiful blue scarf threaded with gold strands. Baba took the scarf and, running it through his hands, wrapped it around my neck and shoulders, saying through Jain, "Blue is a beautiful color for you and you must remember this." Then he put his arms around me and held me tightly, almost lifting me off the ground. We stood like that for a full minute before he let me go, turned, and left, followed by the two monks.

All my life, when times were hard I had whispered to myself, I wish God would put his arms around me and hold me and tell me I'm loved and that everything will be all right. Now, it was as if God had done just that. Working through my guru, Muktananda, the divine had made itself known to me.

At dinner that night Baba said to me, "You have to go back home. You have a film to make."

"No, Baba," I said. "There is no work right now."

Baba smiled and said I had to leave but I should know that not a day would pass when I would not be in his thoughts.

I left the next morning in a manner befitting my profession: in a deluge of tears and over-the-top drama. How I did love to suffer.

I had been home exactly two nights when, just as Baba had predicted, an offer for a film came in. With Alex sitting on my lap I held the phone to my ear and listened to the details: *H-Bomb* would star me and, amazingly enough, Chris Mitchum, with whom I had worked on *Summertime Killer* (not without some issues). The film would shoot in Thailand for three months, and I would have to be there in four days. I decided to take it.

Five days, nine vaccinations, and a twenty-three-hour flight later, Alex and I stepped off the airplane into a wall of sweltering heat and humidity that took my breath away, not to mention being half-blinded by about 200 popping flashbulbs. There are photos online of our arrival; the Thai media, alerted by the film's producers, had made a big show of it. The photos make it look as though Alex and I were mobbed and that Alex was terrified. In truth, he had had a rough flight—as any two-year-old would—and was simply irritable, hot and sticky. Despite what the photos correctly show as a crying toddler and a frazzled actress, I found that everyone was well meaning and very respectful.

Exhausted, the three of us settled into the hotel. Before leaving LA, I had needed to find a nanny for Alex, and with such short notice I had taken the recommendation of an acquaintance. Twenty-three-year-old Maria had said that, although she didn't have references "per se," she just *loved* children.

I began working, fourteen-hour days in temperatures that routinely rose above 112 degrees. It was brutal. It turned out that Chris and I were the only Western actors in the film, and as such we were the only ones who would be speaking English—a fact I learned during a take when the actor who was playing my father stepped onto his mark, looked at me, and spoke his line in Thai. Oh boy, I thought, and struggled through.

Chris and I got on smoothly, thank God. By then, he understood that it wasn't me who'd made our first shoot difficult but Rudy's contract stipulations. (Rudy could really be a tough SOB.) Chris and I hunkered down and made the best of a difficult shoot.

Thailand was magnificent, though. We shot in Bangkok, where the mornings soon became my favorite time of day. People would stop on their way to work at one of the hundreds of shrines that dotted the city. Placing strings of sweet-smelling flowers before the altar, they would bow, say a little prayer, and head off to start their day. I loved the simple idea of that, the beauty of it.

Whenever I had a chance I would head to a small temple that was close to the hotel. There, I would sit among the monks and meditate, thinking of Baba and his promise that he would be sending me his love and light while I was away. Also, in my hotel bedroom I set up a meditation table, something I have continued to do ever since. However, this being my first one, I may have gone a bit overboard. The thing was huge, taking up one whole wall. It was a low table on which I had placed framed photos of Baba, small vases with fresh flowers, candles and incense, and more photos: Jesus, Buddha, and the Virgin Mary. It was lovely to look at, and in the mornings I would sit in front of it and meditate for twenty minutes or a half hour.

A month into filming, I noticed that Alex was losing weight. I could only really spend time with him at night after work or on one of my few days off, which was frustrating. I began to worry. Maria assured me that all was fine and that she and my son were having a great time together.

I worried more. I started talking to the sweet Thai girls who worked at the hotel. Politely, they told me that my "nanny" was spending most of her time by the pool, that she had recently met a tall American man and they were together all day. Alex, they said, was running around the hotel all day, alone and unsupervised. I was furious, but I was stuck. So far from home, I felt I couldn't just fire Maria. (Today, older and a bit wiser, I would have no qualms about letting her go.) Instead, I decided on another solution: I started paying the Thai women at the hotel to keep an eye on Alex, and as soon as I had finished work for the day I would rush back and take care of him. It was horrible, but he did stop losing weight.

Toward the end of the shoot I came down with dysentery. It felt like a huge iron fist pummeling my stomach, grabbing and squeezing my insides. I was vomiting and had a fever of 105, and I was confined to bed. Chris was scheduled to leave before me and begin another movie, but we still had two scenes to do together. Not wanting to delay him, I had a doctor come to the hotel and give me a shot of something. Comfortably numb, I managed to get to the set and do the work, and Chris, happy and grateful, got to leave on time. I've always been proud of that.

The movie, when it was finally released, didn't really cover me in glory and is best left forgotten. I loved Bangkok, though, and the Thai people. Once my work was done, there was nothing left but to take the twenty-three-hour flight back to LA, fire Maria, and look for a new place to live.

Having moved out of the house that Dino and I shared before leaving for Thailand, when I stepped off the plane with Alex asleep in my arms I was something of a gypsy. It was Desi who took us in. He insisted, and seemed all too happy to have us, bless him. He was Dino's friend, of course, but this simple kindness endeared him to me for life.

I bought the groceries and did the washing up while I was looking for a home that Alex and I could move into. It was a vagabond kind of existence, but we made the best of it. Eventually, I leased a little house on Schuyler Drive in Beverly Hills, not too far from Jeanne's. Desi was sorry to see us go, but we would see him all the time.

We settled in, and I made plans to go see Baba. As the founder of the Siddha Yoga Foundation, he had started two major ashrams in the United States: one on the East Coast and one on the West. At that point, he was staying at the West Coast ashram.

Alex and I arrived in the early evening, after Baba had given his lecture and retired to his rooms. As we made our way through the ashram, all the swamis I saw stopped me to say things like, "Muktabai, so good to see you. Baba has been saying all day that his little Muktabai is on her way. That she has been gone for three months. He is so excited to see you." The feeling of welcome, of having been missed and of having a home, was so wonderful. It felt like a sanctuary.

In Thailand, I had bought a large cane chair. They were impossible to find in the United States. It was a low, round chair that sat on a base about two feet off the floor. I thought it might be perfect for Baba because it was wide, round, and open: He could easily cross his legs while comfortably folding in the silks of his *lungi*, the skirt that Indian men wear. I had had the chair upholstered with a beautiful, soft orange silk cushion and sent it to Baba for his birthday. Later, I found out that when it arrived Baba was very happy with it and said that not only did he love it but the person who had sent it was very smart, because now every time he sat down he would have to think of the person who had given it to him!

Later that night, Alex and I were called to Baba's room. He looked up at me, and I felt that bliss, that joy I always felt when I was near him and that I had missed for the past three months.

"I am so happy to have you back safely, Muktabai," he said through his translator.

Alex started jumping merrily on his bed. He always felt so at home with Baba. Noni, Baba's private assistant, was laughing and watching. Today, as I write this, I can still feel the joy of that moment, the feeling of contentment and peace, of being exactly where I wanted to be. It is one of the happiest memories I have.

"You know, Muktabai, I don't think you thought of me enough while you were gone," Baba said with a stern look. I was shocked.

"Baba," I protested, "I thought of almost nothing else, and in between meditation sessions, I made a movie!"

Baba started to laugh and said, "Your meditation table in your room, it wasn't big enough, I think!" And he laughed, a big, full belly laugh. I was dumbfounded. How on earth could he possibly have known about the table? Then, just as quickly, I thought, Well, how could he not have known? He's Baba.

After our trip, Alex and I went home to our little house

on Schuyler Drive and relaxed into a quiet routine. A few months went by, and then I received a phone call. Baba had had a heart attack and was in the hospital. Although the thought of losing him was devastating, I had read that heart attacks are common among gurus, who work with so many people, opening themselves up to their energies; it's physically demanding and takes a toll on them.

After a couple of months, I decided it was time for me to go visit. I wondered what I should take for him. I always loved giving Baba little gifts. He never expected them, and if he felt they weren't right he would simply bless them and give them back. But if a gift was thoughtful and came from the heart, he would appreciate it and keep it. So: what to take this time? In Thailand, I had found a gold necklace with little gold-and-glass Buddhas hanging along it—a Buddha necklace, meant for protection. I had bought it in Bangkok, along with a locket in the shape of the elephant God, Ganesh, which I had also hung from the necklace (I've always had a soft spot for Ganesh, the remover of obstacles). I decided to give Baba the Buddha necklace but take my little elephant off. He was never really supposed to be on there anyway, and I loved him.

Traveling to the ashram I went straight to where Baba was recovering. For weeks, in ashrams all over India, as well as in New York, LA, and other cities, chanting and prayers for Baba's recovery had continued around the clock.

His room was lit only by a muted TV in one corner and a few candles in front of a photo of Baba's own guru, Swami Nityananda, on the bedside table. But I could see that Baba was grinning when he looked at me. When he saw my tears, his grin turned to a big, soft smile. He lifted his shirt. "Look, little Muktabai, look what they did. I have a pacemaker inside me."

I cried more and he laughed more. I showed him the gold necklace. He told me to come closer, right next to his bed, where he took my face in his hands and brought me closer still. We were nose to nose, our faces almost touching, when he said, "I love your gift. I bless you."

When I rose to leave, as I was about to turn the door handle, he said,

"And Muktabai, Ganesh, who stays in your bag, is *my* gift to *you*."

Every day that I feel Baba's blessings, presence, and grace around me I am reminded of how lucky I am to have known him. We all need something to believe in, I think, whether it's the religion passed to us from our parents, a faith found through our own trial-and-error, the fingers-crossed confidence of the atheist, or the enthusiasm of the newly converted. We all seek something larger than ourselves. For me, it was—is—the power of the universe to manifest what you put into it and the grace, goodwill, compassion, and enlightenment of my guru, Swami Muktananda.

You Have to Go There to Come Back

Change. All my life it has been the one constant. Like a powerful wind unexpectedly picking up and blowing in across my life, more than anything else: Change has been the force that has shaped me. My sweet mum first introduced me to it by walking me up a gangway and then across an ocean. Then a mad Italian film director looked at me and made a decision.

Having known change for so long, I have never been afraid of it; indeed, there are times when I have craved it for its own sake. All of this explains why, by the end of 1975, I recognized I needed to make a change and that it needed to be dramatic.

Meeting Baba had given me so much. As well as more patience and a calmer inner voice, he'd shown me how to be kinder to myself, and of course he had given me the gift of meditation. But it was his unerring message of love that had come to mean the most, and it was to that message that I found my heart turning by the end of the year. I missed my mum, I missed my brother, I missed family.

I'd been in Los Angeles for over five years. I had come at nineteen on no one's counsel but my own, and I had made a life. I loved a boy and he had loved me. I had married. I had a baby. Now that boy was gone. That marriage was over. LA is a strange place: a city you come to for the promise it makes you, and now that promise was broken.

Waking up one morning, Alex still snoring in his pillow fort next to me, I looked at him and then I looked around. The light was that crazy clean light that LA has some mornings. It's a cinematic light, all soft blue and sharp white. It made me feel foreign somehow. I felt so English, even if I'm not—not really—lying there looking at the light. I found I missed the gray of a typical London morning.

Why not move? I thought. Back home.

And just like that the decision was made. Once I make up my mind there is nothing that can get me to change it. Whether that's a fault or a virtue I'm not really sure, and, to be honest, I don't really care.

Dino was upset and argued that it wasn't fair; Alex would not be able to see Jeanne and was too young to travel so far. I understood, but I told him that we needed a change and I needed my family and that they needed to meet Alex.

Leaving was simple in the end. I was shocked to find how little I had after five years. A leased house, a closet full of clothes—mostly blacks—and a few random pieces of furniture were my only footprint. I got out of the lease, packed the clothes, and sold the furniture, and that was it; I was standing at the airport stunned at how fast it all had happened.

London was just as I remembered it, and that was both a comfort and source of anxiety. I began to look for somewhere to live and could not believe how expensive everything was. Way out of my budget. Just a small side note: When Dino and I divorced there was no settlement, no alimony, not even child support. I asked for nothing. I didn't want it to seem as though I was using him, and I didn't think it was a classy thing to do anyway. Also, I was proud and didn't want to ask for anything I'd not earned. Dino helped, of course, and a few years later he did start giving me child support, which he was always happy to do. But in the beginning, after our divorce, money was tight.

I bought a Mini and after one drive from Wimbledon to the center of London I sold it; I have never been comfortable behind the wheel, and the chaotic topsy-turvy streets of London were far too much for me. I spent long, quiet afternoons talking with Mum. Alex was a big hit, of course. Drew, who had grown to look so much like the father we never mentioned, loved Alex, and they spent hours playing together.

After a few months, though, I began to feel restless again. Something wasn't right. London felt cold, imposing. It seemed indifferent to me. It felt like, by moving away from the city, I had somehow offended it and now it was closed to me. I didn't feel welcome and I didn't feel at home. Another change was in the works. But what? I thought about Rome, about New York. In the end, however, there was only one place, and I had been living there for the past five years.

LA was home and had been, and I needed to leave to learn that. It's now been nearly forty-five years of living under LA sunshine, and I admit to having a love–hate relationship with the place.

With Dino happy that we were back and Alex starting kindergarten, I thought about work. I wondered where the next job would come from. A good friend, Barry Bergman, would sometimes call. Barry was a photographer as well as the nephew of Jack Haley, who had played the Tin Man in *The Wizard of Oz*. He would call and say, "Olivia, my rent's due. Mind posing for some shots?"

He would then sell the pictures all over the world. I was always surprised when Barry would tell me that the best market for my face was Japan. Apparently, since *Romeo & Juliet*, I had been one of the top three most popular Western actresses there. I remember a photo shoot I did for a Japanese clothing company. I was floored by how much they had wanted to pay me. The shoot had been great fun, and I had especially enjoyed meeting and working with the Japanese crew. What fun to go and visit, I thought.

My Mary and My Vice

One night while I was sitting on the couch drinking a cup of tea flipping through a magazine, the phone rang.

"Darling! How would you like to be a virgin again?"

The accent was unmistakable, and the question was ridiculous.

"I'm doing a miniseries about Christ, and I want you as Mary."

After almost a year of not speaking, Franco jumped in as if no time at all had gone by; we were always that that with each other.

"You look, darling, exactly like Michelangelo's *The Pietà.*" (The statue of Mary cradling Jesus in her lap after the crucifixion. It is on display at St. Peter's Basilica at the Vatican.)

"You must fly to London and meet with Sir Lew. He's producing and wants to have a look at you before he commits." And that was it. Two days later I was dropping Alex off at his dad's and once again taking the ten-hour flight to London.

Sir Lew Grade might have looked like an American

movie gangster from the forties but he was a Churchillian Bulldog through and through and a born showman. As Britain's foremost TV impresario, Sir Lew had been the beating heart of English television for almost twenty years, from the late fifties onward.

Armed always with a cigar, Sir Lew—later Lord Lew—had a completely round, bald head; was jowly; and was thickset, but because he had started out in show business as a dancer, he was quick and even graceful. He was known for his dry, caustic wit; in a press conference he held after the box office failure of his film *Raise the Titanic* he announced, "It would have been less costly to lower the ocean."

He also had the hardness of a millionaire businessman, and like some Russian Premier reviewing troops and watching the missiles roll by in Red Square, he was known to stare dispassionately and with icy coldness when he was in the process of judging something. All of which made me just a little nervous as I sat outside his office door waiting to be seen and, I knew, judged.

As it turned out, I had no reason to be nervous at all. Sir Lew had that easy charm and self-effacing manner that I have always adored in British men.

"Zeffirelli was right," he said, looking at me down the length of his cigar. "Just like the statue." He laughed, and I knew I had the part.

When I was four or five, my mum has told me, one of my favorite games was to play *Nun*. I would walk solemnly around the house, a towel draped around my head, mouthing prayers and raising my pudgy little arms to heaven. I just loved the idea that there was such a thing as a "nun" in the world. I don't why, but they fascinated me. Perhaps it was the force of their devotion, their commitment to something they had no evidence of; just a desire and a will to believe.

Now here I was about to play the Holiest of Mothers, and I was so happy. So happy in fact that I went ahead and signed what had to have been the worst possible contract ever penned—I'm not sure if I even read it. Truth is, I would have signed anything to play Mary and to work with Franco again.

The series would film over eight months—four months in Morocco and four in Tunisia—and it would be a massive production. My only worry was Alex. I couldn't take him on location. After Thailand the thought of Alex in the deserts of the Maghreb for almost a year at some hotel with some nanny during the hot days waiting for Mummy to come home from work filled me with horror. Dino was having none of that, either. He suggested Alex stay with him, splitting his time with Jeannie, but that idea didn't work for me. I needed to be closer to him if the shoot was going to be that long. My mum and I decided, finally, that he should stay with her and Drew in London. He could go to school, and I could take a short flight and see him when I had some time off.

Flying back to LA for a few weeks before the shoot was to begin, I spent some time thinking about the role. I felt a responsibility in taking on Mary. Unlike other roles, Mary was literally *worshipped* by millions. She was, as far as I was concerned, a very real person who shaped the course of Western civilization and whose spirit and story were deeply moving. Also, she was a mother, a mother who lost a child. I was determined, as best as I could, to honor her.

Three weeks later and after a trip to see Baba for a blessing and a stop in London to tearfully drop off Alex, I was standing on the balcony of my hotel staring out across the Mediterranean Sea.

We were staying in a small coastal town about a two hours' drive from Marrakesh, the name of which escapes me now. It was the off-season, so the town was mostly empty of tourists. The entire production had set up shop at the hotel where most of us were staying. Franco and Sir Lew had put together a huge all-star cast, some of whom would fly in only for a day to shoot their part. There were people I had worked with before like Sir Laurence Olivier and Peter Ustinov, and there were many whom I didn't know, actors I was meeting for the first time, such as James Earl Jones, Christopher Plummer, and Sir Ralph Richardson. And, of course, there was Robert Powell, who was playing Jesus.

Robert, with his penetrating sea-blue eyes, was a perfect choice to play Jesus (though an idealized Western European/American idea of him). I remember seeing Robert not long after I had arrived. He was clutching his script and looking troubled.

"I can't find Franco," he said, only half taking his eyes from the pages. "I want to discuss my role, but I can never seem to find him." As I watched him wander off as if he were going to spend his own forty days in the desert, all I could do was laugh.

Days later he took me aside and asked, "Olivia, you've worked with Franco before. When do you talk to him about your role?" I could see Robert was having a tough time; understanding Franco's rhythms could be difficult and frustrating.

"Robert," I told him, "if you were not the perfect actor to play the part, then you wouldn't be here." I went on, "Franco cast you. He knows you are perfect. Just do what you feel is right and then ask him, 'How was that?' I've found that's the best way to work with him." I finished my simple advice with, "He trusts you will do your best work, and that's it." I thought I sounded naïve, but it seemed to help and Robert relaxed a little. I thought he was so moving in the part. He was wonderful.

* * *

Franco was never one to talk about an actor's role; he would talk about what was happening in a particular scene but never really about how an actor should play the part. He did that work during casting. Choosing the right actor for a role is ninety-five percent of the director's job, I think. Franco was always marvelous at casting. Once you had the job, he would give you the space to work, trusting that your choices would be right for the scene. He was wonderful to work with in that way. Even when it was difficult, say during the balcony scene, Franco was always so patient.

Franco and I, I think, had a wonderful understanding. I felt like his muse. I lived to hear Franco say after a take, "Excellent! Let's move on."

I never found that thrill working with anyone else. I only wish we had worked together more. Someone once asked Franco if he had ever been in love with a woman. He said, "Yes, once. With Olivia when we worked together during *Romeo and Juliet*." I cried when I heard that.

I decided that I would wait until I had my costumes set to begin thinking about how I wanted to play Mary. As I was removed both in time and sensibility from her, I found the best, indeed the only, way to bridge time's great expanse was to repeat the same simple phrase that I had found my way into: "It is the will of God." Of course, Mary was pure and innocent, but I decided that she also had an unshakable faith that whatever happened to her was the will of God, and that that faith gave her a deep reservoir of strength to draw on. Later, as she aged, I thought there would be a weariness to her but always a core of iron strength.

Once we began shooting, Franco seemed to love what I was doing. He would say, "Okay, Olivia, we will have the camera here. You do what you want to do." I would reply, "Yes, good," and then almost as an afterthought I would add, "I hope you like it." And that is how we worked.

I like to think that I did manage to get close to what I had in my mind for Mary; along with Juliet it is the work I am most proud of. Today, when people tell me that my portrayal of Mary touched them or that it is their favorite, it makes me so proud. It's corny, but the idea that some of my work might live on after me, that it has affected people, fills me with joy. It's simple really: The highest praise for an actor is to be loved, appreciated, and remembered.

Filming began in earnest: long days under the scorching Moroccan sun and back to the hotel, where it was just the members of the production with nothing to do for four months. The Italian crew were the first to lose it. You think actors can be divas? Try a burly working set of pampered Italian men who have Italian tastes and think Moroccan food is disgusting. They needed their pasta! So within three weeks they had called on the spirit of their distant Roman legion forebears and had taken over the hotel's kitchen, cooking the pasta that they had demanded be flown in twice a week from Rome.

Various members of the cast took it in turns to get good and drunk at the only night spot in town: the hotel's basement discotheque. We felt cut off from the world, and that was probably because we were. I remember about a month after shooting began, going into Franco's hotel room. He had a huge whiteboard sitting on an easel in the corner. It was the whole shooting schedule. Looking at it I would see that there were weeks when I wasn't filming.

"Franco," I'd say, "can't I go to London and see my boy? I am not working for three weeks."

"No, darling, the weather might change and we would then have to shoot some of your scenes."

So weeks would go by where I was alone in the hotel. There was no provision in my contract to be let off when I was not working or even for a car so I could at least get out for a time. The crew would leave before I woke up, and I would spend the day waiting for them to return. I began to drink. A couple of glasses of wine at lunch, thinking it would help me take a nap during the day. It didn't. My body chemistry is such that alcohol metabolizes to pure sugar, and as a result I drink two glasses of wine and it's like I've drunk six. I drink a bottle and I act like I've had two plus a couple of shots. It's awful and self-destructive and can be emotional, but it's also freeing and that's the allure for me.

Alone in my hotel room for hours and hours, I would give in and spend the day with a bottle of wine and tears in my eyes. Nobody knew and it never affected my work, but the drinking that started then would become something that would play a nasty part in the years to come, unfortunately.

There are times, it seems to me, when to make a difficult situation worse, just add men. One of my costars in the series had been a big flirt since day one. Now we began to spend more time together. He told me that although he was still "technically" married, he and his wife were going to separate. I liked him; I even felt, in a rather childish way, that I could love him. After a rare night out and half a bottle of wine I spent the night with him. A few days later he told me that, in fact, the separation was further off than he had supposed and that his wife was actually on her way out to visit the set. I felt sick to my stomach, not only for what I had done—when I met his wife, she was, of course, a thoroughly nice person—but for what her husband had made me think. He had lied to me, blatantly. I sank into a bout of depression and, hating myself, I naïvely vowed to never trust a man again.

The days and weeks of shooting went by. I waited desperately for my scenes to come up; each one would bring me closer to finishing and to getting to London to see Alex. Also, my days off had begun to feel like a prison sentence for me. I was most happy when I was working the whole day on the set, doing my job.

The hard labor of it all was getting to everybody, I think. Franco snapped at me one day. It was a scene between me and the actress Marina Berti, who was playing Elisabeth, John the Baptist's mother. The whole set knew that Franco was in a horrible mood. He was blocking out the scene, methodically staging it step by step. He asked for silence, but the crew kept talking and working. Finally Franco exploded.

"Stop the noise!" he bellowed. "The next person who speaks will be banned from my set!"

Foolishly, about a minute later I leaned in to Marina and whispered something about where I was going to stand when I faced her. Franco's head whipped around and he charged over to me like a bull, eyes glaring. Now the set really was silent.

"That goes for you as well," he seethed. "How many times must I ask!"

He was holding a small cup of water. He threw it in my face. I stood rooted on my mark: A few years earlier perhaps I would have stormed off, but not now. Franco turned and walked back to his DP—Director of Photography—and continued to block the scene. The set was silent. I knew the moment he did it that he was sorry; the pressure on him had been enormous and Franco's nerves were stretched. After a few heavy minutes, makeup and wardrobe came over and dried me off, fixed my costume, and reapplied my makeup. Later Franco came quietly over, stood next to me, and without saying a word took my hand and gave it a squeeze. It was his apology, and it was enough. Knowing Franco as I did, I understood that he would vent like that only with people he felt comfortable with. In a strange way, lashing out like he did was a huge compliment to me and I was oddly happy it happened.

It certainly wasn't all doom and gloom. One weekend the cast and crew were invited to lunch at the palace of King Hassan II. He had been Morocco's king since 1961 and by 1976 he had survived two assassination attempts and one coup d'etat. He was the inheritor of a dynasty that stretched back 300 years. Though an autocrat, whose reign was noted for a poor human rights record throughout the seventies and eighties, King Hassan II played a part in the Egyptian–Israeli peace process as well as overseeing some economic and political reforms in his own country.

I was blissfully unaware of all this as we drove down the huge parade ground toward the Dar al-Makhazen, the Royal Palace, in Rabat. Because this was an Islamic country, there was of course no alcohol served with our couscous and pita, and our crew of Italian divas once again protested at the indignity of having to eat non-Italian food and *Dio maledetto* punch instead of their vino. I sat looking up in wonder at the magnificent geometric patterns of the Arabic motifs and I thought about how lucky I was and what a strange, remarkable life making movies can afford you.

The king was gracious and cut quite a royal figure even as he politely declined to pose in any photos. After a few hours it was time to leave and take the journey back to our little hotel and to the bubble.

*   *   *

After my mistake with the still "technically" married actor, I was upset, and the last thing I wanted was to fall into another on-set relationship. So when the Artistic Director, a gentleman by the name of Gianni Quaranta, began to flirt and pay attention to me, I was far from interested. Eventually, though, he wore me down. He was talented and charming, handsome, and extremely polite. Most important, he was single!

He had worked on Bernardo Bertolucci's *1900* and would go on to enjoy a long and distinguished career working on such films as *A Room with a View* and *Farinelli*. I liked him because he was nice to me and a gentleman. It was wonderful to have a friend at last on set, a confidant with whom I could laugh and commiserate. One of our favorite jokes was about "Mary's many donkeys." Scene after scene I found myself riding on or walking next to donkeys. It became a running joke among the crew. Throughout the long days, whenever there was a lull you might hear one of the crew yell out, *"Dove e il lazinno de Maria?"* Where is Mary's donkey?

Franco had blocked off two days for the filming of what turned out to be the most difficult scene in the series: the crucifixion. For the actors it would be grueling emotional work and for Franco and the crew a technical nightmare. We would shoot at night, turning away from the dust and heat of the desert days. We would try to capture something of the foreboding and deep solitude that was the desert nights. Two massive rain machines were brought in, and there would be hundreds of extras to corral. Meanwhile, I watched as the three wooden crosses were pulled into position, their stakes thudding as they slid and hit the bottom of the holes dug into the ground. I was dreading all of it.

Actors long for *their* moment—the close-up where they

can let it all loose and let it all out. It is the stuff that shiny golden statues are made for, and every actor worth their salt relishes that dramatic chance. And I love being dramatic—just ask my husband—but something about that scene . . . it made me shudder. The thought of looking up and seeing Robert hanging there . . . I don't know, it was really affecting me.

We started filming early in the evening: first shooting the actors climbing our Mount Golgotha and coming to the foot of the cross, then the larger crowd scenes. This was Franco's great talent: bringing big and potentially unruly scenes to life. It took hours and hours. At midnight we broke for dinner.

I sat in a car just a little way from the set with Anne Bancroft, who was playing Mary Magdalene. Anne's a wonderful actress, and we got along very well during the shoot. We were talking about what was coming and how nervous I was: Robert's final death scene. He would be lowered from the cross in the pouring rain and laid on the ground, where his mother would wail over his body. I was telling Anne that I was sick with nerves. That it scared me. That it was too much and I didn't know how I was going to go through with it, to feel what I had to feel. "Olivia," she said, "when I get like this you know what I do? I have a couple glasses of wine to loosen up and get in the mood."

So, an hour and a half later and with three glasses of wine in me, I stood looking up through a machine-driven torrent of rain at Robert hanging between the two thieves. I remember his limp, forgotten body being brought down and left in front of me. A nauseating wave of sorrow welled up inside, and I wept as a mother who has lost her son. I remember kneeling down and lifting him to me, holding him close. I remember a storm of tears. It all felt so distant and far away. I remember being picked up and placed on

Robert's body and then, strangely, I don't remember anything else.

I woke up the next morning to Bianca, Franco's secretary, sitting at the foot of my bed and looking at me. "Franco will be in to see you soon, Olivia," she said, smiling.

I had passed out during the final moments of the shot. I told myself it was because of the wine, and Franco, when he came by to see me, agreed. "Olivia, darling," he said. "You did very well yesterday, *bravo*. But you must never drink when you work. Especially when you have to do an emotional scene that has your nerves on edge, *capisci*?"

After eight months and sixteen days, *Jesus of Nazareth* finally wrapped. The cast and crew packed their bags and left the desert. I helped Franco throw out the whiteboard that had had my weeks of isolation writ out large across it. All I cared about was getting to London and seeing Alex again. I will never forget driving straight from Heathrow Airport to my mum's little flat in Surbiton and walking in to see Alex. He came over and I knelt down, and he put his arm tight around my neck. He said, "I love Grannie Joy and Uncle Drew, but you must never leave for that long ever again." I can still see the look in his eyes. I would never leave him to go shoot something again; Alex would always come with me.

I had also been aching to see Baba. When I had left he had told me it was a great honor to play Mary, Mother of Jesus, and that, although it would be a difficult time, he knew I would do a wonderful job. Now, returning to him, I told him that he was right, it had been so tough. I talked about the crucifixion scene and how I had passed out. When I had finished, he shook his head and said, "No, no, Muktabai, it was not the wine." He smiled. "Perhaps you were there! You were there all those years ago and you did not want to relive it."

I don't know if Baba was serious; he always talked about past lives if he was telling me something that I needed to hear. Either way I left feeling so much lighter; I had been carrying a vague, nagging feeling of guilt since that day, and now it was gone.

Jesus of Nazareth would go on to be a huge success all over the world, with massive ratings in both the United States and Britain as well as the rest of Europe, including Italy where it first debuted and aired to coincide with Palm Sunday. The Pope, Paul VI, endorsed it from the Vatican. It garnered Emmy Award nominations and British Television Award nods. It did meet with a small share of controversy, mostly from the places you might expect, but it never really amounted to anything serious; Bob Jones III, for example, president of Bob Jones University, although never having actually *watched* it, nevertheless declared the whole series "blasphemy."

I was happy for Franco. He was, and still is, Catholic, and I knew how much the success of the series meant to him. Looking back, I feel lucky to have been a part of it. It was hard, lonely work, to be sure, but the end result is something I am very proud of. Mary has stayed with me. Playing that devotion and that strength while giving myself over to simple faith helped me when, thirty years later, I was asked to play another holy woman and I was petrified that I wouldn't be up to the task.

Jesus of Nazareth was over, and now I had a choice to make: Gianni Quaranta and I were still seeing each other, and he asked me to move to Rome and live with him. I thought, Why not? (I seemed to think that a lot when I was younger.) We had a wonderful time together, and I loved Rome. Why shouldn't this handsome, debonair Italian be the one?

I told him, "Yes, I would," and after a few weeks in

London with my mum and brother, Alex and I were landing on a bright, cloudless day at Rome's Fiumicino Airport hoping for an even brighter future.

It lasted ten days. Gianni was lovely but very busy, and I didn't know anybody in Rome. When Alex and I had first arrived he had grabbed my hand and said, "Mommy, I don't think this is going to work," and he was right. I had been impulsive. Desperate to make a new start and not be alone, I had brought us to yet another city far away from our family and friends. I told Gianni that I had made a mistake, and he understood. The truth is, an on-set romance rarely lasts through the opening weekend. They are fun and exciting and can be life-saving, but only in the bubble, it seems. We both knew this, and we said goodbye and parted friends.

It was time to return to what had become—as much as I fought against it—our home, LA. Time for Alex to be with his father and spend time with his family, and time for me to accept that I would be coming home to a very different life than the one I left.

Death on the Nile

Months of quiet followed our return to LA. Slowly, a routine crept around our life, like the thick, green-leaved ivy surrounding the front door of the duplex I had rented in Beverly Hills.

Alex's school day began at eight and ended at three-thirty. That was all I was responsible for. I cleaned and did laundry—I have always been fastidious when it comes to things being neat and spotless (most likely it's something to do with control, but who can say?). And because I had no reason to go out, I stayed in, and staying in made it harder and harder to go out. My agoraphobia, which had been a small but constant itch, was now beginning to rage along my synaptic highways, forging new and deeper connections. I was in real danger of becoming a neurotic and, worse, a stereotype: beautiful young actress achieves fame too early and falls down the rabbit hole of depression and self-sabotage. Boring.

Dino had always been able to help me with my agoraphobia. Sensing that a panic attack was imminent, he would take my hand and whisper, "Breathe. It will pass."

With him by my side, I was able to step into the world. But now he was gone.

In London, I had been introduced to a doctor who specialized in agoraphobia. Dr. Lawson worked on Harley Street, out of the same Victorian-era building that had previously housed Lionel Logue, who had treated George VI's stutter. Dr. Lawson had been helping an old boyfriend of mine, Paul Ryan, who also suffered from agoraphobia and with whom I had remained friends. He thought Dr. Lawson might be able to help me.

The doctor, I remember, was very kind. He told me he had come to study chronic agoraphobia because of his wife. Mrs. Lawson had battled it for thirty years, some weeks winning and some weeks losing. In the end, though, all he could do for me was prescribe Nardil and Librium, "for when you feel a panic attack coming on." Not loving the idea of taking drugs, I carried the pills around in my bag for months.

By the middle of 1978, it had gotten so bad that I had to ask a girlfriend to take Alex to school and go to the market for me.

I picture my agoraphobia as a gloomy, opaque fog that surrounds me and cuts me off from the sharp, clear air of the world. It is the atmosphere of *can't*, and it informs everything I do. The more I tell myself I can't do something, the more impossible doing that thing becomes. I told myself, for example, that I couldn't take Alex to school in the mornings: too many people, too much hustle and bustle. I told myself that I couldn't drive the car and run errands during the day: The city was just too overwhelming. I would drive right into a lamppost. I was afraid of the day-to-day, and I was ashamed of my fear.

About the only thing that could drag me away from this toxic and exhausting cycle was a job. I needed to work. I had to pay bills, simple as that. And, just when I thought it would never happen, another job came my way.

Agatha Christie's *Death on the Nile*—Inspector Poirot's famous case, set against the backdrop of the mystical, sphinx-like atmosphere of 1930s Egypt—would be another long shoot in another exotic location. I was offered the part of Rosalie Otterbourne, daughter of Mrs. Salome Otterbourne, to be played by Angela Lansbury. Also starring would be Peter Ustinov, with whom I had worked, as Poirot; Maggie Smith; Jon Finch; and the wonderfully charming David Niven, who would become one of my favorites. There was also the prospect of working with Bette Davis as Mrs. Van Schuyler, which would turn into a wonderfully daffy ordeal for us all. It was an amazing cast; I was lucky to have landed the role.

Tearfully leaving Alex with his father and now taking my meds on a daily basis—I simply could not afford any panic attacks—I set out for the two-month shoot along the Nile.

"Oh good Lord, it's hot!" David Niven took a long pull on his Benson & Hedges and gazed up at the beautiful Aga Khan Mausoleum at Aswan, its dust-colored limestone walls blending wonderfully with the sand dunes of southern Egypt. "They really were a remarkable people," he continued. "Imagine doing anything in this heat. It beggars belief." He took his free hand down from above his eyes, where, salute-like, it had been blocking the sun, and looked at me. "They didn't even have the wheel. A remarkable people."

It didn't matter that the mausoleum was, in fact, a twentieth-century creation, and mattered even less that neither of us knew this. The point was that Egypt was a magical place for a couple of well-meaning, ill-informed actors to be working.

We were standing on the deck of the *Desert Rose*, a two-deck, seventy-two-meter-long steamship, one of the sets for our production. Sailing south along the Nile, we passed the Old Cataract Hotel (also one of our sets) where, in the early thirties, Agatha Christie had written part of the novel. Occasionally gazing out at the river and waving at the occasional felucca, we were taking a break from being yelled at by John Guillermin, the director.

We had been yelled at by John in some of most magnificent locations in Egypt. He had screeched at us in the shadow of the Great Pyramid and down the crowded streets of Cairo. His profanity, amplified by megaphone, had echoed from five-thousand-year-old temple walls at Luxor and Karnak. Today, after another haranguing, David had walked over to where I was standing idly by the boat's bar.

"Olivia," he'd said, "perhaps a smoke out on the deck, to calm our nerves?"

I had loved David from the moment I first saw him. So charming, so soft-spoken, so English. He seemed totally at ease with himself; an utter gentleman, although he did cultivate a certain roguish quality. His wit and elegance allowed him, I think, to glide on the surface of things. He appeared to be privy to some private joke about the world that rendered him impervious to the petty or the stupid. Also, like me, he was a giggler.

"Olivia, my sweet, our eyes must never meet," he announced on the fourth day of shooting. Upon first hearing "Action!" he and I had taken one look at each other and instantly recognized our problem: I laughed because I was nervous, David because he loved to, and together we couldn't get through a scene. Finally, after the director had given up all hope and begun his metamorphosis into Mr.

Hyde, David had come up with the zero-eye-contact idea. I was to look only at a point in the center of his forehead, while he would stare at my chin. Thus we shot our scenes. If you watch them closely, you can see it: At times, I look as though I'm talking to a lamp or a coatrack.

What fun we had working together. David was cut from old English cloth. Like a perfectly tailored dinner jacket from Savile Row, he was sharp, classy, and never out of fashion.

Then there was Bette Davis. If one were inclined to be generous and euphemistic, one might say that after nearly fifty years in the spotlight Ms. Davis was a touch hard and did not suffer fools lightly. Otherwise, you might simply say that working with her was its own kind of suffering.

Like so many young actresses, I had grown up enthralled by Bette Davis. Staring at her on the big screen from my seat in the back row of the tiny cinema on Coombe Lane in Wimbledon, I had watched and learned and loved. She was strong, smart, and sultry. She killed and kissed and dominated all those fellas in their sharp suits and fedoras. And although her world was black-and-white, you just knew her lips were fire-engine red, her eyes sky blue, and her costars green with envy. I thought she was all a movie star should be. And maybe she was—maybe, even, the last of a breed.

From her three-o-clock gin and tonic, served in a goblet resting on a silver tray, to the way she prowled behind the camera, glaring at Maggie or me like a lioness jealous of her pride, Ms. Davis was a tough old broad. To use a word my rockstar cowboy husband might employ, she was *ornery*. And, although she was never very pleasant to me, for the most part I did manage to avoid the sharp end of her Hollywood hardness.

I was twenty-four and she was seventy, and twenty-four

has no idea what seventy must feel like. Now, I can imagine that it couldn't have been easy for her in that distant location, surrounded by a younger generation of actresses. Still, in the two months we worked together I don't remember her saying one kind or generous thing to me or to anyone else. I was so disappointed that for years afterward I couldn't bring myself to sit through one of her films.

It was the older English men, Peter Ustinov and David, toward whom I naturally gravitated. Their easy, self-effacing charm and paternal warmth relaxed me, made me feel safe. They were also very funny.

The actor Jon Finch and I were the love interest in the picture, and right from the start we got on well. Jon was a well-established actor. His passion had been the stage, but starring roles in Alfred Hitchcock's *Frenzy* and Roman Polanski's *Macbeth* had now made him, for a time, a Hollywood leading man.

Like me, Jon hated to be alone, and on a few nights he knocked on my hotel room door, but it was out of a simple need for comfort and company, and nothing happened between us. He was a darling man and a fine actor.

Six weeks in Egypt passed in a flash. To be honest, I was too young and too inward looking to take in much of the country. As with so many of the places in which I have been fortunate enough to work, I wish I had seen it when I was a bit older. *C'est la vie.*

Six weeks later, the production moved to England and the legendary Pinewood Studios. An hour's drive from central London, Pinewood sits serenely in the picturesque greenery of Iver Heath, Buckinghamshire—how British is that? A quick internet search tells you how important and central a role Pinewood has played in making movies for eighty years. It is best known as the home of the James Bond franchise, but the list of films shot there is staggering. It's a movie Mecca and my favorite lot.

We were shooting on Stages S and R, across from the massive, newly built 007 stage, which would burn down some years later. Working with Maggie Smith, Angela Lansbury, George Kennedy, and the others continued to be good fun, or should have been. My damned agoraphobia kept holding me back (Pinewood is a massive lot, and its size aggravated my agoraphobia). Even with my pills, I would still have the occasional panic attack. I was nervous and couldn't get outside my own head. Then came news that my mum was ill.

They said they didn't know what it was. They said she needed tests. They said not to worry, she would most likely be fine. But when I saw her, I was shocked. She had blown up like balloon. Her hands and feet, her calves and wrists—every part of her was swollen. She was slight, my mum, only five feet one and normally thin, so I was worried sick.

I said, "What about all the swelling?" Again, they didn't know; maybe lupus, although they couldn't rule out cancer.

Working meant I couldn't be with her. I was only an hour away, but it might as well have been thirty million. She was all I had, she and my brother and Alex. And though we had never got on very well, we loved one another. We had endured the inexpressible experience of being poor together. She had worked and we had struggled, and because of her strength we had survived whole as a family when so many others had not. I loved her in spite of our differences; above all, I respected her.

I have a tough-enough time working when other things are fine, but with my mum sick? I was a mess, and the last few weeks of shooting were a total blur. In the end, the doctors discovered she had celiac disease, a digestive disorder that can cause a variety of issues but nothing life-threatening. The news was a relief, of course, but the trauma of those weeks could not help but affect my already strung-out nerves.

One thing could always bring a smile to my face, though: Superman. Every day at lunchtime I would head over to the Pinewood commissary, where the food was surprisingly good. Most days, I would take my tray and head toward a back corner. I must have cut a rather sad figure, munching away by myself and staring off at nothing. One day—I remember it was raining as usual—the commissary doors swung open and in he walked. He had pulled his red cape forward, draping it over his left forearm to keep it out of the rain, and as he walked he let it drop. It was a surprisingly dramatic motion, and so incongruous in the doorway of a cafeteria under fluorescent lights that I laughed out loud. It was like looking at the beginning of a joke: "So Superman walks into a cafeteria . . ."

Christopher Reeve looked magnificent in full costume. (He was filming the first *Superman* movie on the lot, but I had not yet seen or met him.) It says something about him, I think, that even out of context he looked great. I thought, Wow, is he ever perfect for the part! He looks like a superhero! Then he looked right at me. I watched as he grabbed a tray and made his way over to my table. "I love your work," he said. "Mind if I join you for lunch?"

He was a lovely man, and for a few weeks we ate lunch together, always at the same table, chatting away. It wasn't in the least flirty; we just liked each other. We were two working actors having a nice time, he in his Superman costume, me in my 1920s flapper dresses. We must have looked quite the pair. I wish I'd stayed in touch with him; I think we might have become close friends.

While shooting at Pinewood and staying in the little flat the studio had rented for me, I did manage to take advantage of my days off. I saw my mother, and when she was too tired I saw the few friends I still had in London. First and foremost was Linda Deveralle. She and I are still great friends today—no small feat considering we first met on the steps of the Conti Drama School when I was ten. Always ready for a laugh, she's tremendous fun to be around, with her dry, self-deprecating humor and crackling, live-wire energy. I adored her, and soon we'd be traveling together halfway around the world.

Another friend was Paul Ryan, my fellow agoraphobe, who had introduced me to Dr. Lawrence. Paul and I had dated briefly when I was fifteen and at drama school, and now he confessed that he had never really gotten over me. He said he loved me, couldn't stop thinking about me, wanted to marry me. The problem was, he drank. A lot. He carried a silver flask around with him filled with whiskey. I had known him for a long time, and I wanted to help him. I was coming to the end of filming, and in a month's time I would be traveling to India, where I had been asked to open the New Delhi Film Festival. After that, I had planned a trip to the village of Ganeshpuri, Baba's home, which was about a two-hour drive north of Mumbai.

I made Paul a deal: I told him that if he met me in Mumbai and traveled with me to Baba's ashram in Ganeshpuri, and if he asked Baba for my hand and Baba said yes, then I would marry him. In my heart, I knew I would not marry him, but I was determined that he meet my guru. I believed that it would help with his drinking problem. It was a lot to ask and a lot to hope for, but Paul agreed to go without hesitation.

While *Death on the Nile* was warmly received and Peter Ustinov would go on to make a wonderful Poirot in future films, the shoot was for me a mixed bag. I'm grateful to have met David, and it was nice to see my name up on the screen along with Bette Davis, Angela Lansbury, and Maggie Smith, but mostly I remember a time of nervousness and anxiety, of worrying about my mum and feeling helpless and alone.

So overall it was a depressing shoot. For some reason, it felt at times as if some of the actors didn't really want to be there, as if making the movie was a burden. Also, and not to be too indelicate, some of our "big names" were just plain old, and it felt a little like we were making the film twenty years too late. I was glad when it was over.

India

I read somewhere that "for the world's oxygen God gave it the rainforest, and for its soul He gave it India." As soon as I became aware that a place like India existed, I loved it, the idea of it. After having traveled there, I loved it for what it really was. For fifty years, I have chanted Indian songs and prayed to Indian gods. India has been the wellspring of the peace I have known and the joy I have felt. I named my third child—a daughter—India; her middle name is Joy.

Having finished *Death on the Nile* and made sure my mum was being looked after, I made my plans and packed my bags for India. Linda would be my travel companion; our trip would last a month. Paul had said he would meet us in Mumbai after the film festival, but who knew for sure? What I did know was how excited I felt. Not only was I heading to what I had already decided was my spiritual home, but I was also opening the New Delhi Film Festival. I must confess that I had no idea what this job would require—hopefully not a speech. I was sure, however, that whatever it meant it would most certainly be glamorous and exhilarating.

Landing in New Delhi, we were immediately shocked by a swirling vortex of human bodies. "My God, Livi, there are so many people!" Linda exclaimed as we forced our way toward what we guessed was baggage claim. People were pushing in on us, pushing past us, ignoring us. A great wave of humans, all heading to the same exit, threatening to drown us.

With my agoraphobia, large crowds are a no-no, and I had steeled myself for them during the eight-and-a-half-hour flight. Bizarrely, though, once we arrived the crush of bodies didn't bother me. As I stepped out onto the bustling street, I felt relaxed and began to laugh.

I would learn that India has a way of pulling you out of yourself. You are assailed by the life of the place. Its smells, its colors, the tumult and seeming chaos of it almost bully you into being present and outward looking. India tells you—yells at you—to pay attention! I loved it.

Another fact of India that almost immediately confronted us was its poverty. An army of the less fortunate stared back at us as we looked out from the backseat of our car, feeling helpless and guilty. However—and I know this is a broad stroke—I saw a dignity in the poverty that I don't find in, say, the United States. It's shocking, unfair, and infuriating to be sure, but there is less indignity to it, perhaps because there is less judgment. There's something in seeing so many people simply getting on with the business of living that I find inspiring.

Cut to our hotel. The Taj Mahal Hotel belonged to the other India, the India of marble bathrooms and gold leaf everything. Opulent to the point of absurdity, the hotel reminded me of some faded Mughal palace or the dying days of the Raj. It felt silly and tacky to be staying in so swanky a place when the "real India" was living and breathing outside. At least, that's what my young Anglo heart was telling me. Today, I know how much more complicated things are.

I remember going to the window of our suite and looking out over the city. It was dusk, and the sky was a fantastic orange, shot through with streaks of deep red. It looked as if one of Baba's prized silks had been stretched out across it. Below us trees, thousands of them, flowed out for miles from the base of our hotel to four huge, domed buildings that sat solid against the silken sky.

What a place, I thought. It's absolutely perfect.

I went to bed, snug in satin and secure in the knowledge that I was in the right place at the right time. All was well.

What a difference a day makes! At six p.m. on the nose, I was standing in the lobby of the Taj, staring at Linda and feeling an uncontrollable fit of giggles about to come on. We were both wearing new white and gold saris. The doorman was telling Linda that the "celebrity bus" that was to take us to the opening-night gala of the New Delhi Film Festival had just left. Linda was not amused.

"My darling man," she said, "you needn't call it the celebrity bus if in fact the celebrity is not on it. She is standing right here." When things get rough, Linda gets English.

"Nevertheless," the doorman replied, standing his ground.

As Linda became more British and more agitated, I fell back onto *my* default setting in times of stress: nervous laughter.

"But we were told the bus would be picking us up at six," Linda protested.

"Yes."

Long pause, broken only by my giggles.

"It is six now, my good man."

"Nevertheless."

With no end to this little Abbott and Costello routine in sight, another doorman politely put in his two cents: "Perhaps the ladies can still make the bus."

"What's that?" Linda demanded.

"Well, the traffic."

"Yes! That's it!" She grabbed my hand and we bounded out through the gold-leaf hotel doors.

Then we were running down a New Delhi street, our saris, of which we were so proud, hiked up above our knees, yelling at the celebrity bus—which indeed had not gone far—to stop. It was very hot, and we were both sweating. I lost my sandal and went back for it while Linda continued to call out to the bus. Finally, a random car stopped and a rather dapper-looking man popped his head out the window and asked in perfect, lilting English if we might like a ride. Gratefully, we climbed into the backseat, laughing so hard that tears ran down our faces, smearing our makeup and completing the whole crazy picture. It is one of my most treasured memories.

Of course we arrived late. We were shown to seats in the back of the darkened theater. At one point, someone came up and very nicely presented me with a huge bouquet of flowers. And there I sat, a comically large pile of roses on my lap, watching the opening film from my seat in the back! It was strange, disorganized, and so much fun.

After the film, we were escorted to a huge reception room for a lavish twelve-course dinner. I was seated next to Shashi Kapoor and his nephew, Rashi. The Kapoor family were a Bollywood dynasty, with various members working in the industry from as far back as the 1930s, and Shashi was their prized scion. He was charming and confident as well as handsome, and it was easy to see why he was India's favorite leading man. When he asked, toward the end of the dinner, if I might like to take a walk around the gardens, I of course said yes. (Have I mentioned that when I was younger I was, perhaps, a touch naïve? Yes, I've brought it up a few times? Well, that's fine, because it's true, and worth repeating here.)

As I strolled around the gardens, smoking a cigarette and listing to Shashi, I thought, India is just so spiritual. Everybody here is so enlightened and deep. My reverie was broken when Shashi's arms, which had slipped around my waist, began to tighten, and I began to suspect his lips would soon be headed toward mine.

Shocked, I stormed inside, spending the rest of the evening avoiding eye contact and fuming because I felt India had let me down.

Three days and a dozen official appearances later, my duties at the New Delhi Film Festival were over, and Linda and I headed to the airport for our flight to Mumbai. I had declined Shashi's offer of a car and driver, thinking it best not to be in debt to India's favorite leading man with the grabby hands.

Walking up the steps into the plane, I turned and noticed that Linda wasn't behind me. Odd, I thought. At my seat, I leaned to look out the window and saw her coming up the steps at the back of the plane. Her sari, which she had insisted on wearing, had gotten caught on one of the railings. She was almost to the door before she noticed that it was unravelling from her body, the long train of material being gathered up by helpful passengers behind her. When she made it onto the plane she was holding most of her sari in her arms. "Livi, this is not funny," she said. It was so funny.

Standing at a ticketing desk in the Mumbai Airport, Paul Ryan looked rumpled, jet-lagged, and maybe a bit buzzed. I was surprised to see him—shocked, really. I hadn't realized how much I wanted to help him. There are people who hold a special place in your heart; you just want to take care of them. Save them. I had felt that way toward Paul since I first met him when I was fifteen. I knew he had come all this way for me, which was a beautiful gesture, but I had a different agenda: to get him in front of my guru and, I hoped, heal him.

Outside, the three of us were met by a driver standing in front of a white Mercedes. "Compliments of Mr. Kapoor," he said.

"Of all the cheek!" I thought as I climbed in the back.

I am happiest and most at home when surrounded by matters of the spirit. I think that if my life hadn't taken the path it did, the cloistered life of a nun would indeed have suited me best. As it happened, I found Baba and so discovered the life of the ashram—a house of the spirit full of good people tending to their souls. There is meditation and chanting, yes, but also cooking and cleaning, gardening and serving. In some ways—the most important ones—it is really just a place of quiet where you can go deep inside yourself. It contains some of the kindest, gentlest people I have ever known. And for me, an ashram has always meant being close to Baba.

Arriving at dusk, we were told that Baba had retired for the night. But the ashram was still wide awake and lively. The ashram had begun as a hut behind a Shiva temple. Baba's own guru, Swami Nityananda, had wandered into an area near the village of Ganeshpuri in the 1930s, and the locals had asked him to stay. Today, Nityananda is considered a saint in India, and the hut where he lived became the first Siddha Yoga ashram.

We headed over to the *amrit* ("nectar"), the canteen, for tea, and were greeted warmly and told that our rooms where ready. Linda and I would be staying together, while Paul would be in the men's dormitory. Understand, both

Linda and Paul had come all the way to India, and to stay at this ashram, because of me—Linda because she was my oldest friend and loved a bit of adventure, and Paul because he had decided he loved me. Neither one knew Baba, let alone followed him. So when I saw Paul's face turn ash-gray at the word "dorm," I had to laugh—he must have wondered what he had gotten himself into. As I watched him go off to find his room, I crossed my fingers and hoped he would have a good night.

Later that evening Noni, Baba's assistant, came to Linda's and my room. "Welcome, Muktabai," he said. "Baba's been waiting to see you."

I was thrilled to learn that Baba's room was directly below us—I could hear him cough, which was bliss for me. When I was shown into his room, I was struck by its simplicity. This was Baba's main residence, where he spent most of his time, but you would never have known that, it was so sparsely furnished: a low wooden cot and everywhere framed photos of Swami Nityananda. Baba was sitting cross-legged on the cot. We ate some *prasad*—food that had been blessed—and smiled at each other. My heart swelled with bliss at being near him again; I loved him so. After a short time, he asked, "So you have brought people with you?" I told him about Linda.

"Yes, yes, I know. The other one."

"Oh, that's my friend Paul. He has come to ask you for my hand in marriage." I said it tentatively, as though I was talking about someone apart from myself. Baba reached out and gestured for me to come closer. He took my face in his hands and stared deep into my eyes,

"Bahut acha," he whispered, "very good." Then, more loudly, "Now get something to eat and go to bed. I will see you tomorrow."

I floated back to my room, where I told Linda that Baba

was happy we were here. She looked at me and said, "Livi, the bathrooms."

They did take some getting used to. They were down the corridor and they were public, but, worst of all from the point of view of a Western woman, the toilet was nothing more than a hole in the floor. Though Linda could handle almost anything and loved India, those toilets were almost too much for her. (In subsequent years, as the ashram grew, everything, including the bathrooms, was updated.)

In my cot, after our giggles had finally receded, I was overcome by the familiar, but all too rare, feelings I have when I am near Baba: sublime happiness and an inner knowledge, calm and clear, that I am where I should be. As I listened to his coughing, I gave thanks for his presence in my life, slowed my breathing, and quietly began to recite, *"Om Namah Shivaya,"* "I am that I am." I was asleep in two minutes.

We woke to the melody of the *Guru Gita*, "Song of the Guru," being chanted around the ashram. Listening to the beautiful rhythmic sounds, Linda and I began slowly to climb out of our cots. It was six a.m.

Although it was still dark as we walked out into the courtyard, people were already going quietly about *seva*, selfless service in the form of chores. We sat in the canteen drinking chai tea and watching as the main ashram gates were opened and hundreds of people who had been waiting to see the guru began to enter.

In the main hall, men sat on one side and women on the other. Baba always joked that the separation allowed people to feel God, rather than each other. It was an important day on the Siddha calendar, I remember, and there were now a few hundred people crowded together. I hadn't seen Paul yet.

The *darshan* line began to form. Baba sat on an elevated, wide-backed chair so everybody could see him and, holding a huge peacock feather, greeted people from the line one by one. In *darshan*, your exchange with the guru could be anything from a small smile as you rose from your bow to a conversation about who you were and why you had come. Baba would then pass his peacock feather over you.

Linda grabbed my arm. "There's Paul," she said.

He looked dazed and irritated, like someone who had just walked into a room where music was turned up much too loud. He also looked a mess: He was dressed all in white, but for some reason one of his pant legs was hiked up to his knee. His hair was mad, half of it pushed straight up. We watched as Malti, Baba's translator, gave Paul some kind of instruction. We were too far back to hear anything, but we saw Paul kneel down in front of Baba, and we watched as he rose, turned to go, and was called back. Malti spoke to him, whispering in his ear. Then Paul seemed to melt away into the crowd and the lights dimmed.

In the now-darkened hall, people began their meditation. Baba walked around and touched people's foreheads—as he did mine—or said a blessing. I always found meditating in his presence a powerful and mysterious experience.

After the morning program, Linda and I finally found Paul at the *amrit*. He looked pale and confused.

"Paul, how are you?" I asked.

"Olivia," he said, his eyes looking through me, "I love you, but I have to go."

"What?" I said, shocked. This was only our second day.

"Please don't ask me why, but I'm leaving this morning and flying back to London tonight."

Stunned, all I could do was nod. The next thing I knew, I was waving good-bye at a taxi's taillights. Paul was gone. He had been in India less than forty-two hours.

Linda and I stayed for three weeks. I was in heaven. Linda, though she did come to respect and admire Baba greatly, made the best of it. A friend indeed.

As soon as I got back to London, I picked up the phone and called Paul. I was nervous. We spoke and arranged to meet.

A month to the day after I had last seen him, looking worn and pale and stepping into a junky taxi in India, he walked through the door of the trendy Kingston café looking calm, healthy, and happy. I was shocked.

"My God, Paul, how are you?" I said.

"Lucky," he said. "Olivia, I can't thank you enough."

And he told me what had happened at the ashram and why he had left so suddenly. He had spent the first night alone, talking to no one and secretly drinking from his flask. In the morning, while he followed the crowd to the hall he rehearsed what he would say to Baba: "I have come all the way here because I love Olivia. I want to ask you for permission to marry her."

But when he entered the hall and made his way up the *darshan* line, he felt his words slowly leave him. As he knelt in front of Baba, all he could say was that it was nice to meet him. Then, numb and feeling a fool, he turned to leave, and Malti introduced herself. "When the lights go down," she instructed him, "Baba wants you to raise your hand up high, so he can find you."

"So what happened when the room darkened and he found you?" I asked.

"He breathed into me."

I didn't know what to say to that. I just stared.

"I sat in the dark with my hand up for a few minutes,

feeling stupid. Then suddenly Baba was there. He held my lips together like a child who won't take his medicine, and he shouted inside my head that this was nuts. Then he slapped the back of my head, and when I opened my mouth to protest he bent down, cupped my mouth with his other hand, and blew a long, deep breath into me." This is one of the one of the ways Baba would occasionally give spiritual initiation.

"Jesus, Paul," I said.

"After that," he went on, "I just had to leave. I went back to the dorm and packed. I didn't feel anything. I came down, saw you, and said good-bye. I got back here and for three weeks, day and night while I lay in bed, I saw a bright blue light in the center of my forehead. Three days ago, I climbed out of bed and called Dr. Lawson. When I saw him, I told him I was an alcoholic and wanted help. He asked me when I had last had a drink, and I stopped. Olivia, I have drunk every day, all day, for a long time, but as I sat there in his office I had to search for the answer. Finally, I said—I couldn't believe it—'Three weeks ago, Doctor.' Three weeks, Olivia. Not since Baba. Not since the ashram!"

This was my friend Paul's miracle. We stayed together for a while after that. He even came out to LA with me. We never married, but we remained friends until he died many years later from lung cancer. He had drunk every day, all day, until he met my guru. Then he never drank again.

Thank you, Baba.

What's My Line?

"**O**h, Jesus, I'm so sorry. I've forgotten the damn line again!" Eight days after returning to the United States from England, I was on my first-ever American television location forgetting my first line. As the crew was again forced to do the same shot over again because of me, I could feel my embarrassment turning slowly to panic.

"Okay, everybody. Back to one," the Second Assistant Director yelled for the umpteenth time.

We were filming in Los Angeles, on a huge estate called Greystone Mansion in the center of Beverly Hills. The scene was a ball, with extras, dressed in late eighteenth-century costumes, dancing as the camera tracked to a few of the principle actors, who had overlapping dialogue. It was for a TV miniseries called *The Bastard*. In 1978, the miniseries was a new concept for U.S. television, and the shoot had a two-worlds feel to it. On one hand, it felt like a movie, with huge sets and a fairly big budget. On the other, it was being shot at TV's breakneck pace and with a somewhat small-scale sensibility. It was all new to me.

I had been back home with Alex for only about a week

when the offer came in. I thought, Great, I'll be a little jet-lagged, but I'm sure I'll have a few days to get up to speed. Oh no. U.S. TV is fast; I had no idea just how fast. And, because of unions, shooting is very structured and regimented. Not at all like the chaotic but leisurely European shoots I was used to.

The series starred some wonderful actors, although it certainly was an eclectic group, from a young Kim Cattrall and me to Tom Bosley, Donald Pleasence, and William Shatner. In the lead was the actor Andrew Stevens, the son of Stella (herself a veteran of TV as well as film), who went on to be a successful writer and producer. Also, there was the incredible Patricia Neal, who had had a cerebral aneurysm some years before, when she had even been in a coma. She had battled through, and continued to work. She was classy and kind, a total inspiration.

Years earlier, Zeffirelli had dubbed me "One-Take Hussey," and over the years I had been proud of my reputation for knowing my lines, hitting my marks, and not needing many takes. I knew it happened to every actor; I'd heard a hundred horror stories, but it had never happened to me. Until the ball scene, my first day on the miniseries.

When I arrived on set, the shoot was in full swing. I was immediately fitted into the most amazing costume: a low-cut, tight-waisted dress and—my God—a powdered wig. It was simply fabulous. The designer was Jean-Pierre Dorléac, and we would become good friends. I loved his designs, although once on, they did take a team to manage. Linda, who would come to the set with me, had to help me with my costume when it was time to use the restroom. Now, that is friendship.

Since filming had begun weeks before, the cast and crew had already found their working rhythm. When I came onto the set, the director, TV veteran Lee H. Katzin, immediately started telling me what the shot was, where I needed to be, and who was included. I nodded and thought, Holy hell, he's talking fast. Then, after a quick run-through, we were rolling. I was jet-lagged, I was new to the shoot, I was—I admit—frazzled. (That's what I tell myself now, at least.)

The camera moved past those dancing extras for the first time, came to me and—blank. "Back to one." No big deal, Olivia just needs to settle. Focus was off in the camera anyway.

Camera moved past extras dancing and Olivia—blank. "Back to one!" This time, maybe with a bit of an edge.

Camera moved past extras dancing and Olivia—blank. This time, with, "Back to one!" my mind started to go. I could feel the heat rise in my cheeks. Sweat began to form at my temples.

The camera moved past extras dancing—Oh God, Olivia. What's the line? The camera came to rest on me and—blank. God, please. No, no, no. Stay calm. Ask for the line. "Back to one!"

Camera moved past extras dancing—I was in full mental meltdown. In my head, a red haze. No words.

I don't even remember the next five takes.

Eventually, my two—*just two*—lines had to be done in a pickup shot. Humiliating. I went round to every single crew member, every extra, and the other actors in the scene and apologized. I went home convinced that the only thing left for me to do was to quit acting.

The next three weeks went by just fine, though, and I decided that maybe I wouldn't quit my day job after all. Ironically, after this U.S. TV baptism of fire, my next three projects were all for television and very different.

During this time, I bought a house. For the first time in my life, I bought a house.

Nestled in a quiet corner of Hollywood, the "village" of Larchmont had a small-town feel: Old Hollywood homes with high ceilings and crown moldings lined sweet, well-tended, tree-lined streets. It would be a wonderful place for Alex to grow up. When we moved in, it felt just right.

After finishing *The Bastard*, I settled into a new routine, one of my own making. I had Linda with me, and though we were now just friends, Paul was also staying with us. We rescued a dog, Dylan, which would begin my lifelong love of animals, especially dogs. (At one point, I would have thirteen running around the house and was not allowed to visit animal shelters anymore!) Life was simple and good. Dino would come around every weekend and pick Alex up. We got on, as we always did: me with my moods and drama, and Dino with his sunshine grin and his halo of golden effortlessness. Somehow, we understood each other; or, rather, we understood one another's limits. That let us be friends.

So things were good. Soon Paul would move out and head back to London. He was a special man and a great friend; I would miss his sense of humor and his sensitive soul, but it was time. Linda stayed, much to Alex's delight. He loved her, and we all lived happily together.

A few months after *The Bastard*, I was offered another role in a miniseries. This one sounded like it would be fun. Based on the novel by Harold Robbins, *The Pirate* would have me tan, short-haired, and firing a machine gun. I was in! It also starred the Italian actor Franco Nero, whom I had met years earlier by the pool in Spain while shooting *Summertime Killer*. There was Michael Constantine, who turned out to be wonderful to work with. Years later, I was delighted to see him in *My Big Fat Greek Wedding*. And I got to work a little bit with Christopher Lee and the wonderful character actor Ferdy Mayne. The three of us learned that we shared the dreaded giggling disease, and I had great fun telling the two of them all about David Niven and our struggles on the set of *Death on the Nile*. Christopher, for whom the greatest sin was lacking a sense of humor, commiserated with my difficulties. Lord, the old guys were the best.

There were boys, as well. When I was younger, I was never really happy or healthy when I was alone, so I tried not to be. *The Pirate* was set in the Middle East, so the actors were of the tall, dark, and handsome variety, like Armand Assante. Armand has had a tremendous and well-deserved career, but back then he was just a young, hungry actor who was very serious about his work and looked great in fatigues. We got on well, liked each other, and went out a few times.

But Franco Nero . . . well, he was Italian, after all. I loved his intensity, his passion. He had flirted with me all those years ago in Spain, but I was married then and not interested. I had, however, always remembered how charming and charismatic he had been. So we had fun together for a few weeks. But, although I hated being alone, I never really liked dating, especially dating for dating's sake. So when, after about a month, I felt that Franco wasn't really looking for something serious, we ended it.

I had a good time making the series. The lead character was loosely styled after the Saudi Arabian billionaire businessman and international celebrity Adnan Khashoggi, and after the series aired I heard that his daughter, whom I portrayed, loved my performance.

Japan with the Toad

For reasons having to do with both class and dignity, and in the interest of not getting sued for defamation, we'll just call him "Toad Man," or simply "the Toad."

I met him toward the end of filming on *The Pirate*. He was five-foot-nothing tall, with nothing blond hair and the wide, toothy grin of a reprobate. He cut an almost transparent figure, as if there was no one there. Linda despised him immediately. I should have listened to her.

He went on and on about how my career had been completely mismanaged—how I needed to be in every meeting for every big part in Hollywood and how he could make that happen. Funnily enough, since moving to Los Angeles I had yet to be given the full, "I can make you a star" dog-and-pony show. I had been either managed by Rudy or not managed at all. And I had never spent time with the über-Hollywood types, with their flashy cars, endless promises, and vacant eyes. I fell for the Toad's line.

First thing on his agenda for me: Japan, where *Romeo & Juliet* was, apparently, still a popular film.

The Toad suggested that I record a single for release in Japan.

Okay, I thought, and said, "But, you know, I don't really sing."

"Doesn't matter," the Toad replied as he leaned in. "We'll make sure it's something you can handle."

I had done a photo shoot for a Japanese clothing company and had enjoyed the day I spent with their crew, not to mention the amount they'd paid me. I thought, Why not? I've never done anything like it before. Might be fun.

Two songwriters were flown in from Tokyo. The song was to be sung entirely in Japanese, and apparently needed to be two keys higher than anywhere I was comfortable. Recording it turned out to be a fun adventure but, thank heavens, the recorded song can't be heard anywhere today.

The Toad was not through with the Land of the Rising Sun. He negotiated a deal with a Japanese cosmetics company called Kanebo. I was to do a commercial, followed by a small promotional tour. This was 1979, well before serious Hollywood celebrities had figured out that they could make a bundle doing ads in Japan while keeping their credibility intact at home.

I agreed. I was excited to see Japan; I had wanted to go for years. I shot the ad in the States and got the old suitcase out for another trip across the world, this time heading west.

What I didn't know, and learned only a week before Alex, Linda, and I were set to leave, was that the Toad had screwed me. He had made the original deal for me with a huge Japanese advertising firm named Dentsu, but I had signed a contract only with the smaller company, Kanebo. As a result, I was paid a fraction not only of what he was to receive but also of what I should have been paid for the work involved. I would get nothing for the use of my image nor any royalties on anything that was used later. In short, I was getting paid scale for two days' commercial work, but I was obligated to do three weeks of promotion.

The truth is, I have never been any good with money. You might think that, growing up as I did, I would have a sharper sense for it and how to look after it. The truth is, though, that my years growing up in London with Mum and Drew, living as we did, only showed me the value of escape—and acting was my means of escape. I could step through the doors of my drama school and into the kind of life I wanted. So it was the acting—the work—that was important, not the money that came along with it. That was always an afterthought with me.

Besides, I have never been a spendthrift. "Stuff" has never been all that important to me. I don't really care about cars or clothes or being rich and showing off. All that is ephemeral and disappears like smoke. If I had enough to live comfortably on, that was perfect; I wouldn't spend any more time thinking about it. It would only be years later, after half a lifetime of airily not thinking about cost and consequence, that I would learn the real value of money: security. Security for myself, my kids, my health, and my home. Money can keep you safe.

So instead of firing the putz, I decided I would just ignore him, going so far as to have Linda—who already loathed him—sit between us on our long flight to Japan.

As angry as I was about the deal, I couldn't help but feel a thrill as the plane touched down at Tokyo's main airport. Waiting for us as we got off the plane was a huge reception: TV cameras broadcast our arrival live, hundreds of flashbulbs popped, and a line of suited men bowed as Alex laughed and pulled on my arm. Into the limo we went, and all the while I was shooting dagger looks at the Toad. His presence cast a pall over what should have been a wonderful moment.

My schedule was mad, detailed down to the very last half hour. Far from being overwhelmed by this, I marveled at the huge amount of work that must have gone into organizing the meetings with company executives, the dozens of personal appearances, and live TV presentations. There would be hundreds, if not thousands, of hands to shake and bows to make. We had fourteen bodyguards (I counted) looking after the three of us. They were there to "protect" us, but I had the feeling their main job was to keep us on schedule— including strictly timed ten-minute bathroom breaks.

All of it did make us feel like strangers in a strange land. The people we met were wonderful but also, I felt, impenetrable. A mask of civility and professionalism was pulled down over every exchange and every new introduction. The distance this created was great for my agoraphobia, though. Although we were living in a fish bowl, I still felt I had space; I could be alone even when I was surrounded. Still, it was hard. I had my little crying fits alone or with Linda. I was angry and scared—angry because the Toad was ruining the trip, and scared because I knew I had to go back to LA, fire him, and once again be without any management.

I called Baba.

"Baba, I'm scared!" I was crying as I said it and as I heard Noni translate. "This awful man is here with me and Alex. He's cheated me, stolen from me, and I see him every day. I don't know what to do."

"Muktabai," Baba said through Noni, "last week I performed twenty-six weddings, and I see that you are next on my list."

Um . . . what? "No, Baba. That is not right," I said, a little shocked. "Not me, Baba. I'm never. Ever. Going to marry again. Besides, Dino and I are only separated; we're not divorced yet."

"Ah, my Muktabai," he said, "I love you. I bless you. All will be well." He chuckled in the way that always made me feel so good, and hung up.

Up in our hotel room, Alex sat transfixed by the cartoon he was watching. It was called Pokémon, and it was brand new. I sat with Linda, taking deep breaths and laughing at what Baba had said during our call. I dreaded the idea of getting dressed up for yet another event, but what could I do? A concert of sorts was planned for me a few hours later. I would walk out onstage while the singer who had sung the song for the commercial I had shot performed it. I would listen, and at the end make a little bow and walk off. At six sharp, I kissed Alex and stepped into the hallway with Linda. Three bodyguards walked us downstairs.

Later, standing in the wings of a huge concert hall waiting for the signal to go on, I was sick with nerves. I could hear someone speaking onstage, but of course I understood nothing. The audience laughed and applauded. Then the music began, and the singer came in. What a voice, I thought. So beautiful. So clear. So strong.

A stagehand waved to me, and out I stepped.

At first, a blinding glare: spotlight in the eyes. Need a moment to adjust, I thought. Wow, this man can sing. There we go, I can focus now.

The glare receded and I looked across the stage. The singer turned and looked at me. His voice, filling the hall, flooded my head. He smiled and, through the white light of the flood lamps, I looked at him and fell in love.

Akira

He made everything stop that kept me out of the moment: my nerves, the voice in my head that told me to be afraid, my agoraphobia. I was there on that stage looking at that man and nowhere else. He had the most perfect smile, enveloping and comforting. Oh God, it was love—right there on that stage in front of a few thousand people and real as a heart attack.

The song ended. I accepted flowers brought out by a little girl and walked offstage. Linda was there, and as I passed her I said, "Lynn, I'm in love." Then, "Do you think he speaks English?"

In the dressing room, I was so excited I felt I might come apart at the seams. I was pacing, and all I could do was think of that smile. "What do I do, Linda? I have to speak to him."

"Then you shall." With that, Linda said she needed a walk. A little while later, she came back with her report: Akira was down the hall in his dressing room, and now would be the perfect time to go see him. Taking a deep breath and Linda's arm, I opened my door and stepped into the hall. The bodyguards looked nervous; this wasn't on the schedule.

When I knocked on the dressing room door, a man opened it: Akira's assistant. *"Choto mate kudasai"*—Please wait just a minute—he said, and stepped away from the door, leaving it open.

Akira walked out from behind a changing screen and smiled. I didn't think I could fall any deeper, but I did.

Suddenly, I was talking, in a kind of crazy pidgin English. "I like you," I said. "Do you like me?" I had never in my life been this forward before. I was using crazy hand gestures, trying to convey my meaning, although I think it was obvious.

Akira nodded.

"Maybe we could eat something together, then?" I said, bringing my hands to my mouth and miming a knife and fork.

"Okay," he said. Later, we would both say that right there, we knew.

I left, having made no definite plans but feeling that we absolutely would see each other again, and soon.

Akira Fuse was one of Japan's most beloved singers, with something like 27 number one hits since his debut in 1965. He had grown up in Tokyo and at seventeen had won a singing competition. Asked to attend the La Scala opera house in Milan—he could sing in any key—he declined and signed instead with Japan's biggest multimedia management firm, Watanabe Productions, headed by Shin and Misa Watanabe. From there, he recorded hit after hit and sold out live shows all over Japan.

The day after I met him, I was scheduled to do about six interviews. I remember floating through them as if in a dream; all I could see was Akira smiling at me from across the stage. Later that night, a big dinner for executives and notables from the cosmetics company was planned at one of the huge, glitzy hotels that clustered around downtown Tokyo. The Toad would be there, of course, but somehow I didn't seem to care. All I could think was that maybe Akira would join us.

Sitting at the head of the table, I leaned across and asked one of the translators if the singer from the commercial might be coming tonight. "Ah, no, Mr. Fuse has another dinner tonight at the hotel across the way."

I've never eaten so fast in my life. Coffee was just being served when, abruptly and no doubt rudely, I stood up and announced, "I'm sorry, but I have to go." And with Linda leading the way I headed for the doors.

She had found out the hotel where Akira was, and we headed straight there. Walking in, I saw him. He looked up and didn't seem at all surprised, as if it were the most natural thing in the world for this young actress to barge in on his dinner. Without hesitating he made room for us at the table. His English was broken at best, but I understood every word. After he had finished his dinner, I asked if he would like coffee at my hotel.

That night, after Linda had gone to bed in her room and Alex was happily tucked away in his, Akira and I spent our first night together. It was filled with laughter and talking and falling in love. You only get a few of those nights, and the memory of them stays with you for the rest of your life.

By the time Akira left at six the next morning, we both understood that our lives had changed forever.

The tour was coming to a close. I glided through interview after interview, while all I wanted was to see Akira again and be near him. Two days before we were set to leave, he came to my hotel room, stopping first to see Alex. He had brought him a toy truck and a question: "Alex, I like your mother and I want your permission to see her more." What a thing to do. It told me so much about him.

Later, Akira and I talked. "I love you," I began, "all I want . . ."

"Stop," he said. "Let me say this." He took my hand. "I love you too. And in the proper time we should marry."

He was so calm and formal as he said it. Thank goodness, because I was . . . well, an Aries. All I wanted to do was run right out and get hitched, move to Japan, and retire from acting so I could be with him.

"Olivia, be patient," he said reassuringly. "We will do things all in good time, you'll see." He was confident and he was right.

At the end of my official visit, Akira and I arranged to sneak off to Guam for a few last, precious days. Alex, Linda, and I flew into the tiny U.S. territory and met Akira, who had come in the day before. Three days together and I saw what kind of man I had fallen for. He was the kindest, strongest person I had ever met. I felt safe when I was with him, and I couldn't believe how lucky I was to have met him.

Flying back to LA, I cried hard into the cheap airline blanket, knowing it would be months before Akira and I would see each other again. How would I survive?

After Dino, I had been in a couple of relationships; I had even convinced myself that they were real. But no; not since Dino had I felt anything like this. It carried me through my meetings with attorneys to dissolve my contract with the Toad. At the end, I was given a check for some miserly amount in exchange for agreeing not to use his name in public. The whole thing was toxic and should have sent me spinning into a terrible, dark mood, but it didn't. My love for this incredible, talented Japanese man was complete. These were happy days.

Akira made a trip to LA, his first, and it couldn't have gone better. Alex loved him, and the three of us had a quiet time together. A month later, I flew back to Japan, leaving Alex with Linda and back at school.

Akira and I were still trying to keep our relationship secret. The glare of the public spotlight and the pressures it can add are anathema to new love. So when a photographer caught Akira and me getting into a car together and took some shots, and Akira ran after him, pushed him down, and took the film out of his camera, we knew we were in trouble. I loved what Akira did—what woman wouldn't?—but the paper demanded an exclusive or they would sue him. We agreed, posed for some pictures, and a week later there was a huge spread complete with bold headlines announcing that actress Olivia Hussey—*Juliet*—was seeing popular singer Akira Fuse. So the story was out. It was a big deal in Japan, but I didn't care. I was head over heels.

Another few months passed with trips back and forth, and it felt so right, so easy, and so safe. I knew it was time to call Baba. I had explained to Akira that, as far as I was concerned, Baba was a very great being. That he looked after me and made me feel happy, and I loved him. Akira had smiled and said he looked forward to meeting my guru, so after I had greeted Baba I put Akira on the phone.

"Muktabai is a daughter to me. I love her," Baba said from his South Fallsburg, New York, ashram. "Have you a date for the wedding?"

"We were thinking February fourteenth," Akira replied.

"*Bahut acha!*" I heard Baba yell, "I bless you! And we will see you here in February!"

I was getting married!

Later, Akira would tell me that at that point he had some apprehension about Baba; a guru was a totally foreign concept to him, and he wasn't at all sure what to expect. As it turned out, he needn't have worried. He finally met Baba when, after eight months and a lot of air miles, we traveled to the South Fallsburg ashram for our wedding. At their first encounter, Baba hugged Akira and held his face. He acted like a father meeting the love of his daughter's life and liking him. After we left, Akira looked at me and said, "Yes, he is very special."

But I could see that Baba's *shakti*, energy, had hit him hard. He felt dizzy and exhausted. "It's good for you, I promise," I said as I put him to bed.

On Valentine's Day 1980, Akira Fuse and I were married. The whole thing was beautiful. The Japanese press had been invited, as had all of the two thousand or so people attending the ashram. Akira threw himself into it with his whole heart, and Baba was magnificent. He hugged us, blessed us, held us close. He made it spiritual and intimate, and we both felt blessed to have him perform the ceremony. As for me, in my flowing white and cream sari and long, ornate necklace—both gifts from the ladies at the ashram—I was the happiest I had been in a long time.

We left as husband and wife, with no idea what would happen next.

Long-Distance Love

For the next few months, my new husband lived sixteen hours ahead of me. My late-night long-distance calls met his middle-of-the-afternoons, which led to his late-night "Sorry I missed you, but I was out all afternoon" calls to me in early morning LA. We lived for stolen, twenty-minute conversations—hurried, loving talk between his meetings or before I took Alex to school.

And then Alex and I went to Japan. It was the early eighties, and Japan was *the* new economic superpower. Efficiency, discipline, and a borderline-insane work ethic had made Japanese businesses the envy of world markets. Tokyo was the epicenter; you could feel the power of the place pulsing all around you. Although I loved the city, with its end-of-Silk-Road otherness, living there was hard. Alex was away from his dad and the whole Martin family, and I knew he missed them. Meanwhile, I was struggling with my Japanese.

Languages have generally come easily to me. I think I have an ear, and as far as the Romance languages are concerned, once you're fluent in one it bleeds into the others.

With my knowledge of Spanish, Italian and French were easy. Not so Japanese. At first, with its rather straightforward phonology—there are only five basic vowel sounds—its two tenses and non-gender-related noun forms, Japanese appeared doable. And I wanted to learn it so badly, for Akira and for myself.

But after getting lost in a thicket of pronouns, after realizing that there are subtle but profound differences in both organization of thought and in the relationship between speaker and listener, and after getting a migraine every time I stared down at page of Kanji (written characters), I decided life was too short. And, well, Akira and I understood each other perfectly well; we were in love.

For the next two years, that was how we lived: trips back and forth, some extended stays and massive telephone bills. Somehow, we made it all work. Akira and I booked a job together, a campaign for Fujifilm, which was so much fun. I did three films: The first was ridiculous but a wonderful experience; the second was very good; and the last, guaranteed to be a huge success, wasn't. In addition to all this, I lost Baba: For the first time in my life, I experienced the emptiness that follows the loss of someone close.

Turkey Shoot was the perfect name for the film, but for some reason, when the reviews came in it was renamed *Escape 2000*, only to be inexplicably rechristened *Blood Camp Thatcher*. I knew it was a B movie right from the start; I just didn't want to tell my director.

It came to me as a straight offer, which meant I didn't have to audition. It would shoot in Australia. It would star the actor Steve Railsback, who had done a great job in a wonderful film called *The Stuntman* with Peter O'Toole.

Reading the script told me *Turkey Shoot* was a pretty

apt name; there would be a lot of running around looking terrified. There would be gore. The whole thing was clearly going to be campy and silly. Worryingly, though, it called for some nudity.

So I met with the director, Brian Trenchard-Smith. He was a lovely man, very sweet and kind. He said everything would be tastefully done and that the film had the potential to become a real cult classic. As I listened to his carefully-thought-out ideas for the film, it struck me that I was per-haps not taking it quite as seriously as he was. When I met Steve, and saw the meticulous notes written all over his al-ready well-thumbed script, I remember wondering whether I had the same script as everybody else. I most certainly did.

I hadn't worked in a while, and I was nervous. Akira said not to worry; he would travel with me. (Alex was in school, staying with Dino.) We flew into Sydney, where I would have liked to spend more time, and then took another flight to Cairns in the north of the country, up in Queens-land. Exhausted and jet-lagged, we nevertheless wanted to meet everybody and see the set, so we took a car. It was hot and humid. We found Steve, who had started work the week before, suspended six feet above the ground, locked inside a cage and wearing an ill-fitting yellow jumpsuit. He looked concerned. The first thing he said to me was, "You knew all along what kind of movie this was going to be, Olivia, didn't you?" I burst out laughing.

Not surprisingly, the production was beset by problems; right away, the first twelve to fifteen pages of the script were simply thrown out. Never a good start. Soon, an odd duality set in. On one hand, the movie, with its outrageous dialogue, schlocky horror-movie effects, and campy makeup, became more ludicrous every day. As with Steve in his cage, some kind of escape was essential.

Fortunately for us there were, on the other hand, won-derful people involved in the shoot—the Australian actors were a pleasure to work with, so good and so profes-sional—and we had time off to spend with some of them. Akira and I adored Steve and his wife, Jackie. The four of us spent most of our time together. During the day, Akira would work on his music; at night he would put together amazing meals for us. He had brought a suitcase full of his favorite Japanese ingredients, and he took a childlike de-light in seeing what he could come up with.

Once we knew what kind of monster the film was, it be-came easy to make sensible choices. I asked not to do any nudity, and a body double was brought in. The scene was terrifically deranged. It took place in the camp shower and boasted some of the worst, most cringeworthy dialogue I've ever heard. The Aussie actor Roger Ward and I toiled through it. Ironically, when I saw the film, and saw what the body double looked like, I wished I'd done the damned nudity. I had a much better body than she did.

Another choice was not to be eaten by crocodiles. One morning, Steve and I were sitting in makeup when sud-denly these huge explosions went off. "What on earth is that all about?" I asked, and was bluntly told, "That's for your scene today, Mrs. Olivia. Production is just setting off bombs in the river to scare all the crocs away."

"All?" I said.

"Well, it is the outback."

The outback had started to look a bit demon-haunted to me. I had convinced myself that it was full of actress-eating animals and giant, creepy-crawly things just wait-ing to creep and crawl all over me. So when I heard talk of crocodiles and bombs, I quite naturally panicked.

The scene called for Steve and me to swim past the cam-era as fast as we could. I demanded that the crew sit along the riverbank with their legs in the water. My thought was, Let's give the crocs some choices besides Steve and me. The crew loved it and had a good laugh; I was deadly serious.

Brian yelled, "Action," and, under his breath, Steve began to hum the theme from *Jaws*. More panic. For years afterward, whenever I ran into Steve he would greet me by humming John Williams's immortal two notes.

About three weeks into the shoot, the Australian actors came to Steve and me and said they hadn't been paid. We stopped working until things got sorted. After all, actors have got to stick together.

All in all, *Turkey Shoot/Escape 2000/Camp Blood Thatcher* was fun to make and an absolute nightmare to watch. The trailer lives on YouTube, for all to see and laugh at!

The polar opposite to *Turkey Shoot*, Walter Scott's classic *Ivanhoe* was a solid, dignified, and professional production. It knew what it was and where it was going. The TV movie would shoot in and around London and the English countryside. It starred Anthony Andrews as Wilfred of Ivanhoe, together with Sam Neill, Ronald Pickup, and Michael Hordern. I was playing Rebecca. Most exciting of all, my father would be played by James Mason.

The cast assembled in late summer 1982 for the first table read-through, which is just what it sounds like. It has taken me a long time to really understand how I work, and I know that I am no good at readings. I need to spend time thinking about what I am going to do. I need to feel my costume. I need a shoot to be up and running to find my feet. Only then can I start to feel things. For me, the line runs from thought to feeling to acting. So I was all adrift at that first table read, and it showed. I remember Douglas Camfield, the director, coming up to me afterward and saying, "Olivia, you seemed very unsure. You will be all right?"

I could see that he was nervous. Asking an actor if she will deliver is an awkward conversation. "Oh, yes, Douglas, I'll be fine," I said, "I just don't know what I'm going to do yet."

Three weeks later, I shot my first scene. It was set in a long, damp stone hall. My character was answering questions from a group of men. I had a page-long monologue, and I nailed it in one take. After yelling, "Cut!" Douglas came over. He was all smiles. "Brilliant, Olivia!" he said. "I never would have guessed from the table read."

"It's all about feeling for me," I said, and understood for the first time how true that was.

Ivanhoe was a happy, albeit chilly, shoot. Fall had swept in with a freezing-cold wave, and there were days and days of outdoor filming.

Sam Neill and I had a very complicated scene together. It can be hard to shoot scenes that involve a lot of movement. Eye lines change, and continuity between camera angles becomes critical. Also, it can difficult for the actors. With so much extraneous technical detail to worry about, you can lose the emotion attached to the situation. Sam and I rehearsed a few times, and when we shot it the scene flowed perfectly. It was all done in one shot, and we nailed it on the first take. We got a nice round of applause from the crew.

Although James Mason and I had worked together on *Jesus of Nazareth*, and had met a number of times over the years, it was still a thrill to come onto the set knowing I would be working with him. He was one of my favorites, one of the old guard of English actors for whom I will always have a soft spot. With his distinguished repertory of films, from *North by Northwest* to *Lolita*, he was, simply, a legend. And he didn't for one moment act like one.

"Olivia, how are you today?" he asked one particularly cold, wet morning.

"Oh, I'm freezing," I said. "How are you?"

"Achy. At my age, Olivia, that's about as good as you can hope for."

He was always charming and kind. He never complained or was late. He knew everybody on set by name and would speak to anybody who wanted a word. He was a dear man and a pleasure to work with.

Ivanhoe was a success, receiving positive reviews and high ratings in the States as well as Europe. Apparently it is considered something of a classic in Denmark and is aired annually on Danish television.

Akira was with me often during the filming, flying in and out when he had a chance and his hectic schedule would allow. It was such a comfort to have him close by. He had a way of calming me and keeping me centered and strong. So it was always traumatic when he had to leave. Saying good-bye, if only for ten days, felt like the end of the world to me. Lines blurred; I felt abandoned, like the little girl I had once been, locked in a room with her younger brother somewhere in London.

Then, a few weeks after filming had wrapped, we found out I was pregnant. We were so happy, so excited. For me, the news helped make those separations bearable. Now, a part of Akira was always with me.

On January 5, 1983, my second son, Maximilian Hussey Fuse, was born. It had been a hard pregnancy. I had been ill every day, but now Max was born and he was beautiful. But Akira couldn't be in LA for the birth and had to send a friend to the hospital to take pictures and wire them. That was very hard for me.

Three weeks later, he did come out and meet his son for the time. We sat for a photo shoot with a big Japanese magazine, proud parents introducing their boy to the public.

For years, I had been asking my mum to come out to LA and live with me. I missed her, and I thought the golden California weather would be good for her. Finally she agreed—I should say relented—and about a month after Max was born, my little mum moved in.

Not long after the delivery, I was offered a good role in what promised to be a big TV miniseries. *The Last Days of Pompeii* would film in Italy; in Pompeii, in fact. It would boast an all-star cast, including Ned Beatty, Ernest Borgnine, Brian Blessed, and Sir Laurence Olivier, whom I had not seen in over a decade. It would be a big-budget, sword-and-sandal spectacle with a huge amount of press behind it.

Truth be told, I had no business saying yes to the job. I was sick. I had lost a lot of weight during the final weeks of my pregnancy, vomiting every day and feeling nauseated all night. It had been brutal, and I was run-down. Also, though I didn't know it had a name, after Max was born a postpartum depression had descended like the setting of the sun, leaving everything black. I felt as if it were always four o'clock in the morning.

To add to that, for the first time since we'd met, Akira and I were struggling. The long separations and constant travel had taken a toll. It was a low-boil kind of frustration, but it was affecting my state of mind.

Nevertheless, and against my better judgment, I took the part. I wanted to work in Italy again. I wanted to see Sir Larry and share a scene with him. I wanted Alex to see Pompeii. What an amazing experience for a boy, I thought.

Five months after having Max, I wrapped him in his swaddle blankets and, with his brother and grandmother in tow, set off to Italy for six weeks.

The sets and locations for *The Last Days of Pompeii* were incredible. Entire Roman towns were built. The detail was fantastic. For Alex, it was a dream. He would wander around the sets in Pompeii with his little wooden sword, imagining epic Roman adventures and soaking up the place. For my mum, the trip provided a chance to go to Rome, to Vatican City. She stood in the crowds on Wednesday afternoon and saw the Pope. It was a dream for her. Who knew that in a few years I would be starring in a film written by Pope John Paul and would have the opportunity to meet him and be blessed by him?

For me, filming *The Last Days of Pompeii* was like a homecoming. Along with Sir Laurence, there was my old flame and friend Franco Nero. I was in Italy, with a European crew. It made me think of *Romeo & Juliet* and all that had happened since.

One day, I was sitting in the hair and makeup trailer while Mark Nelson put the finishing touches on another gorgeous, elaborate hairstyle. Mark was head of hair, and as he worked on me I said, "You know, I am so looking forward to seeing Sir Larry again. He's such a nice man. Do you think he will remember me? We worked together years ago."

Later that day, I ran into Mark again. "Sir Larry was darling," he said. "Do you know what he said to me? 'I'm working with Olivia Hussey today. I wonder if she will remember me, Mark.'" So humble.

Sir Larry and I had a little scene together. He was older now and very frail—a few years after *Pompeii*, he would pass on. But he still carried himself with all the grace and aplomb his years and years on the stage had taught him.

His line was something like, "Oh Ione, so good to see you again." (Ione was my character's name.) The director called, "Action," and Sir Laurence looked at me and said, "Olivia, so good to see you."

By take five, calling me Olivia each time, he turned to the crew and said, "At my age, you must take what you can get."

Through the laughter, I was struck by his vulnerability. Here was Sir Laurence Olivier, one of the seminal actors of British theatre and a living legend, throwing his hands up and apologizing, essentially saying, "What can you do? I'm an old man." Time and age catches up to us all, and whether you are an Oscar-winning actor or a guy driving a bus, it doesn't discriminate.

The poet W. H. Auden wrote, "Time watches from the shadow / And coughs when you would kiss." I am always aware of how fleeting it all is. Actors who bluster and are self-centered, whose egos are so fragile they demand to be treated differently from everybody else, seem to forget this simple fact of life. You may get your moment, true enough. But it will be only a moment. And it will pass. Then you are left with who you are and how you treated people on your way up, because, believe me, they'll all be there on your way down. I will never forget Sir Laurence's kindness and honesty in the face of his own fragility.

Pompeii was six weeks of costumes, pasta, and postpartum depression. In a way, going straight back to work after having Max was the best thing I could have done. Alone at home, waiting for Akira to call, would have been much worse. Still, it was a grind for me. I fought my little demons. I cried a lot. I drank.

After all these years, I understand that a part of me will always be vulnerable and alive to the vibrations of life's changing frequencies. I have no filter and I have no guard.

I take everything to heart, from a harmless comment made in passing to huge, life-altering events. It all affects me. Also, I have a terrible habit of taking life's slings and arrows and turning them in on myself. Blaming myself.

Unfortunately, for all its star power, magnificent locations, and exploding mountaintops, *Pompeii* was a ratings dud. American audiences just weren't interested. They tuned instead to a sci-fi miniseries called *V* that aired opposite *Pompeii* and became a massive hit. The future clobbered the past.

In between *Ivanhoe* and *The Last Days of Pompeii*, Baba died. I was six months pregnant with Max. I had known Baba was ill, although I didn't know how ill. During his illness, traveling to India and staying at the ashram obviously wasn't an option. Instead, we spoke on the phone.

"Baba, I'm sure I'm having a girl," I would say. "Please bless her." He would laugh his big belly laugh and reply, "I bless your *son*, Muktabai." Every one of our conversations ended the same way: Baba would say, "I love you. I bless you and everything about you." Then we would hang up. But our last conversation was different. At the end Baba paused, then said, "I love you. Bless yourself."

"No, Baba," I said. "I want you to bless me."

Baba laughed and repeated, "I love you. Bless yourself."

We hung up, and I started to weep. That was the last time I would speak to him. I knew it. He was leaving soon. I just knew it.

Swami Muktananda—Baba—passed away on October 2, 1982. This was the first time that death had touched my life, and the finality of it was shocking. For a year, I could not bring myself to say Baba's name. I couldn't go anywhere near the Siddha Ashram in Los Angeles. The candles on my little prayer table stayed unlit. Like a Victorian widow, I was in mourning, carrying myself with a kind of detached, glassy-eyed sadness. I missed Baba and wished I could see him again.

And then I did.

When I think of it now, it still seems more real than anything real that has happened to me, a dream so simple a five-year-old might have had it. I'm sitting on the edge of Baba's bed, looking over my shoulder and down at him. He reaches up and takes my hand.

"I love you, Muktabai," he says. "And I will never leave you. I will always be in your heart."

I woke with a start, still feeling Baba's warm hand over mine. The weight of his loss was gone. It had completely disappeared, and in its place there was only certainty, certainty that I had not lost him forever, that death was not the end. Certainty that when it was my time Baba would be there, waiting, and I would not be afraid.

In the years to follow, death would come again. First, it was sudden and tragic, then inevitable. Each time, I felt the pain and the loss, but I was never overwhelmed. I was never despondent. I could be strong for my family, helping them through because I knew death wasn't the end. It was simply a part of the life cycle—maybe even its own beginning. Baba had taught me that.

Up, Up, and Away

The year 1985 found our eclectic little family together but starting to buckle under life's mounting pressures. We had sold my cozy Larchmont house and leased a huge, old-Hollywood-style home in Los Feliz that had been built by the LA philanthropist Dorothy Chandler. My mum, who had never taken to Los Angeles, began to have health issues again. She missed England. She missed my brother. Worse still, I think, she hated seeing her daughter struggle.

Akira and I were fighting hard to make it work. After seven years marred by more and more separations, we had drifted apart. Akira was becoming increasingly frustrated as he was forced by work to spend more time in Japan. When he flew in to see us, he felt like a stranger in his own home. He was a Buddhist and by nature calm, so we never really argued—indeed, what was there to argue about? I had to be in the United States for work and Akira had to be in Japan. Slowly—it felt inevitable—the two of us were pulled apart. We were like twin galaxies in an expanding universe, moving farther and farther away from each other, with a dark, widening void between. We stopped knowing each other.

In 1986, my mum moved back to England. Akira was spending months working in Japan. Here I was, alone with my two boys, living in a huge house on a Hollywood hill. There was a tennis court nobody used. A pool nobody swam in. A giant dining room seating twenty people that never held a dinner party. The master bedroom was miles from the boys' rooms. The place was designed, it seemed, to separate us.

No, I thought, this doesn't work. We moved two weeks later.

I found a house in Malibu, high on a mountainside overlooking the sea. It was small and simple and just what I thought we needed.

During this time, my work was unremarkable. I did a Hallmark Hall of Fame miniseries, *The Corsican Brothers*, and an episode of *Murder, She Wrote*. That was it for almost two years. There was a lot I could have done: so many projects I talked my way out of, so many missed opportunities. I look at the work choices I made and think, If only I had been more focused. Had thought more in the long term. Planned better. If only I had been tougher, saying no to the wrong people and yes to the right people.

But I always follow my heart. I made the choices I made because they felt right at the time. Nothing I did was ever calculated, and to expect anything else would be like asking a rock to sing. For me to have had a different sort of career, one with perhaps more gravitas and a few more hits, would have called for me to be a different person. And who can manage that?

But that year was different. I didn't work because I couldn't: I had my hands full. I was raising my boys and struggling with my marriage. I was worrying about my mum and trying simply to live day to day.

Max was a darling baby boy, and aside from the time when he almost drowned in the pool he was always bright, always happy. Alex was having a tougher time. He was twelve years old and couldn't read. He was having a bad time in school and lagging behind his classmates. There was one bright spot, though—his father.

As Alex got older—honestly, I should say as Dino got older—his dad became more hands-on, and the two of them grew much closer. Now, instead of picking Alex up on the weekends and taking him to Jeanne's, Dino would take him back to his own swinging '80s condo, where they would spend the weekend watching movies, with breaks at the Hamburger Hamlet to drink milkshakes. I could not be more happy.

Dino was still Dino, of course. A few years before, he had joined the U.S. Air National Guard. He wanted to fly jets—God, how he loved speed. Discovering he was too old to join, he did something he loathed doing: He asked his dad for a favor. Naturally, because Dino never did anything small, that favor involved the president of the United States. So after a few calls, one coming directly from the White House, Dino was off to the U.S. Flight Academy in Alabama to train to be a fighter pilot. That man never let anything stand in his way.

I talked to him about Alex's problems at school. We took Alex to see a whole host of doctors. They tested his eyesight, his hearing, his hand–eye coordination, his IQ. Eventually, a well-respected psychologist, Dr. Jack Wetter, diagnosed Alex with dyslexia. Every week, we would meet at Dr. Wetter's office, where, after Dino and I had talked briefly with the doctor, Alex would happily go in for his own solo session. Left in the waiting room, Dino and I would talk. And, just as the sixteen-year-old Dino could make me laugh and flirt with me and always manage to pull me out of myself, the thirty-five-year-old could too. Dino was always special to me, and I think I was to him too. Our souls clicked. No matter the changes life had wrought on us or the time that had passed, we could always fall back into that easy, natural familiarity that comes from a deep love and a deeper understanding.

Over the years, one of Dino's favorite lines to me was, "When we're thirty-five we're getting back together, you know."

I would laugh and say, "In your dreams, Dino!"

"You'll see, Olivia. And it's Dean Paul now."

"You'll always be Dino to me, Dino."

One day in the waiting room, neither one of us was laughing. We were sitting across from each other, magazines spilling over the table between us.

"You look so well, Olivia. Still the most beautiful woman in the world," Dino said.

"Still the most shallow but handsomest man in the world," I responded. But this time my teasing fell flat.

Walking to our cars after the session, we were both quiet.

"See you next week, Dino," I said inside the garage as I moved toward my car.

"Of course."

After getting Alex into the backseat, I buckled his seat belt, closed the door, and stood up. Dino was still standing where we had said good bye. The underground garage's fluorescent lighting gave everything a strange, greenish glow. Dino was pooled in it. He was watching us.

"Are you okay?" I asked. He looked so alone.

Smiling, he said, "Yes." Then, "I love you both very much. Take care of yourselves."

"You too, Dino." He walked off.

My God, I thought, maybe we really will get back together.

That was last time I ever saw him.

A week after that doctor's visit, Alex was standing at the curb outside our Malibu home, waiting for his dad to pick him up. The two of them were heading out to Edwards Air Force Base, and it was a long drive so it was early in the morning. It was only Alex's fourth time seeing his dad fly, and he was excited to be waiting outside by the curb.

Akira was in town. We had made breakfast for the four of us and were playing with Max and not talking about what had happened to our marriage. When Dino pulled up outside, the low growl of his Porsche was unmistakable—the car had once belonged to Steve McQueen. It was pea green, always in the shop, and the love of Dino's life.

With Alex off, I puttered about, watering plants and drinking my morning coffee while Akira worked in his home music studio. By five p.m., the late March sun was casting long shadows across our backyard swimming pool. I was sitting at the kitchen table, watching the shadows dance back and forth on the water, when the phone rang. When I picked up, Alex said. "Mom, I don't want you worry, but my dad's jet went off the radar and they can't find it."

Life drained out of me while my soul ached for my little boy, who sounded so brave giving his mother news he should never have had to give.

"Listen, Alex, I don't want you to worry, okay? I'm sure everything will be fine." But my mind flashed to Dino, standing alone in the parking garage. "Where are you?"

"At Nan's." He was at Jeanne's house in Beverly Hills.

"Do you want me to come get you?"

"No. Not yet. I think I should say here. Nan isn't coming out of her room, and people are coming over."

"Okay. I love you. Everything will be fine."

A pause. "I love you too." And we hung up.

Oh God, please, no. Please don't let this be happening. Not to Alex. Not to all of us.

A few hours later, it was all over the news. Dino's F-4 Phantom jet had gone missing somewhere over the San Bernardino Mountains. The weather had been awful, and the reports were saying that search-and-rescue planes were having a hard time staying in the air.

I kept saying that if anyone could walk away from this, it would be Dino. Somehow, some way. Dino was too full of life. There was just no way he could be gone.

I felt helpless. Waiting by the phone for Alex to call back with news, I replayed all the times I had had with Dino. All the fights, all the forgiveness, and especially all the love. The tenderhearted golden boy, who had waited so long for the girl he fancied, might be gone.

I couldn't bear it. I needed to do *something*. I turned to what I've always turned to, the thing I knew best: faith.

A few years before, I had attended a talk by a swami from Hong Kong. I had liked him. He was soft-spoken and had a lovely, caring energy. I thought, why not call him? He could pray for Dino and his safe return. Who knows? He might help with my anxiety, my fear. It certainly couldn't hurt.

He had given me his contact information, so I phoned. When he answered, I said, "Hello. This is Olivia Hussey. We met when you were in Los Angeles. I'm the actress you spoke with."

"Oh, yes, Olivia," he said. "Of course I remember. How wonderful to hear from you. Are you well?"

Kind words from a kind man, I thought. I told him what was happening. Maybe he could send a blessing. After a pause, he said, "Call me back in an hour."

I waited, feeling sure he would tell me everything would be fine, that he had said his blessings and that I should be strong. But still. An hour passed, and I called again.

"He has passed, Olivia. He is on the other side," were the swami's first words. "And because it happened so fast it has been difficult for him to adjust. I am sorry. I will give you some words to chant and meditate on."

I wrote them down. I thanked him. I hung up.

Please God, don't let it be true, I thought. Let this man be wrong.

He wasn't wrong.

Years later, Alex would tell me that although he was young and his memory of those three days was more images than coherent narrative, he remembered when the doorbell rang: A current of fear flowed from all the adults in the room straight to Dean Sr., who was sitting in a living-room chair staring straight ahead. Someone opened the door, and in walked a man in a tailored blue air force uniform with shining silver eagles on the shoulders and a black-brimmed hat held firmly under one arm. Alex remembers the officer standing still in front of Dean—the rest of the assembled family now just bystanders—and delivering his message: "Mr. Martin, the United States Air Force regrets to inform you that your son has been killed in the line of duty. You have our deepest sympathies." Then he turned smartly and left.

The manner in which he handled this terrible job, telling a father his son was dead, stayed with Alex. The officer had been respectful and dignified. He had been a credit to the air force and had taught Alex something about being a man.

Akira and I picked Alex up from Jeanne's a couple of hours later. Sitting in the backseat, I held my son close in my arms. Akira was driving, silent and somber, an outsider on this most private of family occasions: Dino was gone. There would be a huge funeral. There would be news crews and TV specials. There would be an investigation into the accident. There would be people who barely knew Dino coming around just to be close to the loss. For my son, there would be a whole life spent without a father to rely on, to look up to. But all that was to come. For now, my boy needed to be with me. Needed to be home. We spent the next two days crying together, looking out over the ocean.

Dino's life touched so many others. For some, he was simply a Golden Boy who, like the cherry-red hood of the Ferrari he drove when he was seventeen, was shiny and bright and all smooth surface. Others saw the actor, hardworking and always on the brink of hitting it big. Still others saw the tortured prince, trapped forever in the shadow of his father's fame. People projected onto Dino what they needed to, and for the most part he was okay with that. Everyone felt special around him.

I didn't see any of those Dinos. Dino was my first love, my first best friend. He was my first glimpse of America, that elevator door opening and all his sunshine pouring out. I knew Dino as a boy and as a man, and a piece of my heart died when he left us.

He was always unapologetic about who he was and the privilege he came from, but he was also fearless in his pursuit of his own identity. Ultimately that pursuit, that drive to define himself on his own terms, cost him his life. That was tragic. But for the people who loved him most, memories remain. Wonderful memories of a wonderful man, whose energy, spirit, and love of life made the world a more colorful place and gave a young, moody actress so much happiness and so much laughter. I miss you, Dino.

A few months later, we had something to celebrate: Dean Sr.'s youngest daughter, Gina, was getting married. She and her longtime boyfriend, Carl Wilson, had decided to make it official, and I couldn't have been happier for them. Gina had always been the apple of her father's eye. She was all sweetness and laughter, a wonderful girl, and now she was marrying one of the gentlest, kindest men I had ever met.

My memory of Carl is of his manner. He had the softest, most caring way about him. His sincerity was almost transcendent. He and his brothers had started one of the biggest bands in the world, the Beach Boys, when they were teenagers. The price they paid for the immediate success of their genre-defining sound had been, I think, very high. Carl had battled through it and had come out on the other side with a kind of peacefulness inside him. He possessed a tranquility that was palpable. You felt it when you were with him, and it always felt good. Like Dino, he was taken from us—from Gina—much too soon, and like Dino's, his passing left a hole in this world.

The wedding was held in Vegas, and I was so happy to be invited. Gina looked beautiful as she and her proud father walked down the aisle. After the pain of the past few months, we all needed this. It was a chance to laugh and to party, to forget, if only for a night, the man who wasn't there. I remember thinking that the minister who performed the ceremony said some wonderful, healing things.

Yet I couldn't help but be drawn back to another wedding, with my slim white dress and Dino's baby-blue suit, the ring Jeanne had given me. The memory of that day and of the happiness lost welled up as I sat at the reception table, my chicken getting cold in front of me. All I wanted to do was run into the bathroom and cry my eyes out. I was not pleased when I saw the minister walking toward me. Oh God, I thought, not now. The last thing I needed just then was to have to make small talk.

The minister sat down, placed his hand gently on mine, and said, "It's so nice to meet you, Olivia. This must be a hard night for you. Memories of your own wedding must be strong." My tears nearly fell then, and I fought hard to hold them back. "I want to tell you, Olivia," he went on, "that Dino is at peace now. He had a hard time at first. The suddenness of it made it difficult for him to—what's the word—adjust."

As I sat there listening to what was almost word-for-word what the swami had told me during those awful three days of waiting, I felt a heaviness bear down on me. As we spoke further, though, I started to feel better. The weight that had threatened to crush me lifted, and by the end of our short conversation I felt freer, more lucid, and less burdened.

The minister was John-Roger, founder of the Movement of Spiritual Inner Awareness. Carl was close with JR, and after our brief conversation I could understand why.

I've always thought the term "closure" was vague and used far too often; it's a catchall word that has been drained of meaning. However, that night was a sort of ending for me. After months of heartache and some regret, I could at last look past Dino's death—or, rather, through it. Today, I see a part of Dino every time I look at Alex, and I smile, remembering the force of Dino's personality, the bright burning energy of his life, his humor and courage, and finally his love. I am grateful that in his all-too-short life he experienced what it meant to be a parent. He lives now in the hearts and thoughts of the people who loved him most, and I know that when my time here is done, after I shuffle off this mortal coil, I will laugh with him again.

Let the '80s Be Over

Dino died in March of 1987, and by October Akira and I had split up. In a little under a year, I had lost the two great loves of my life.

Akira and I were friends. We understood that it had been distance and circumstance that had ruined us. That it simply could not work for two people, however much they might be in love, to live and work thousands of miles apart for years at a time. And, given that Akira and I were both artists, with artists' hearts, susceptible to caprice, wild swings of mood, and gnawing wanderlust, it's no surprise that we could not make it work. If anything, it is a testament to how much we cared and loved one another that we lasted as long as we did.

One of the last things we did together was buy a house. Akira wanted us—me, Max, and Alex—to be secure and have something real that we could count on. The house was in the Hollywood Hills, off Mulholland Drive in a gated community called The Summit. Akira paid in cash—I helped a little—and we bought it outright, full and clear.

"It's a nest egg for your future," Akira said.

A little over a week after we moved in, an offer came in that grabbed me. The script dealt with four young friends, their relationships, and how they were connected to a small, local jeweler's shop. Oh, and it was written by the Pope.

Pope John Paul II—then Bishop Karol Józef Wojtyła—had originally written *The Jeweler's Shop* in 1960 as a three-act play set in his home city, Kraków, Poland. The play had been translated into twenty-two languages and had sold an estimated fifty million copies worldwide.

I thought it was a beautiful script, and I immediately said yes to the offer.

Another attraction was the film's cast. The fine actor Ben Cross, whom I had adored in *Chariots of Fire*, had been cast as one of the four friends, and I thought we would work well together. However, it was the chance to work with another actor that really sealed it for me: Burt Lancaster was one of the all-time greats, and the idea of sharing the screen with him delighted me. I had grown up watching Mr. Lancaster's films, from *Birdman of Alcatraz* to *Trapeze*, and adoring him. He would be on set for only two days; essentially, he was doing a cameo in the film as the jeweler. Not that it mattered to me. He was a marvelous actor, a true Hollywood legend. From what I had heard, he was also a wonderful man and a pleasure to work with.

The Pope, a trip to Europe, working with a movie great? What was there for me to think about? And considering what the past few years had been like, I was desperate to get back to work. *The Jeweller's Shop* not only afforded me that opportunity but also had the potential to be something special, a work of quality. I wanted a project I could believe in, and here, it seemed, the universe had given me one.

Unfortunately, it also meant being on location in Kraków.

It might have been my harried, fragile state of mind, but even as I arrived in that most Eastern European of cities, I knew it would depress me. Kraków, like most of the Soviet Union's abused and bitter satellites, wore a palette of grays and browns, of dirty windows and peeling yellow paint. Cars infamous the world over as some of the worst in history—Trabants, Zaporozhets, and Yugos—clanked and coughed as they splashed through inky-black puddles next to roadside heaps of trash. Everywhere you looked, the strained, hollow faces of a people too long misused looked right through you. The fall of communism was three years away, but you could tell it wouldn't last. Nothing seemed to be working.

A sooty dark mist enveloped the city center. When I asked my translator what it was, she replied simply, "Dirt."

Wonderful, I thought. Just wonderful.

There was a curfew throughout the city, and by ten o'clock, when the car pulled up to our enormous gray cinder-block hotel, the streets of Kraków were deserted. In the lobby, the all-Italian crew was loitering with intent, which instantly put me at ease. Waiting to be given their rooms, the crew members looked around the fraying lobby with raised eyebrows and whistled low to themselves. There were murmurs of *"Questo sarà un lungo tiro"* "This will be a long shoot" and *"Cosa devono fare le stanze essere come?"* "What must the rooms be like?" from the key grips, line producers, best boys, and PA runners. I thought it was all hysterical.

My suite, when at last I saw it, was less funny. About the size of a prison cell, it comprised one small room with a cracked window, two cot-like sleeping things, a small wooden desk, and a hot plate.

"Lord, and this is the *suite*," I muttered, looking around.

There was a fine patina of grime covering everything. When I ran my finger along the desk, my fingertip turned black. I shuddered. Please, let the food at least be decent, I thought.

Meals were served in a huge banquet hall attached to the hotel lobby. Covering one wall was a mural of happy, marching workers, their eyes turned upward and out, toward the future and the hall. I wondered how they liked that future.

There were, I'm not kidding, 170 items on the menu. Going down the list, you might pick an appetizer, only to be met with *"Nie, nie mamy, e pozycja dost pna"* "No, we don't have that item today" from a smiling waiter. Or you might ask for, say, the soup called *Bigos*: *"Nie, nie mamy, e pozycja dost pna."*

Grilled lamb?

"Nie, nie mamy, e pozycja dost pna."

The chef's special salad?

"Nie, nie mamy, e pozycja dost pna."

Finally, exasperated but dying to see how this little episode would end, you'd ask, "Well, what *do* you have?"

A flush would come over your waiter's face as he swelled with pride: "We have turkey!"

Just as Jack Nicholson had always been the caretaker at the Overlook Hotel, so we would find that turkey was what was *always* for dinner at our Cinder-Block Hotel, Kraków.

The Jeweller's Shop turned out to be one of the most enjoyable film sets I'd worked on. Michael Anderson, who had directed films such as *Around the World in 80 Days* and *Logan's Run*, helmed the production, and he was delightful to work with. Michael was unassuming and polite, and he knew exactly what he wanted—a great blend for a director. As I suspected, Ben Cross and I got on right away.

It was a pleasure to find we shared a similar sense of humor—something close to gallows humor.

The film had a representative from the Vatican on set every day, one Monsignor Janusz St. Pasierb, who was close friends with Pope John Paul. He was assigned to ensure that the film's themes were being conveyed in a manner that would meet with the Pope's approval. It sounds very ominous, but Monsignor Pasierb was in fact an absolute pleasure to be around. He was a proud Pole, an essayist, and a fine poet. He had a beautiful, resounding laugh that broke out all the time and was completely infectious. I had to do a Polish accent, so a top-notch coach, Anna Korda, was brought in from Rome. The three of us became good friends. We ate lunch together every day: the Monsignor laughing and talking about Polish history, Anna fanning herself—she was forever too hot—and me committed to staying in my accent while on the set. It was the happiest I had been working for a long time.

Back at the Cinder-Block, however, it was still communist cliché raised to the level of farce. In my room, one of my sleep-type cots was far too soft. I called downstairs and asked if they might place a board under the mattress to firm it up.

"No worries. Yes, yes, later today."

I came back that night and jumped onto my cot for a test run. There was indeed a wooden board there, solid and strong. However, it had been laid down *on top* of the mattress and the sheet thrown over it.

On the set, I finally met Burt Lancaster. When he shook my hand for the first time and flashed his smile I nearly died, I was so happy. I had seen that smile so many times in so many great movies, and now it was directed at me. I was starstruck.

"So nice to meet you, Olivia," he said. Oh God, that voice.

It was a short scene. The Italian actor Andrea Occhipinti, who was playing my future husband, and I come into the jeweler's shop and meet Mr. Lancaster, the owner. Although it was small, the scene was pivotal, and Mr. Lancaster had a page-long monologue to deliver. The problem was that he got through a few lines and then he dried. Because it was such an important speech for the film, he couldn't do it as a pickup and continue from where he had forgotten his line; he had to start again from the beginning. Andrea and I felt terrible. We wished we had some lines so we could help prompt Mr. Lancaster. Hour after hour went by, take after take. At three o'clock, a break was called. Cast and crew headed to the craft-service tables for coffee and a bit of food, or stepped outside for some fresh air. I was standing by the monitors when Mr. Lancaster walked over. He had asked that I call him Burt, but there was no way I could.

"I am very sorry, Olivia, that this monologue is taking me so long," he said. "Please accept my apologies."

Without a moment's thought, I looked him straight in the eye and said, "Mr. Lancaster, there is nothing, absolutely nothing, to be sorry about. You have touched every one of us with your work for so many years, and if it takes us the whole day and night to finish, then it is our great good fortune to be here with you and to watch you work. Truly."

He smiled and, without saying a word, walked away. We worked late into the night.

When I arrived on the set the next morning, we still had the last part of the scene to cover. Just as I was settling into hair and makeup, Mr. Lancaster arrived. He was holding one red rose. He walked over, handed it to me, and said, "A rose for a rose." Then he kissed my hand. I swear, it was one of the greatest moments of my life.

After shooting in Poland was complete, the production was to pull up stakes and move to Montreal for three final weeks of filming (during which I would have my boys with me). I left Poland thinking the people were warm if a bit worn out, and my hotel—Cinder-Block Plaza—had been the greatest worst hotel I would ever see. Taken together, I had had a wonderful time.

Unfortunately, after it was finished *The Jeweller's Shop* was caught up in litigation. Some kind of dispute broke out between the two companies that coproduced it. This happens all too often in the movie business, and it can leave good work—great work—orphaned, consigned to a shelf somewhere on a Hollywood studio's back lot.

The film was screened at the Vatican, though, and a few months after returning home I received a call inviting me to Rome. Regretfully, because of the boys and the short turnaround involved, I had to say no. I heard the screening was a fantastic experience. Six thousand priests and nuns filled Vatican hall. Bishops and cardinals had flown in to join them. Apparently, afterward, when Pope John Paul was introduced to the cast, he asked where the rest of the cast was. One of the producers replied, "She could not be here, your Holiness, due to family commitments." The Pope had asked about me! I always regretted not going. Years later, though, I would have an opportunity to meet him.

On June 24, 1989, my sweet brother, Andrew, phoned from London to tell me that our beautiful mother had passed away. After almost a lifetime of smoking, the emphysema she had battled for years had finally won.

I had spoken to her only three days before, and before we hung up she had said, "I love you, Livi. I'm very, very tired."

I told her I would visit soon. It was tough, with the boys in school. "During their holidays," I'd promised.

But I was too late. My mummy had passed and I hadn't been there. When I got off the phone with my brother, I started to cry. "I'm so sorry I couldn't be there with you, Mummy," I said aloud. Crying turned to sobbing as I thought of my mum and of her wanting to see me one last time. I thought of how different we were, and how those differences had made our relationship challenging at times. I wished I could have told her that, for all the differences, I loved her dearly. I admired and respected her, and I needed her. She had been my conscience, speaking calmly to me truths I hated but needed to hear. And when I pushed and pulled and tore at my life, as I often did, she never panicked, or judged the violence of my actions or my whims; she listened and loved and always tried to understand. She was the rock I could break against, and I miss her every day.

What a shitty few years this has been, I thought. By July, I wanted nothing but to see the back of the 1980s and start fresh. Still, I couldn't believe the decade was ending, and with such sadness. Then something surprising happened.

Part IV

A Song, a Harley, and That Hair

Ilook up from my computer screen and there he is. He's sitting—I should say slumping—as though he might at any second slide right off that old leather chair of his. His beloved Gretsch White Falcon rests high across his chest; he noodles away on it. Nothing specific, just bits and pieces of old songs, stuff he's written or just bluesy licks and minor chords. Honestly, it drives me crazy at times, or it would if I didn't know what it did for him. It's his meditation. I have my candles and incense, my pictures of Baba. David has his guitars.

We've been married almost twenty-eight years now, and have been together for thirty-two. Today, when he's almost sixty-five, people still tell him he's a dead ringer for Neil Young. He gets stopped on the street by folks wanting a picture with him; they give him disbelieving looks when he assures them he's not, in fact, the great, grizzled troubadour. In truth, David is much better looking than Mr. Young; three decades ago, when I first caught his eye at Jerry's Famous Deli in the Valley, he was a stone-cold rock-star hunk.

I'd been back from filming *The Jeweller's Shop* for a few months. The haze of sadness that had hung around me—around my family—for the past few years was, at long last, clearing. I was lighter, happier, and more my old self. We are built to heal, I think. It's part of our DNA. It's almost easier to come back from the big ones—loss, illness, the freak unforeseen trauma—than to keep from getting worn down by life's grinding, day-to-day disappointments and stresses. Anyway, I was happy.

I had started seeing someone who was fifteen years younger. He was sweet and fun and he absolutely adored me. (I should also say that he, too, was an amazingly talented guitarist.) It was a relationship that had nothing but light, sunny breezes blowing through it. We laughed and watched TV. I didn't have to think too much.

On a lazy Sunday, the two of us were driving down Coldwater Canyon Avenue. I decided that instead of making a left at Ventura Boulevard and heading to the salad place, we should go right. I had an urge for deli food, and Jerry's Deli was a Valley staple. It served huge portions of guilty pleasures, the kind of meal you need to go home and nap after. And because I had a craving—it's a cliché, I know, but it is mind-blowing how your life can change with of the smallest thing—a right turn instead of a left.

On Sundays, Jerry's is packed. You are greeted by shelves of desserts in their see-through glass cells and, on the walls, posters of long-closed Broadway shows. The place is all colors and smells and noise. There's even a bowling alley, and the crash of pins underscores every conversation.

We sat down. If it were a movie, the shot would be:

<u>MEET-CUTE</u>.

INT - JERRY'S DELI - DAY

A couple sits down at a table. The man facing the woman who is seated with her back against the wall, looking out at the whole restaurant.

WOMAN'S POV:

CAMERA looks over, past the man's shoulder. We see the crowded dining room. Every few moments someone passes in front of the CAMERA, blocking the view and filling the screen with blackness. WITH EACH PASS THE CAMERA JUMP CUTS CLOSER AND CLOSER TO . . .

Biker boots laced up and leading to skin-tight black leather pants. The belt with its huge silver buckle is adornment only; a tsunami couldn't blow these pants off, they're so tight. Over the ripped tank top, a leather jacket announces that the wearer rides a Harley. Chains hang loose from the jacket. The look is "Rock God," and it all draws a line straight up to the face. Framed by a flowing, blown-out lion's mane of blond hair—glam-rock style—the face is surprisingly soft, its features touched with a kindness that belies the hard-rock, hard-drinking, hard-living look.

```
DAVID GLENN EISLEY, lead singer, stands
at the front of the restaurant frozen,
staring at the woman like nothing else in
the world is happening or, if it is, he
doesn't notice, he doesn't care.

WOMAN looks back. Their eyes lock...

The biker is shown to his table far
from the woman. Jolted from his reverie,
he keeps looking back as he is led away.

END SCENE.
```

That's how it happened. I'll never forget seeing David across that restaurant. What struck me most, I think, was his hand: It rested across his heart, fingers spread wide. For all the leather, the chains, and the hair, it was the gentleness of his hand that stayed with me. As in the famous painting by El Greco, *The Nobleman with his Hand on his Chest*, it was a soft gesture, so honest that it cut straight to the heart. It said, "Wait, there's more here than you might think. Look deeper."

At one point, my boyfriend turned and looked over his shoulder and back at me. "What do you keep staring at?" he asked.

I kept quiet, but I was feeling a karmic connection with the man across the room. It was so much more than simply being recognized by a fan. But, my God, karma works in mysterious ways: This man could not have been more different from the men I was used to. What a confusing, wonderful universe we spin in!

Over the following days, life elbowed its way back in, and the image of the biker rock star faded. I would be leaving soon for Hong Kong; I had booked a film and would be gone for a month.

A week or two after that initial encounter with the biker, my boyfriend and I were driving back from the market. Winding our way up Mulholland Drive, we came around a bend on the crest of the mountain road and my eye caught the gleam of shining chrome. There, parked to enjoy the scenic view, a lone biker sat square in the saddle of a huge Harley cruiser.

It was him. The rock star. He sat looking out over the vista like a Viking at the prow of his ship. No way this is a coincidence, I thought—we couldn't have been more than a quarter mile from my house. Clearly, my imagination was running away with me, but I flushed with excitement as we passed.

Over the next few days, I kept coming back to that image of the biker on the mountaintop. The mystery intrigued me, and I kept turning it over in my mind. Then, a month before I was scheduled to leave, the mystery deepened. In my mailbox one morning I found a small box. It had been sent over from my agent at the time, and at first I thought it was something to do with the upcoming film: a set of director's notes, perhaps, or costume ideas, or an updated shooting schedule. But inside the box, I found a note—not from my agent and not for the film—attached to a cassette tape in a clear plastic case. . . . I rushed back inside, rummaged around for my portable player and headphones, slapped the tape in, and hit Play.

A huge voice, pulsating with emotion, sincerity, and deep passion, poured into my ears. I closed my eyes. One song was called "Olivia." I rewound and hit Play again. And again. And again . . .

After three days—during which I took my Walkman with me everywhere, playing the song over and over and picturing the singer—I thought, It's only right that I send him a thank-you note. In the note, I thanked him politely, cautiously said I had enjoyed the song, and let him know that I was seeing somebody but loved his gift. I included my home address.

Sending a thank-you note was one thing, but to include my home address? I was hooked. I was well outside my comfort zone, but that song, the biker on the mountain, the whole buildup—it was all so exciting.

Three days later, a letter came from him. "Miss Hussey," it read, "I can't believe you wrote back. Thank you. My band is heading to Woodstock, NY for a few weeks to record a record. Please call, day or night." He included the number. Later, he told me that after he had mailed the note he said to his band, "Not a chance in hell she'll call."

I called. It took a while to build up the courage, and I was more than a little disappointed when the voice on the other end of the phone said, "Bearsville Studios." Then, "No, the band is coming in tonight. Want to leave a message?"

"Yes, please tell David Eisley that Olivia called."

That night, at 2 a.m., David was given a stack of pink sticky notes with his messages. Reading them over, he came to a name and looked up, wild with anxiety, his eyes like saucers. Grabbing the night watchman and pinning him up against the wall, he stammered, "Did she have an English accent? The woman who left the message."

David loves telling that story.

Hours and hours of late-night phone calls followed. Our relationship began at a distance, and that was lucky, I think. The stark opposition of our styles—demure English actress versus hard-rock musician—would have confounded us before we had a chance to get to know each other. Talking on the phone allowed us to see beneath the surface, to focus on who the other person really was. There is a line I read once, "The shock of other people's lives amazes and thrills." David was—and is—what you see, a tight-panted rocker, but what I learned in those first late-night conversations was that he is much, much more. His kindness, his humor, his gentleness, and the simple, straightforward way he sees the world ran through everything he said.

He was born and, except for a stay in New York in his early childhood, grew up in LA. He studied drums and martial arts (he's a black belt in tae kwon do). He loved baseball and was even scouted by the San Francisco Giants. But music was his first love, and the music he loved best was loud.

His father, Anthony Eisley, was an actor—he'd appeared onscreen with Paul Newman in *The Young Philadelphians* and worked with Karl Malden (my costar in *Summertime Killer*), in *The Desperate*, in addition to appearing in dozens of other TV shows and films. (Once I got to know him, he had a great response when I told him that a movie I had made was voted the tenth worst movie of all time: "Well, Olivia, I was in the other nine.")

David's mother, Judie, was a Pisces like mine. Strong, caring, and confident, she had an openness that came from a deep understanding of the difference between right and wrong, a quality she passed down to her son. She also took the first photo of David and me together. I remember sitting in the shade at Anthony and Judie's Palm Desert home, watching my son Max splash around in their pool, and laughing as Anthony told one of his old work stories again while Judie rolled her eyes and poured more ice tea. Sadly, she passed away three-and-a-half years after David and I met. She held on long enough to cradle her granddaughter in her arms; look down at her with her soft, gentle blue-green eyes; and give her a kiss. She was so strong. We miss her every day.

In one of our late-night conversations, David told me

that his father had once asked him who he thought the most beautiful woman on film was. Without a moment's hesitation, David said it had to be Olivia Hussey as Juliet. He told me that he had seen the movie at least fifty times over the years. He was a fan. And now he was becoming my boyfriend—and would later become my husband.

On the day I was to leave for Hong Kong, David was scheduled to arrive back in LA. He came in an hour or so before me, so we arranged for our limos to rendezvous in a parking lot in Studio City, where David would transfer to mine so we could drive to LAX together. In my limo, we held hands like awkward high school kids. My longtime manager, Rudy, sat across from us staring in ill-concealed bafflement, his expression reading, "What on earth is Olivia doing?" I confess that I, too, had the same thought, if only for a moment, but then I caught a glimpse of David's watch. It was a vintage Rolex like the one Dino used to wear. I thought, Well, I can't be that nuts.

In the airport lounge, I asked David to fly to Hong Kong with me. He laughed and said he couldn't. We hugged. We kissed. We looked into each other's eyes. I was sick with excitement.

I was in love.

All I remember about Hong Kong was my $6,000 phone bill and David's voice on the other end of a crackling line. "You should come up to the house the day I get back," I said.

"Won't you be jet-lagged?"

"You're kidding, right?"

Giddy with anticipation, my unopened suitcases still standing by the front door, I sat at my kitchen counter waiting for David. I had given him the private gate code, and at seven-thirty on the dot a Harley-Davidson thundered into my driveway. I literally ran to the door. I opened it and there he was. That was thirty-two yrs ago. We haven't been apart since.

It was an easy fit. David has a natural ease with ople, something I totally lack. He is relaxed and disarming onest and unapologetic. He accepts the world as it is an expects the world to do the same for him. My boys respoled to this. They loved him from the start, and that was I wanted.

It was Christmas when we came together, David and I, time to give thanks and be grateful. A time to love and be loved, with the promise of a new year. I felt blessed with this new happiness, with the gift of love. I thanked Baba. I thanked God. I thought of my mum and wished she was with us. I was happy. I was grateful.

Reality

There's a Dylan lyric where he sings about money not talking but swearing. For years, I was deaf to whatever my money was saying, profane or not. I had always worked; I had always made money. It was something I was proud of. When a paycheck came in, I happily sent it off to whomever was taking care of my finances at the time and thought nothing more about it.

But dealing with fame is a skill, I've learned; without the right tools, it can overwhelm you. One of those tools is reading people. In my life, I have known hucksters and swindlers. I've laughed in the face of seducers, and, to borrow again from Dylan, known people who "disappear like smoke." I've met fools and charlatans and smiled sweetly at both. I've spent time with rogues and revolutionaries, dazzled by their self-confidence and romanced by their sincerity. Some have tried to buy me, some to sell me. Some have simply orbited me, and I've never really known what they wanted. Ask anyone who has been touched by fame or stands in the public eye, and they'll most likely say the same.

In a business that's all about being looked at, it's often easier not to return the look. You skim people's surfaces while they stare at you with all their hopeful knowing. You let them have their expectations, their biases, so as not to embarrass them. There are always people who want, and sometimes looking at their surface is enough. But sometimes, by not looking beneath the surface, you can get people terribly wrong. I've only known evil once, and it nearly destroyed my life. Jay Lawrence Levy was evil. His wife Rochelle was evil. And I got them both horribly wrong.

I had met them through a girlfriend's brother-in-law. I remember asking him, "Do you know any business managers who are honest?"

"There's a couple I know who are just great," he said. "They work with tons of celebrities. You can't go wrong with them."

Jay and Rochelle drove out to my house to meet me. Jay was charming and talked a lot, while Rochelle was like a comfy quilt, all soft and cozy, so easy to get on with. It was a great tag-team performance, and I bought it. I hired them, and within a month they were taking care of everything.

I know it was my fault. I know I should have been more hands-on, more responsible. Hollywood is brimming with stories like mine. The town floats on a vicious undercurrent of slime: It bubbles up, it seeps through. It's made of the people who survive—flourish—by stealing from others, playing on their egos or their naiveté. And it's not just ditzy artists that get taken in. Smart people—business people, doctors and lawyers, studio heads and directors who run 200-person film sets—fall prey and lose it all. People play a brutal game here, and they play it well—I know, I've worked and lived here a long time. You don't last long if you don't have a talent. Jay and Rochelle's talent was to *smile and smile and be a villain.*

My pension, my savings, all my bills. They took care of everything. Rochelle became my friend, confiding in me that if not for the business she would leave Jay. He was cheating on her, she suspected. He had a cocaine problem. At her son's Bar Mitzvah she told me I was her closest friend and she thanked me for my generosity. She would call me, crying and saying she wanted to pack a bag and walk out the front door.

Eight months into my relationship with Jay and Rochelle, David asked if he could sit in on a meeting in their swanky office on Santa Monica Boulevard. He had a feeling something wasn't right. Once a week, one of Jay's minions would drive to the house and drop off cash for me to use the following week. "You know, Olivia," David said, "that seems like a strange way to do things."

"It's how they work," I said.

"Yes, but no bank accounts? No checkbook?"

"I suppose," I replied.

I had the weirdest feeling as we walked into the reception area. Everybody was watching us. It was subtle but unmistakable, from the woman who greeted us to the assistant who sidled up to us as we headed down the hall to Jay's corner office. They shot furtive glances sideways at us and looked away again much too quickly. It was like one of those spaghetti westerns, where the dust-covered cowboys ride into some small, forgotten border town and are greeted by shutters slowly closing and an air of brooding malice and creeping danger.

Jay sat behind his desk; Rochelle leaned against a table and bit her nails. David asked some simple questions. It was all nervous and jittery and didn't last long. When David had heard enough he simply said, "Well, thanks. I was just curious about the people taking care of Olivia."

We left. In the parking garage, I asked him what he thought.

"I smell a rat, Olivia," he said.

I still remember his fingers on the steering wheel as we drove through Beverly Hills toward my bank, the knuckles turning chalk-white because he was gripping so hard.

They had taken everything. Cleaned me out. My savings account, money I had saved since *Jesus of Nazareth*, was gone. My SAG pension, which I had been paying into since I had first started working and which was to be my safety net: gone. Worse still, my home, the home that Akira and I had bought together and that I owned outright, was essentially gone: They had forged my name and taken out three huge mortgages on it. I now owed the bank hundreds of thousands of dollars! After nearly thirty-five years of work I was left with nothing.

Words abandon me; even now, I cannot truly express the impact. I sat frozen at a bank manager's desk, David a furious blur beside me. As document after document was put in front of me, my name—but not in my hand—notarized and official at the bottom of each page, numbness ran through me and I felt nothing. How do you process something so calamitous? The betrayal of it. The news arriving out of nowhere. No lead-up. Nothing. The oddest thoughts ran through my head: But it's sunny outside. How can I be told I have nothing when it's sunny outside?

David was apoplectic with rage. He wanted to drive back to their offices and throttle Jay. The sheer scale of it overwhelmed him. The numbers. The way it was done. All of it was so foreign to him. He had no frame of reference, no way even to begin to understand how it could have happened.

It wasn't just me, of course. They had stolen from all their clients, some of whom were well-known. There was a successful German jewelry designer who, when she learned she had been made destitute by Jay and Rochelle, drove to their home in Beverly Hills and rammed their cars over and over with her Mercedes while they hid inside like cowards. We spoke to many of their other cheated clients and learned their stories. We hired lawyers. We spent a year trying to get back some of the money they had stolen. Some was in Belize, we learned. Some probably went up Jay's nose. Most was simply gone—hidden in a global matrix of ones and zeros. With an attorney's bill nearing six figures and no money coming in, David and I struggled to form a new plan.

I was forced to sell my beautiful home. Looking back, I wish I had found a way to keep it. I'm certain there must have been a way, but with the pressure we were under we just couldn't see clearly enough what choices were the right ones.

With what was left after selling the house and paying our bills, the mortgage, and our lawyer's fees, we moved to Topanga, a secluded community of artists, graying hippies, and eccentrics hidden deep in the canyons overlooking the Pacific. I was in shock. David was solid and unwavering. Alex, my oldest, had moved out a year before, and Max was too young to understand what was happening, although I know something of that terrible time must have filtered down to him.

It had been almost two years since I had last worked, on two TV projects. One, *Psycho IV: The Beginning*, a prequel to *Psycho* with Anthony Perkins and Henry Thomas, was shot in Florida. It was a happy shoot; Anthony and Henry were wonderful to work with. I was playing Norma Bates, Norman's mother, the fount of all her son's "troubles." As soon as I got the part I began thinking about how I would play it (which came in handy when, on the first day of shooting, Anthony walked over and asked how I was planning on playing her). You can't play "crazy." It will always come across as phony, and it's insulting to an audience. The key—and this is true for all good acting—is specificity. The more specific you are with your character, the more believable your performance will be. Fortunately—rather unfortunately—for me, I had some experience dealing with a troubled mind. So Christopher Jones became the template for my Norma. I recalled that even at the height of his madness, when he was lashing out at me at the top of his lungs or seething with rage, there was a panic in his eyes, as if some part of him knew he was out of control and was as terrified by it as I was. I pictured that part of Christopher as a tiny controller sitting at all the levers and switches and shocked that they were unresponsive. I explained this to Anthony that first day, when he asked what I was planning. He nodded gravely when I had finished and said, "Yes, a striking image and an apt one, I think. Thank you for sharing it, Olivia."

Anthony, though very quiet and intense, was a total professional. During the shoot I did wonder why he kept coming back to play Norman. Was it simply about money? Possibly. But I doubted it. From our conversations, I came to think he was emotionally invested in the films, he cared about them, he might even have felt responsible for them. Like me, he had come to *Psycho* early in his career. And, like me, he had had the privilege of working with a visionary director in Alfred Hitchcock. Such experiences don't come along often and, of course, they do come with baggage: type-casting, fame at a young age, and so on. But for me being a part of *Romeo & Juliet* had always been an honor, and I thought Anthony felt the same about the *Psycho* franchise. Whatever the truth, he was fantastic to work with. His beautiful wife, Berry Berenson, would come onto the set and they would sit together in a corner talking. (Sadly, she would die on 9/11, a passenger on American Airlines Flight 11.) The other was a miniseries, *It*, starring Tim Curry, John Ritter, and many others. It was a tougher shoot, although John's humor and kindness made it easier and Tim was a pleasure.

Clearly I needed to work, but I didn't care. I was ruined, and I don't just mean financially. I felt finished, spent and empty. My money was gone. My career was over. I spent days thinking about the mistakes I had made and the opportunities I had wasted. I told myself I was done with people. There was no more trust left in me for anyone new. I had my boys and I had David. That was it. I had run my course.

Then, on a cloudless Tuesday afternoon, my body gave me some news: I was pregnant! A brand-new little life was on its way, maybe even—oh, how I hoped!—a baby girl.

The news of my pregnancy arrived exactly when it needed to. There's that maxim "The universe never gives you more than you can handle." What hogwash! In my experience, the universe may pile the weight of a planet on you at any time. It will load you up till your knees buckle and you can't see through the sweat in your eyes. But I have found that the universe also loves balance. Seeking equilibrium, it deals both the trials that hurt so much and seem so unfair *and* the joys and loves and fun that make life explode with happiness. I believe the universe listens, and you can call things into your life. Easy/hard. Love/loss. Friend/enemy. Balance. Always balance.

Being pregnant brought me back. I was energized, vitalized by the gift of a new life. All at once, David and I shed our dire defeatism and went about the business of getting better as well as getting ready. This would be David's first child, and I had such fun watching him twist himself in knots worrying over his new daddy role.

It was again a hard pregnancy. I was sick almost every day. I was emotional (by now you know that's hardly surprising) and puttered around the house, forever tidying up. I watched daytime TV. I tried knitting.

On October 29, 1993, my third child was born, a precious baby girl. She was perfect, and we named her after two of the things I loved most in the world: India Joy.

A month later, a job offer came in: three weeks in Canada for a TV show called *Lonesome Dove*. All I wanted to do was stay home with David and Max and our new little colicky bundle of joy, but I was in no position to turn down a job.

We had found a wonderful nanny, Lola. She was Guatemalan, loved babies, and soon became part of the family. Carrying India with one arm, she would help me feed my ever-growing brood of canine friends—at one point, we put the dog count at thirteen. I felt comfortable with her. I trusted her and, as I didn't have any choice, I packed my bags and left India in her more-than-competent care. David would fly with me and stay until I was settled.

It was there, in Canada, on the fortieth floor of my Calgary hotel, that David and I were married. We had been together for four years and had been through hell and back. With our luck, we told each other, we would most likely go through much more, but we knew we wanted to face it all side by side. David is the third great love of my life. And, like Dino and Akira, he is a deeply kind man. It may seem strange, but I feel I have been lucky in love. These men, though so different in their ways and not without their flaws, have all been good, strong men whom I am proud to have been with. Plus, if I'm honest, I'm no picnic. I'm moody, stubborn, sensitive to the point of neurosis, and racked by insecurities and peculiar vulnerabilities. It's no easy thing to be loved by me, I know. It says something wonderful about these men that they came to me and loved me.

From my nondescript hotel room, with a hard wind howling and blowing snow sideways outside the window, David and I called the front desk with what, from their point of view, must have seemed an odd request: We needed a justice of the peace. We had Ulla, the costume designer on the show, and Henry, the waiter from the Chinese restaurant down the street, bear witness. Afterward, we had dinner and bought matching cowboy boots. It was one of the most romantic nights of my life.

Under Siege

I don't want to write this; it hurts too much. If I could, I'd take a buzz saw to these memories. I'd slice through them, bag them, and leave them outside on the curb next to the recycling bin. But I have decided to write this book and commit myself to telling my *whole* story.

The years following Jay and Rochelle's crime were bleak. Disasters followed one after the other. After three years, we lost the house in Topanga when we could no longer manage the payments. We moved out into canyon country, north of Los Angeles near the Vasquez Rocks in the shadow of the Sierra Pelona Mountains. The rocks were a famous backdrop used in dozens of old Hollywood westerns, but perhaps best known now as the surface of countless distant worlds in the first *Star Trek* series.

We needed land. By then, we had an ark full of adopted animals. Along with all the dogs there were two huge pot-belly pigs, Pork Chop and Bruce, and an old gray mare, Mabel—who, after eight years, died peacefully in David's arms. There were three cats skulking around the house, plus a rabbit named Oscar, a guinea pig called Rex, and an

African gray parrot, Popeye, who has been with us now twenty-two years and speaks in an English accent.

Once rescued, my animals are never left behind. I had a vet tell me once that when he died he wanted to come back as one of my pets. I would go to shelters and clean them out. I made the animals' suffering mine. Call it a coping mechanism, projection or transference of whatever pain I was going through. Call it whatever. These helpless souls needed a home, and I gave it to them.

Each morning, when the desert air was cool and the sky was tinged baby blue, you'd find me walking with my bucket and my feed bag. By noon, the heat would level off at a suffocating 105 degrees, and the pig sty, if not watered down, would harden. My pigs would have no way to cool off, and they would literally cook under the blazing sun. So I'd take the hose and, moving back and forth as if I were planting seeds, I'd soak the whole enclosure. Then I'd fill the bucket with the feed and announce in my best Shakespearean voice that breakfast was served. The boys would waddle up and the morning feeding would begin.

Something about the process, or the morning air, made me meditative. And retrospective. "Well, this has been quite a journey," I'd say out loud, remembering: the seventeen-year-old at her command performance, bowing to the Queen of England. Dinners at Franco's villa when, sitting outside with the wine going to my head, I'd listen to the rustle of the wind in the cypress tress. Gossiping with David Niven while we sailed down the Nile. Laughing with Elizabeth Taylor. Flirting with Fellini. Calling Dean Martin "Dad." I remembered standing on my mark waiting to hear, "Action!" and looking Sir Laurence Olivier in the eye—and he winked at me. Knowing Baba, a fully realized human being. Hugging him; feeling the power and the mystery teeming inside him. Being called "Mother" for the first time.

All these moments, all the way back to when I was a little girl bounding up the steps of the Conti Drama School—was I still that girl? The answer, of course, was no. After a lifetime of experience and change, what was left of Juliet?

Desert life suited me: Simple and clean, it took me away from L.A. and the business that had been, by turns, so cruel and so kind to me. However, it was not to last. Again, it was down to money. David kept us going: He toured, he did commercials—including a big campaign for Budweiser, with Ringo Star. He played Merlin with what little money we did have, paying our bills, keeping our credit solid, and making more appear where there was less. Bless him.

No amount of magic, though, could abracadabra away the crisis we had been left with, and after another year we were forced to move again. This time it was to the mountains. For years, David had kept a little cabin just south of the San Bernardino mountains, in a small community near Lake Arrowhead. He had built the cabin himself. Set hard against a hillside, it was meant as his little getaway place. It had just two rooms, with a freestanding wood fireplace and snow shovels leaning against the front door. It was perfect for a tough, single guy looking to get off the grid for a while. Now it became our home.

This would be our most difficult time. Work was impossible: We couldn't just hop in the car and drive into L.A. for a meeting; we were hours away. Besides, there were no meetings to take. We were in survival mode, and I had withdrawn almost totally from public life.

Two months in and we were hit with the worst snowfall in twenty years. Mornings would find us snowbound, trapped in the house and snapping at each other, all patience lost.

"This is why I left London!" I'd yell.

"I know, Olivia. It's just for a little while," David would say soothingly.

We had to slide down the hill and dig out the car to take India to her first day of kindergarten. From the start, she had a terrible time at school. All the moving had been hard on her; she couldn't make friends. Kids were cruel, bullying the pretty new girl. She was left with nothing but to withdraw into herself. It broke my heart to see and, after eighteen months, I had had enough. "We have to leave here, David," I said. "I can't do it anymore."

"We can't afford it yet," David replied.

"You need to find a way."

And he did.

Back to the desert: Agua Dulce, northeast of Santa Clarita. Another eighteen months. It was a terrible time. At one point, between moves, we were forced back into L.A., staying in temporary corporate apartments. While the Rodney King riots raged across the city, our family slept two to a bed. There were moments of absurd gallows humor: David sneaking our potbelly pig Pork Chop into the apartment complex in a piece of luggage. Never being able to find anything in our ever-expanding universe of boxes. Forgetting where we left the car.

Brief though they were, these flashes of levity were solace to the soul. You couldn't help but see the funny side. Left with nothing else, the tragic becomes the comic, and although these were some of the darkest, hardest days I have ever known, I had David. I had India, Max, and Alex. We laughed through it all. We laughed because we didn't want to cry.

There would be more moves: Palmdale to Sunderland. Sunderland to the Valley. Cruel moves. Friends, even relatives, who left us or, worse, betrayed us. Then, in 2003, things began to turn around.

Mother Teresa

In 1977, during the publicity tour for *Jesus of Nazareth*, an Italian interviewer asked me what roles were left, now that I'd played both Juliet, Shakespeare's most romantic heroine, and Mary, mother of Christ. What character did I dream of portraying? I thought for a moment, and a single image came to mind: a simple white sari bordered with three blue lines.

"Mother Teresa of Calcutta," I replied.

"Really? Why?" asked the reporter.

"Because I think she is the woman I admire most in the world."

I was twenty-seven years old.

I had stumbled across her story while flipping through the pages of a magazine. The article focused on her early religious life: She had been given the name Teresa as a novice nun and sent to India at nineteen, taking her first vows there in 1931. She was a teacher until a revelatory 1946 train ride from Calcutta to Darjeeling, when she received a "call within a call." She must leave the convent, she was told, leave her old life and live and work among "the poorest of the poor."

She began in the Calcutta slums, first opening a small school, then tending to the very ill, the destitute, the forgotten. Years before, she had been turned away from a hospital when she arrived with a dying elder woman she had taken off the street. Told the woman was an untouchable and could not be admitted, all Mother Teresa could do was hold her and pray for her while the woman passed away in her arms. No more: In a country where tradition cut deep through the heart as well as the heartland, where the caste system, though officially banned, still divided people, the Missionaries of Charity order she founded would care for all.

Receiving Vatican approval, the order soon attracted volunteers. Young women came to Calcutta as if called there. Wrapped inside the simple act of kindness, such power resides, limitless and life-changing. In giving yourself to the well-being of others, you proclaim what surely must be the most self-evident of truths: that all life has dignity, another's life is worth your own, and no one's sin is beyond redemption. Mother Teresa changed the world through this simple service. Her empathy, the force of her will, and the clarion call of her message was so clear to me that by the end of the article I was sobbing. What a story. What a woman. What a part to play.

Time and again over the years, I would corner some writer or producer and tell them Mother Teresa's story. Time and again, I looked for any opportunity to play her. I kept an eye on trade magazines and called Rudy to ask if he'd heard that her story was in development anywhere. I would phone Franco, begging him to make the movie.

"But, Livi," he would say, "who wants to work in India? So hot. So crowded. Besides you, my darling, you are much too beautiful to play Mother." It seemed it would never happen.

Then, in 1990, I saw a chance. A production company out of Canada was considering making her story. My name came up. Years earlier, *Time* magazine had reported that Jackie Onassis had told Mother Teresa that the only actress who should ever play her was Olivia Hussey, and that not only had Mother known who I was but she had agreed. I was deeply touched by that. The producers were less sure. They were considering Cher for the role.

I consigned it to the fates. If it was not meant to happen, so be it. It was hardly in keeping with the life of Mother Teresa, I felt, to be selfish about playing her. In the end, the production never got off the ground, and after a few months it receded into the background, as so many Hollywood projects do. I continued to wait.

Bruised and battered, we stumbled and fell into 2003. David was exhausted, shattered from all the moves and worn down by the pressures of keeping our family one step ahead of disaster, while I was concentrating on our daughter, India, working hard to raise her the best way I could. She was already a stunning girl. Possessed of my dark, brooding features and David's tall, slender build, she was turning into a knockout. But what was more striking, and far more important, was what was going on underneath. She was, clearly, an old soul. She had a calm and an intuition well beyond her years. What's more, she had—has—an eye for people. She can spot the good at a glance and warn me of the bad just as fast. I learned early on not to dismiss her instincts, and by the time she was fourteen she was my closest friend. She still is.

I had endured almost a decade of rough seas since losing everything, and I was resigned to the fact that my luck had well and truly run out. There would be no silver lining, no happy ending to my career. This was it, so get used to it. Then a phone call came.

Lux Vide, a well-respected Italian TV production company whose films included biographies, adaptations from literature, spiritual films about the saints and apostles, and stories from the Bible, was putting together a project on the life of Mother Teresa for Italian television, to coincide with her beatification in Rome. They wanted me for the part. I had two weeks to prepare.

I had waited twenty years for the opportunity to play this remarkable woman. I was determined to give her every ounce of my soul—to play her with authenticity and a whole, vulnerable heart. In this way, I felt I could honor her. I wanted to be proud of this work, which I considered the most important of my career. However, if my soul and mind were willing, my body was not. I was sick from the moment filming began.

First, I suffered ear problems—a dull ache, followed by a constant ringing. Then my throat swelled, restricting my breathing and inaugurating a procession of brutal, sleepless nights. I had digestion issues that left me dizzy and weak throughout the long days of shooting.

Then there was our first location. The problem wasn't the island of Sri Lanka itself. A teardrop rolling off the tip of the great Indian subcontinent, Sri Lanka was what, perhaps, that massive, ancient neighbor would be like if it ever decided to take a vacation from being so massive and so ancient. Sri Lanka was more laid-back, easier on itself; swept as it was by more southerly breezes, it was slower and more user-friendly. Think of rolling hills, open green plains, and a single fisherman out on the ocean, legs coiled around a long, leaning wooden staff projecting from the water.

The problem was that I never saw any of that. I was stuck in the capital, Colombo, or on location in some unhealthy spot, locked into an unrelenting shooting schedule. The film had to wrap in time for Mother Teresa's beatification by the Vatican in eight weeks' time, and there was so much to get through. We spent fourteen-hour days out in the heat and humidity. The crew were ill; I was ill. The difference was that I couldn't stop; I was in almost every scene. While some crew members were released to recuperate back at the hotel, a doctor was brought on set to pump me full of antibiotics just to keep me upright.

I remember waiting for a shot one day. Lumps of course, damp sand were blowing hard across my face. I had a temperature above 103 degrees. Great waves of nausea sloshed through my guts. I closed my eyes and prayed.

"Please, Mother," I implored, "I am desperate to honor you through my performance. Give me the strength to do this." I felt then a calmness, a warm, peaceful light around me. I thought about Mother Teresa: how she had come down with malaria when she first began her mission, yet with no help, no treatment, no respite at all, she had carried on.

I thought, Here I am, an actress! Surrounded by a whole crew of men and women here to help me. I have doctors to treat me and medicine to mend me. What am I complaining about? I can do this!

I didn't take a single day off for the six weeks we shot in Sri Lanka.

David and India, who were with me, weren't about to stay safely in the hotel, so they went on hair-raising adventures in the countryside. These usually involved a local driver. When, in typical fashion, driving hell-for-leather, he got them through a twisty mountain pass to visit Pinnawala Elephant Orphanage, I was glad they survived.

* * *

Our last week of shooting on the island finds us deep in the rain forest. A low canopy of the most vibrant green I have ever seen shades us and keeps us cool. It's humid, of course. Everything is wet; our damp clothes are heavy and uncomfortable. The soft ground gives a little as we step. Huge beetles crawl everywhere. Slithering things slide past, catch my eye, and send shivers up my back. Mosquitos land. Our director, Fabrizio Costa, is bitten. His blood is taken and sent for testing: dengue fever. Nurses arrive. Fabrizio is flown back to Italy, where he spends three weeks in intensive care. Our time in Sri Lanka is over.

Though the circumstances were horrible—we were literally waiting, day by day, to learn if Fabrizio would pull through—his illness afforded me a much-needed break. The production had moved to Rome, where I spent a week in bed and ate pasta until it was coming out of my ears. David and India had had enough of adventure; they clung to all the tourist spots: Trevi Fountain, the Forum, the Spanish Steps.

The work in Rome went smoothly. Fabrizio had recovered, thank God, although he was still very weak. We shot for another three weeks. Still, I was not feeling myself. I chalked it up to my immune system being overloaded— I was just run-down, I told myself. I ignored a creeping feeling that had begun to work its way into my head and terrify me.

Mother Teresa premiered on Italian television on October 19, 2003, the same day as Mother Teresa's beatification. The film was generally well received—the reviews were mostly good, the ratings high. At the prerelease Vatican screening, members of her order told me it was like watching Mother herself. I was deeply touched by the compliment. I had the opportunity to meet Mother's only living relative, Aga Bojaxhiu, and she also felt I had done her auntie justice. We spent a wonderful afternoon together, having lunch with Franco, sitting outside on the terrace of his magnificent villa. It had been a totally satisfying experience that culminated with Mother Teresa's beatification and with my all-too-brief introduction to Pope John Paul II.

Beatification is the first and most difficult step toward canonization, which is official recognition by the Holy See of sainthood. Beatification proclaims the individual's right to enter heaven as well as her ability to intercede with God on behalf of those who pray in her name.

On October 19, 2003—a Sunday—after the shortest vetting process of modern times, Mother Teresa was beatified. Thousands massed between the embracing arms of the colonnades of St. Peter's Square, held tight in the shadow of the great basilica. All had come to bear witness, to be part of the ceremony. There were suave Italian men in shiny designer suits, clutching rosaries and hoping their wide-framed Euro sunglasses hid the tears in their eyes. Some of them were holding hands with some of the old ladies—mothers, grandmothers, great-grandmothers—who had flocked there, women with black shawls draped over their heads, wearing long wool skirts and cable-knit cardigans, with deeply lined faces and sad, seen-it-all eyes. There were legions of priests and nuns, cardinals and bishops. I will never forget the image of a group of Greek Orthodox bishops lined up in front of me with their tall black hats, their thick chains, and black-and-red vestments. Each one had a cell phone to his ear.

It was as much celebration as it was a ceremony, and throughout the crowd there were bursts of laughter, smiles, and wishes of goodwill.

I had invited Franco, and as we pushed through the crowds I heard him whisper, *"Santa Maria, Madre di Dio, prega per noi peccatori."*

"Amen," I said.

When you practice something for six hundred years, you get fairly good at it. The Church is expert at ceremony. As we sat among the thousands under a gray sky, flags and banners snapping in the sharp wind, I was swept away by the pageantry. The day began with a prayer, solemn and sincere. Then a series of speakers: cardinals, priests and Missionaries of Charity spoke to Teresa's compassion, her devotion, and her dedication.

All the while, people would come up to me and, leaning in close, tell me they had seen my performance and thought it was wonderful. It was embarrassing, but still, I couldn't help but feel some pride.

As the beatification concluded, Franco and I were escorted inside through a long corridor lined with huge Renaissance tapestries depicting the life of Christ and the establishment by St. Peter of the Church in Rome. Again, I was awed.

We were invited to join the line to be received by Pope John Paul II. The line was long, and people spoke in hushed tones, their faces reserved and deferential. At last, I stepped up to the Holy Father. Pope John Paul was by 2003 very ill: He was suffering from Parkinson's disease, he had survived two assassination attempts, he had crippling osteoarthritis, and he could barely hear. Still, he had those kind, forgiving eyes, that fatherly smile, and his aura that radiated compassion and intelligence. As I bent down to kiss his ring—the Ring of the Fisherman, St. Peter's trade—I thought I caught a flash of recognition in the Holy Father's face. Of course, I cannot be sure. But as I walked away through the grand Vatican hallway and made my way outside to stand again with the thousands, I chose to believe that I had been recognized, that the Holy Father had, indeed, remembered me and why I was there, and that he had been most pleased by it.

Cancer

For five, maybe more, years it grew—ignored, undiagnosed, and unchecked. I had pushed away the feeling I had had during the filming of *Mother Teresa*, that inkling that something wasn't right inside me. I'd pushed it so far down that I'd all but forgotten it was ever there. But of course it was there. It was real, and no amount of wishing would make it go away.

A few years before I was finally diagnosed with stage 4 breast cancer in the summer of 2008, something strange had happened to my meditation. Since I'd recovered from Baba's death, I had taken twenty minutes each day to sit, close my eyes, and begin my breathing. Always, a calming blueness would appear and I would relax into it. It was my connection to Muktananda. It brought me back to myself, to all the parts of myself I loved best.

Then, one day it was gone. I closed my eyes and saw nothing, felt nothing. There was only blackness. When this continued, I started to feel very alone; for the first time since I'd met him, I felt no connection with Baba. I would call out inside myself, "Can you hear me? I don't feel anything anymore. I'm scared."

This mantra became my new prayer, and I wondered if it would be my last.

Then I received a phone call from an actress friend of mine. We hadn't spoken in months. "Olivia," she said by way of greeting, "how are you?"

"Good," I lied.

"It's funny," she went on, "I've been working with a healer out in South Carolina who's been helping me with my fibromyalgia. He called me the other day." She paused. "He asked if I knew the actress Olivia Hussey. When I told him I did, he said he needed to reach you."

"What's this about? Why does he want to speak to me?" I asked.

"He says he has a message for you," she said. "I told him you're a private person, Olivia, but that I would tell you he wants to reach you. His name is Howard Wills, and he's incredible." She gave me his number.

Three days later, I called. When Howard Wills answered, in a soft voice full of caring, he knew who I was. As soon as we'd exchanged greetings he said, "I have a message for you."

"Yes, my friend told me," I said, hesitantly.

"Are you sitting down?"

I sat down.

"Baba says that he hears you."

"Excuse me?"

"Your guru, Swami Muktananda. He hears you when you pray. We all do. Olivia, you are never alone."

Sitting cross-legged on the floor, I began to sob.

"Baba has told me," Howard said over my crying, "that I'm to look after you now, and that's what I'm going to do."

Howard Wills's unexpected arrival in my life was a godsend. He reconnected me with Baba and has been a huge part of my life ever since. He has been my teacher, calming me and showing me the power and the value of living in the moment. He has been my friend, someone I can count on. I pick up the phone, we speak, and instantly I feel better. After I was diagnosed, Howard gave me the strength to fight what was to become my toughest battle.

This brings me back to 2008 and the changing dynamic of my life. India was now a working actress. David and I had at first been reluctant to encourage her—or, perhaps, too weary to. I knew all too well what working in the business at a young age could do, the effects it could have. But India was determined. It wasn't simply a case of her growing up not knowing anything else. She wanted it for her own sake, and she was adamant. It was her passion.

I talked to her about the risks, the life it might entail. We talked about the rejection, the constant waiting, and the long road ahead. I was as honest as I could be. "You will only get the jobs you are meant to get," I told her, "so just relax, and always keep moving forward." Then I told her I loved her with all my heart, that I would always be there for her, that we would keep it fun, and, finally, that I supported her 100 percent.

After a couple of years of almost weekly auditions, India landed her first big project, a series for ABC Family, *The Secret Life of the American Teenager*. The series, created by Brenda Hampton, centered around a teen pregnancy. I felt it was powerful stuff, and if done right it would, certainly, resonate with audiences. Few young adult shows deal with hard questions. And fewer still treat their teenage viewers with respect. Judging by the first scripts we read, it was clear that Brenda was determined to meet both those challenges. It would be a lot of work for India. David would spend every day on the set, helping her adjust, making sure she was being taken care of and keeping her mood light;

like me, India has a streak of the serious and sensitive running through her. It became their routine. Meanwhile, at home with the animals, I had my own routine, and it had begun to scare me.

Since *Teresa*, I had been fighting waves of tiredness. I was fatigued, it seemed, all the time. I was run-down and achy. Then, in 2007, I felt a small lump in my left breast. I told no one. What a mistake. By May 2008, I was terrified.

Why was I keeping it from my family? I would ask myself. Why haven't I been to the doctor? Was it because I was afraid that if I said it out loud, if I named it and gave voice to it, I would somehow make it real and be forced to deal with it? I was scared. It was as simple as that. Scared to confront something that could destroy my life, the life we had worked so hard to rebuild. Also—and this was very difficult to deal with—I had always been healthy: emotionally fragile, yes, but physically as strong as an ox. Never having been really ill, I didn't think I had the mental strength to cope with it.

But I decided it had now gone too far. Scheduling the doctor's appointment, I told myself there was nothing to be afraid of, everything would be fine.

Mammograms are a drag. You feel exposed, vulnerable. You are quite literally laid bare. They are a necessary evil, though I always put them off. Luckily, they only last ten to fifteen minutes, or they always had. This one took forty minutes, and at the end it was decided that a biopsy was needed.

"Biopsy."

The word hung there between the doctor and me, then landed like a spider and crawled all over me. I was terrified.

"We'll get the results back in a few days," the doctor said.

I waited. Did chores. Waited. Fed the animals. Waited. Acted strong. Waited. And always, out of the corner of my eye, watched the phone.

"Everything will be all right, Olivia," David said. "You'll see."

No, it won't.

Two days later, we received the results. The lump was malignant: I had cancer. It was fourteen centimeters, the size of a large, rotting lemon filled with black bile, and sat snug inside my chest as it worked its evil on me. I wanted to be sick. I *was* sick.

We made an appointment to see a specialist in Glendale. It was a nightmare. Everything in the office was pink. Pink ribbons tied to fat, little potted plants. Pink frames on the walls enclosing photos of smiling women. Pink gift baskets lined up against the wall, waiting to be handed out. I wanted to yank the pictures down and smash them. I wanted to kick the baskets over. Most of all, I wanted to punch the women who spoke so condescendingly to David and me right in the face.

"Yes, you know, it's unfortunate, but I perform these kinds of procedures all the time," she said.

Unfortunate! It's my life. Looking up at David, seeing the tears in his eyes, I felt my own. We cut her off midsentence and left, with a pink bag forced into my arms.

My children waited outside. Max and India buried their faces in the folds of my coat, sobbing and holding me tight. Alex was a rock. Having already lost one parent, he took the news that he might lose his other one with a calmness and maturity that even today breaks my heart and makes me proud. What a reservoir of strength he must have, shaped as it must have been by his father's passing. It was to his strength that we now turned. We had to follow him as he slowly drove his own car out of the parking garage. David was in shock. He couldn't focus. Such a strong man brought so low by life's cruel turn. My heart breaks again, thinking about it.

But we are built to carry on. Of course, I was scared, and worried sick for my family, but having been told the news, and having had a few days to let it sink in, the reality of it took over and we moved forward. We made appointments with doctors. We did our research. Howard gave me the names of homeopathic healers and natural doctors and worked on me himself, although my cancer was too far advanced for him to heal. Still, his insight, his opinion, his comfort helped me so much.

"Olivia," he said, "a natural path is always open and positive, but there are some things Western medicine excels at. You need to find a doctor you believe in and trust."

Alone most days save for the animals, I had more than enough time to think about myself. India had to work every weekday and, as a minor, had to have a parent present. That was David's job, and he would call me dozens of times a day.

"How are you feeling?" he would ask, trying to keep the worry from his voice.

"David, I'm fine. Just feeding the dogs."

"Okay . . . Yeah . . . Good. Well, I'm here with India if you need anything."

People don't know how to talk to you, not really. Even the ones who love you. Especially the ones who love you. I fell into this uncomfortable truth two weeks after the diagnosis. It's strange: You are sick—really sick—yet you are the same. You have this wicked thing eating away inside you, but slowly. I looked the same. I felt the same. But people began to tiptoe around me, not knowing what to do. At the edges of their conversations I felt a hesitancy, an awkwardness, an apology. My family and friends cared, and that caring now colored everything they did and said to me.

David might ask, casually, if I wanted to go down to Whole Foods, but his eyes would say anxiously, "I can't lose you."

India and I would run her lines for the week, but her expression read, "Please, please don't leave me. What can I do?"

No, no, I thought, this isn't right. I'm the one who's supposed to be there for *them*.

It's terrible—maybe the hardest thing—to see the pain your illness has on your family. You know you are the first thing they think of when they wake up: *My mother is dying. My wife is dying.* You know that all they want to do is to make you better. You feel the strain they're under; you sense the havoc your illness is wreaking on their souls. And it tears you to pieces.

Cancer doesn't just spread inside your own body. It infests everything and everyone around you—a cancer of the heart.

I liked Dr. Armando E. Giuliano from the start. His bio, when distilled, was simple: He was considered one of, if not the, best surgical oncologists around.

A researcher as well as a surgeon, Dr. Giuliano had been at the forefront of the fight against breast cancer for thirty years. His research had helped shape the way doctors and patients approached cancer. He was widely published, heavily honored, and highly respected. Women flew in from all over the world seeking his care. I liked him because he listened. He had a wonderful nature, a surfeit of empathy, and understanding that almost made him fatherly. Also, if I were casting the role of world-renowned surgeon for a movie, I'd cast him. He looked the part.

Howard had said, "Olivia, you have to have the thing out." And now, as I sat in Dr. Giuliano's office at Providence St. John's Health Center in Santa Monica, he said the same. We needed to schedule a mastectomy immediately, he told me, followed by an intense round of chemo and radiation therapy.

Let me be clear: I speak only for myself. I would not presume to judge anyone else or the choices they feel they need to make (there is more than enough of that already). I can speak only to the choices I have made. And I just couldn't see how exposing my body to poison would help me. I wasn't rash. I accepted the surgery, and I didn't reject the chemo and radiation lightly—when doctors you trust and respect say it is necessary, you listen. It would be stupid and dangerous not to. But in the end, it is your decision. It is your life and yours alone. I put my faith in something Howard had told me during one of our many conversations: "Olivia, the doctors will see what I already know: The cancer has not spread. The malignancy can be treated with surgery alone."

So I made the decision not to undergo any postsurgery therapy. I decided I would stay true to the path I had always traveled, that I believed in and was now made manifest in Howard. A natural path of holistic healing and love, of faith and meditation. It is in times of crisis that your beliefs are tested, and I was not about to abandon a lifetime's reflection and discovery because I was scared. Perhaps I was wrong, I thought seriously, but I had put my life's journey in the hands of the universe, and the universe had always held me close and pulled me through.

I spent David's birthday, September 5, 2008, in surgery. The last conversation I had before they wheeled me into the operating room was with Howard. His voice calmed me and called me to that familiar blue light that had always been my shelter from the storm.

For nine hours, the expert hands of Dr. Giuliano did their job. Thirty years' experience with Western medicine were brought to bear on my tumor. At the same time, somewhere beyond reasoning, centuries of another kind of wisdom did their work. As I came out of the anesthesia, images rose to meet me. I found a place of quiet, calm, and spiraling consciousness. Baba was there. Howard was too. People I had loved and learned from came to meet me and help me.

Then came pain. A pain I had never known before. Lying in intensive care, dozens of tubes and wires spiraling out of me, I felt as if I were being turned inside out. All the questions came flooding in, confused and disjointed: Was the surgery a success? Was Howard right, or had the cancer spread? Then the questions were blotted out by the searing pain. I closed my eyes and tried to slow my breathing. I listened to the low hum of the machines: the *beep, beep, beep* of my heart monitor, the *drip, drip, drip* of my IV.

The questions don't matter. Not right now, Olivia, I said to myself. This pain is what matters. It means something. And, realizing what it meant, I closed my eyes and started to cry.

I'm alive. Thank you.

Six days after returning from the hospital, I tried to stand up. I have no recollection of what happened when I got to my feet—if I even made it that far. The part of me that protects my conscious self drew a veil, blocking out the avalanche of pain that must have overwhelmed me.

When I woke up, I was lying prone on my rumpled bed, sweat running down my whole body. A thought shot through me: Oh Lord, I'm stuck.

My surgery had been a success. Having removed a lymph node as part of the mastectomy, Dr. Giuliano found that the cancer had not spread. It had happened just as Howard had said it would. I was, for now, cancer free.

I am still deeply grateful for that. An eight-year reprieve (and still counting). Time to spend with my children, my husband. Time to watch all my English television shows. What more could I ask for? What more is there? Still, it would be a long road to a full recovery, and it was going to be rough.

I have always had a lot of energy, although at times I have channeled it toward unproductive ends, like cleaning and worrying. I have always been an early riser, getting up to start the day's chores and not stopping until everything is done. At work, I am always on time and, if anything, overly prepared. That has come down to me from my mum, I suspect. Her youthful vibrancy turned, over the years, into a steely work ethic. She was a powerhouse of energy, and that became my inheritance.

Now, I was stymied. For weeks after the surgery, I couldn't manage even the simplest task. It all fell to David. For me, not being able to make lunch for myself, play with the dogs, or go to the movies was torture. All through the holidays, I was healing. India was on set all week, and David did all the errands and chores, all the things you do to keep a household going. All the while, I lay ensconced in a mountain of pillows and down quilts. I needed help with eating and dressing and taking a shower. It was ridiculous. I grew cranky, irritable, and depressed.

So hours turned into days, and days turned into weeks.

Around Christmas, India went on hiatus, and that was a blessing. Now it was the two of us lying in bed, surrounded by our dogs. David brought us our lunches on two matching TV trays. Oh, how he must have loved that.

Toward spring, I began to get my strength back. David, always one to see simple solutions, came into the bedroom one afternoon with a suggestion: "Why don't we drive down the hill and buy a couple of bicycles?"

"Bicycles?" I said from somewhere inside my pillow fort.

"Yeah, it'll be fun," he said. "Some fresh air and light exercise. I think you're ready for it."

"Bicycles?"

"Olivia."

"You *have* met me, right, David?"

But he was having none of it. "Come on. You'll see," he said.

And I did. Strapping the helmet on, I had the vague feeling that I might look like an idiot; catching my reflection in the little side mirror confirmed my suspicion.

"David, I look like an egg riding on two wheels," I called out. David laughed and cycled away. We were in a park just off Moorpark Avenue, one of the wide boulevards running east to west through the Valley side of L.A. It was a small, tree-lined, kidney-shaped park, flat and an easy ride. At first I was at sixes and sevens. It had been, I don't know, thirty years since I was last on a bicycle (apart from a magnificently awkward ride in the miniseries *It* that Richard Thomas and I shared). Slowly though, I began to find my way. I started to smile. Once I was out of bed and using my body, it responded. Air filled my lungs. The moment grew on me. It was silly and fun, two things I had not had a lot of in a long time.

My three-times-a-week rides became part of my routine and an enormous help in my recovery: laughing with David and India, grabbing lunch at our favorite Thai restaurant, making our way home with our bikes strapped to the car. We were the very picture of happy domestic life. It was careless, easy, and free. It was just what I needed.

Taking a Backseat

India's tenure on *The Secret Life of the American Teenager* lasted four years. For me, they were quiet ones. I moved comfortably into a new supporting role, one I found I was born to play. India was the lead now, and her happiness and well-being were the climax toward which we worked. Over those four years, our tight troupe of three grew, if that was possible, even tighter. My boys were older; they had their own lives. All of us were close, of course, but for David, India, and me, it was different. The three of us had been through so much together. We relied on one another in ways we didn't even understand.

David's meat-and-potatoes approach to life, and the ease with which he interacts with the world is wonderful, and it provides a balance for India's and my more, shall we say, ethereal approach to life. When I look at my daughter, I see deep veins of similarity between us. We are both sensitive creatures, bound to *feel* our way through this life. We take things hard, and are harder still on ourselves. Knowing so well how capricious life can be, I do worry that she is a bit too much like me. If only she was less raw and alive to all the slings and arrows, less likely to take it all to heart. But then I look and see the woman she is becoming and I think, No, I wouldn't change a thing.

By 2012, India was starting to make real inroads in the business. One difference between mother and daughter could be seen in the audition room: India was good at auditions. She was wowing casting people and directors. She was going in for *big* roles in *big* films and we felt it was only a matter of time before she landed one. We were right.

I am loath to write in too much detail about the particulars of the three months we spent in London during the summer of 2012. The phrase "burning bridges" comes to mind and, honestly, dishing dirt is not really what I want to do anyway.

India had treated the audition process for the project like any other. We worked together on the scenes and kept our expectations in check. It was a great part in what would be a huge film. Over the course of three weeks and a half-dozen meetings, India grew more confident. After an exhaustive two-hour meeting with the film's director, the three of us were having coffee at a little place on Ventura Boulevard when we got the call. She had landed the role.

We were elated. We felt this could be *it*—the job that changes everything. There's a tipping point in an actor's career, a point—it might come more than once if it's a long career, or not at all—when your work gains you the privilege of choice and you are *offered* roles instead of having to fight for them. Scripts arrive at your agent's daily. Directors and studio executives call, begging for you to be in their pictures. This is the holy grail, the moment when you can start to build your career and shape it the way you want. Of course, it comes with its own set of challenges.

Make a few bad decisions and you'll find yourself right back at square one. However, those issues were a long way off. India was at the beginning of her career, and we felt everything was about to change.

As I said, the film would shoot in London. India was scheduled to work for two months, maybe three. In our excitement, none of us noticed what else was happening that summer in the English capital: the Olympics. The city was about to become the center of the world's attention.

There's an image that springs to mind when I think of that summer in London. It's a silly image, but it symbolizes perfectly the utter futility and frustration the three of us came to feel: London's wonderfully foppish mayor Boris Johnson dangling halfway down a zip line. He's stuck: Hanging there, clutching two Union Jacks and wearing a tiny helmet, he has nothing to do but call down to the assembled crowd in good-natured banter while they delight in his folly. Boris, with all his calculated dishevelment, natural wit, and charisma, had no trouble pulling it off, but still the visual is striking. I can't help but think of the lead-up. It must have seemed such a good idea: to celebrate England's first gold-medal victory in the games by zipping down the wire in front of a massive crowd—only to realize, halfway down, that it's all gone terribly wrong. This was our experience, too, although ours lacked Boris's happy landing.

After a lifetime in this business, I have no illusions; I've seen it all and know how things work. Still, this shoot was a tough one. When you find yourself working on a movie that's in a state of perpetual flux, there's a good chance it's still being rewritten; the script changes daily. The studio execs have to have their say and, if there are big names attached, you better believe they'll have theirs too. The director is looking at the dailies—shot footage from the day before—and assessing, debating, or perhaps bowing to pressure beyond his or her control. With so many chiefs, it's a wonder the thing ever gets made at all.

Over the course of two months, India worked a total of fifteen days. The city was bedlam: Crowds thronged everywhere. We were hustled and bustled every day. The general craziness reflected India's state of mind. She felt that something was off with the shoot; things were happening on the set all around her and they had nothing to do with her, yet they had everything to do with her. She felt uneasy. She was stressed, and I began to worry.

On the positive side, India did have a chance, finally, to meet her family. I had not seen my brother, Drew, for nearly ten years. Shaped as we both had been by our shared childhood; our complex relationship with the father we never spoke to, or about; and our similarly stubborn natures—though Drew is more cerebral—there's always been a tension between us. Our lives have been so different. Mine skyrocketed into this strange, exotic stratosphere, and I always hoped that my brother could see past that. I hoped he never felt resentment or envy. But who knows? I don't apologize for my life, and I like to think that, had I never stepped in front of the camera, had I stayed in Wimbledon and led perhaps a less unorthodox life, I would still be exactly the same person I am today.

I was overjoyed that India and David had a chance to meet Drew; his wife, Cate; and their children, Jack, Phoebe, and Leonora. For India, it was heart-expanding. Here was family, at last. All her life it had been just David and me—and her brothers, yes, but that's different. She had never met my mum. She had lost David's parents when she was so young. She would never meet my father. I knew how desperate she was for family, and as I watched her talk with her cousins I nearly burst into tears.

Drew and I found our way to some solid ground, and it was so good to see him.

We saw them all a few more times that summer, and those visits made up for all the showbiz madness around us.

I could hardly travel to London without seeing the boy whose relationship with me had started it all.

Late afternoon on a Friday, and the three of us are riding the tube. Swaying rhythmically back and forth, we keep an eye out for the Hampstead stop and enjoy the party. England has just taken another gold in rowing, and there is a patriotic glow in the faces of our fellow passengers. Some are singing, some laughing. All are in a fine Victorian fervor. Pushing past people, we make our way up to the surface and emerge into the bright summer daylight. I am a bit nervous; it's been a long time, a long life.

Looking across the street, I think, maybe we can all go over to the park. We can look at the skyline. I'll ask what he thinks of the Shard.

At Gayton Road, we make a left. David has his cell phone out and is following directions. We find the house. A short flight of stairs, and we're knocking.

"Coming, just a sec." The voice is familiar; the accent, even after so many years, is still there. I hear the clicking of the lock, the turning of the knob. I take a deep breath and smile as Romeo opens the door.

Leonard and I had always kept in touch, if only peripherally. Like siblings, we could go for years without speaking but still feel close. Our friendship grew as the years rolled by, though. We emailed, we occasionally called. Once, when he was in L.A., Leonard spent a week with us, swimming in the pool, laughing with David and filling the house with his jocular cockney energy. Leonard has always had a firecracker personality, if tempered slightly now by his own share of hard times. I can't help but see reflections of my life in his, and in the past that has made me a little uncomfortable. Not anymore, though. You could say we took the long way round to close friendship. Leonard has become dear to me, and I love him after a fashion.

His wife isn't too bad, either. Lynn waited a long time for her man and, as far as I'm concerned, Leonard is lucky to have her. She has a joyful presence that makes you feel safe and well-looked-after. And for Leonard, her innate maternal energy has a calming influence. She's good for him and, fortunately, he didn't wait too long to see how special she was.

We walk in, exchange hugs, and Lynn busies herself making David, India, and me comfortable. Tea and sandwiches, to which every English person turns when there's ice to be broken.

"Livi, look at you. You look wonderful," Leonard says with broad grin.

I can't quite meet his eyes yet. Bound as we both are to our pasts, it will take a bit of time to warm to the present. Instead, I look around the room.

Their flat is cozy and warm. All around there is evidence of a life spent in movies and the theater. Framed production posters, photos with friends whose faces I recognize instantly, scripts and awards—the actor's accumulation. Other photos testify to another life, a life well-lived far from the trenches of the business: Leonard's beautiful daughter, Lynn's family, vacations abroad. I feel right at home.

Then I respond to his compliment. "Oh, Leonard," I say. "Do I? You know it's been quite a long time."

"Please, Olivia, you haven't changed a bit." He laughs.

The truth is that I have, of course. We both have, and we know it.

"And India, lovely India. How goes the work?"

India rolls her eyes, and Leonard laughs again. "That well, eh?"

India bursts out laughing, which is all it takes. We are in the present.

We walk to a little café across the street. We talk about our lives. We gossip. We tread carefully around the past, avoiding potential potholes.

Back at their flat, we have coffee. All is relaxed. Then I see it: a sweep of his hand, his little-boy smile, and I fall down the rabbit hole. Leonard catches my look and knows instantly what lies behind it. Maybe he feels it too.

"Oh, Livi, it's okay. I know," he says.

Tears well up as he stands and takes a few steps toward me.

"I know," he repeats.

Then Romeo takes Juliet in his arms and hugs her tenderly. The long way round.

Our time in London was proving to be a roller coaster, so in late August when the production company told us that India could travel back home, the three of us couldn't help but feel relieved. She had filmed almost all of her scenes and would have to return only for the odd pickup shot or small insert scene.

Arriving back in L.A., we barely had time to unpack before David's cell phone rang. It was the film's director. He needed to speak with India. I still remember watching my daughter's face as she listened; it betrayed nothing of what she was being told. After about a minute, she said, "I understand. Thank you for the call." Calmly, she ended the call; I saw that her hand was shaking.

"I'm not going to be in the movie anymore," she said.

"What?" David said.

"They have decided to go in a different direction."

Tears rolled down my little girl's cheeks. David stood in shock while I became angrier than I'd ever been in my life. It wasn't just that it was happening to my daughter—who, despite appearances, was still just a teenage girl—it was the manner in which she got the news, the way she was being treated.

These things happen, I told myself. It's a tough business. But not like this. For two months, India had worked. She had done her best. She was professional and easy to work with—all the things I had taught her to be. She did all this knowing from day one that something wasn't right. Clearly there had been some tension behind the scenes, a power struggle over control of the film's direction. India had become a casualty of that struggle.

Why couldn't they have told us something of what was going on earlier? Why let her go to work when the knives were out? All she had heard were good things: The director was happy with what she was doing, the producers had no issue, the other actors adored her. Still, India had felt some sort of threat, and in the end she was right.

She was absolutely gutted. She felt she had failed. She felt she had let us down. Who knows how many opportunities she had missed over the past months, how many jobs, auditions, and meetings had gone begging?

She's too young to become jaded by this industry, I said to myself.

To her credit and my relief, once the tears had dried, her passion for acting, her love of watching and making good movies, and her kind, open heart remained.

The film was released in 2014. We didn't see it. We heard, though, that it was far from *Magnificent*.

India has worked regularly since then, and has had some wonderful experiences. She and the great Samuel Jackson costarred in a film and loved each other. She has met some talented directors, fallen for a few handsome actors, and done some work she thinks is not half bad. She's had the opportunity to travel to places she'd never seen: New York, South Africa, and of course South Carolina with me to see Howard Willis. And wherever she goes, David and I are right behind her with support, advice, and, always, with love.

Today

A cypress tree grows outside my bedroom window. Some mornings, I slide open the glass doors and let Baba run around it, rubbing himself silly against it. Baba is my baby. He has been since we first locked eyes on each other at the shelter.

"You, my little sad darling, are coming with me," I'd told him when I found him in his cage. "I'm going to look after you now. You're going to have a home."

He'd nodded in agreement.

Baba's an old dog now. Half-blind and stone deaf, he spends most of his days curled up on the bed next to me, making sure I'm aware of his total love and dedication. I lie with him, surrounded by my Buddhas, my Ganeshes, my Marys, the paintings and statues I've collected over the years. There are photos everywhere: of the boys, of David and me on his Harley, of India as a baby, of my brother with his family. There's an old shot of my mum, framed and resting easy next to a photo of my other Baba, my Indian Baba.

A few weeks ago, I received a call from Matilde, my father's wife of fifty-six years.

"Olivia," she said, "last night your father passed." Her voice faltered then, if only for a moment. Over the past few years, my father and I had begun to speak again. Our conversations were always polite, always formal. He would ask after his grandchildren: "Do any of them speak Spanish?"

"Not yet," I would reply.

He would ask if I was well, if I was happy, if I ever thought of him.

"Matilde, I don't know what to say."

"At the end, he said your name, Olivia, and he called me Joy." Joy, my mother's name.

He was eighty-eight.

I lie here in my comfy bed and think of my father, but only for a moment. India and David are in town, at another audition, but they'll be home soon. Later, India will cook one of her healthy pastas and we'll all sit in front of the TV watching some obscure English drama and loving every second of it. But that's later. For now, it's just me. I look out at my little cypress again and recall others, tall and beautiful, framing an elegant terrace garden.

Franco's villa: It takes shape now, and I can almost hear the laughter competing with the wind, the clinking of glasses, the record player spinning out a Verdi opera. I can smell the heaping bowls of pasta and taste vintage red wine. I think of Franco but, again, only for a moment.

"I hope you are well, Maestro," I say out loud.

I think of another place in Italy, in another time. It's a fiction drawn from the mind of a genius, but real to me. I've known it all my life. I am there now. I can see the girl on the balcony. She is me but not me.

Juliet.

I imagine her looking down, seeing me standing there.

She smiles and raises her hand. A look passes over her face: a question.

"It's because of me, you know," she seems to say. "I brought you all of this. I hope it's been worth it?"

I smile as I answer her. "Of course it was worth it. Yes, all of it." And as I wave good-bye I say, "Thank you."

Acknowledgments

My mum would always say if, when you are in the last stage of your life, you can count your real friends on one hand, then you are very lucky. I am a very lucky woman, indeed. I want to acknowledge the following handful and say how grateful I am for their support, friendship, and love.

Swami Muktananda; Howard Wills; Gurumayi Chidvilasananda; my brother, Andrew; his wife, Cate; and their children, Jack, Phoebe, and Leonora; Bob & Darlene Delellis; Leonard and Lynn Whiting; Linda Deverell; Bonnie Colodzin Moffet; Kevin Reid and Doug Lebelle; Kelsey and Kayte Grammer; Franco Zeffirelli and Pippo Corsi; Liberte Chan; Akira Fuse; Matilde Attene; Michael and Oriana Parks; Frank and Carole Blundo; Omar Sappietro; Elfi Roose and John Gueyikiam; Larry McCallister at Paramount Pictures; Brian St. August; Laura Mcintyre; Ciro A. Morales; Maureen and Greg Penn; Desi Arnaz Jr.; Jeanne Martin; Yuriko Reyes. My literary agent, Rob Kirkpatrick (thank you for taking a chance); Paul Horne at OliviaHussey.com; and all the great people at Kensington Publishing; my wellness team: Dr. Michael Castro, MD; Dr. Ari Gabayan, MD; and Dr. Soram Singh Khalsa, MD.

And a special thank you to Signe Hammer, whose patience, expertise, and clear-eyed judgment helped a first-time writer turn his scribblings into something his mother could be proud of.

David, Alex, Max, India, Megan, and Greyson. You are always in my heart and forever with me.

I live in gratitude and love every day because of all of you. Thank you and bless you.